A PATH TO LEADERSHIP

The Heroic Follower

Robert Palestini

Rowman & Littlefield Education
Lanham, Maryland • Toronto • Oxford
2006

Published in the United States of America
by Rowman & Littlefield Education
A Division of Rowman & Littlefield Publishers, Inc.
A wholly owned subsidiary of The Rowman & Littlefield Publishing Group, Inc.
4501 Forbes Boulevard, Suite 200, Lanham, Maryland 20706
www.rowmaneducation.com

PO Box 317
Oxford
OX2 9RU, UK

British Library Cataloguing in Publication Information Available

Library of Congress Cataloging-in-Publication Data

Palestini, Robert H.
  A path to leadership : the heroic follower / Robert Palestini.
      p. cm.
  Includes index.
  ISBN-13: 978-1-57886-297-9 (hardcover : alk. paper)
  ISBN-10: 1-57886-297-3 (hardcover : alk. paper)
  ISBN-13: 978-1-57886-319-8 (pbk. : alk. paper)
  ISBN-10: 1-57886-319-8 (pbk. : alk. paper)
  1. Leadership. I. Title.
  HM1261.P35 2006
  303.3'4—dc22

                                                              2005017177

$\otimes^{TM}$ The paper used in this publication meets the minimum requirements of
American National Standard for Information Sciences—Permanence of Paper
for Printed Library Materials, ANSI/NISO Z39.48-1992.
Manufactured in the United States of America.

CONTENTS

LIST OF TABLES

LIST OF FIGURES

INTRODUCTION

Hundreds, maybe even thousands of books have been written about leadership. What are the characteristics of an effective leader? What leadership behaviors lead to success? What is the very best leadership style? These and many other questions have been posed by countless scholars attempting to find the one leadership style or approach that is most effective.

What the literature on leadership fails to include, though, are the traits of an effective *follower*. After all, what good is a leader without followers? What is lacking, therefore, is a book on what characteristics and behaviors are manifested by good and effective followers. Because there are many more followers than there are leaders, it seems to me that a good number of individuals would find such insights invaluable. This book provides the vast majority of the population—the followers—with this information.

One might ask, why would anyone want to know how to be a good follower? One answer, I believe, is that being a good follower is the path to becoming a good leader. On the contrary, if one is not a good follower, there is little chance that that individual will ever develop into an effective leader. In fact, we will see that virtually every characteristic of a good, make that *heroic*, follower is reflective of that possessed by a successful leader.

I have written four books on various aspects of leadership. In those books, I elaborate on the habits of highly effective leaders. In this text, I offer six habits or behaviors of highly effective followers, the most heroic of whom will become leaders. Heroic followers should be:

1. Purposeful
2. Responsible
3. Communicative
4. Flexible
5. Trustworthy and respectful
6. Sensitive

Each of these habits or behaviors is treated in detail in this text. Acquiring and enhancing these habits leads us through the personal and professional path from dependence to interdependence, and finally, to intradependence. Further, these habits are distinguishable by their effect on the follower's mind or heart. I will suggest that the heroic follower follows with both mind and heart. The habits of the *mind* include purpose, responsibility, communications, and flexibility. Mastering these habits leads us from dependence to independence. The habits of the *heart* include trust, respect, and sensitivity. Honing these habits leads us to the ultimate stage of personal and professional development, that is of intradependence and heroic followership.

I have been fortunate enough to be in one leadership position or another for almost forty years. Over that time, I like to believe that I could be described as a reflective practitioner. I studied, researched, and thought about leadership almost every day. I have written several books and many articles on the topic of leadership over the past several years; however, I have been focusing my most recent research efforts on the follower. I have visited and spoken to a number of successful leaders in various fields and asked them what characteristics or behaviors they sought in their followers. Because I anticipated some self-serving responses, like blind loyalty to their bosses, I asked them to include only those behaviors that would make followers effective leaders one day. After literally hundreds of interviews and a thorough review of the literature on this topic, the six behaviors in this book represent those most mentioned in the literature and by the leaders. Because all of these leaders were once followers, they were able to respond from both perspectives.

The first chapter of this book sets the foundation for the path to heroic followership. Here we deal with the organizational development theory on which our assumptions regarding the effective follower are based. We look at the contributions of Scott Martin, Stephen Covey, Chris Lowney, and Robert Spitzer, as well as to my own thoughts on the habits and behaviors of the heroic follower.

The second chapter addresses the requisite habits of the *mind* that the follower must develop and considers the need for a follower to be *purposeful*, that is, to have an end in mind before he or she begins. It speaks to the need for followers to develop their own personal and professional mission and vision. This chapter also includes an exploration of what it means to be a reflective practitioner as well as the need of the follower to clearly focus on the ultimate goal and to persevere in attaining it.

In chapter 3, the need for an effective follower to be responsible is examined. Here we address such subtleties as attribution and locus of control, and how important it is for heroic followers to hold themselves accountable for their behavior.

The need for the highly effective follower to be *communicative* is addressed in chapter 4. In this chapter, we stress the importance of the effective follower to first understand before expecting to be understood. The concept of active listening, for example, is explored in detail in this chapter.

In chapter 5, we look at the habit of adaptability or *flexibility*. Charles Darwin pointed out in *The Origin of the Species* that the plants and animals that survive are those that are able to effectively adapt to their environments. In the same way, the effective follower must adapt to the environment and nurture in her- or himself a high tolerance for change.

In chapter 6, we begin looking at the habits of the *heart* and address the need for followers to develop a sense of *trust and respect*, both self-respect and respect for others. To be taken seriously, the heroic follower must surround him- or herself with the aura of trust and respect. Here we discuss such issues as personal integrity, behaving out of an ethical framework, and appreciating the gift of diversity.

The need for the highly effective follower to be *sensitive* to the feelings and beliefs of others is explored in chapter 7. Just as an effective leader needs to lead with both mind and heart, so the effective follower needs to possess and exhibit an emotional dimension to his or her behavior. Here we will investigate the ramifications of emotional intelligence and its impact on the heroic follower.

In chapter 7, we suggest ways in which the six habits of a heroic follower can be honed and perfected so that the highly effective follower will indeed develop into the highly effective leader, maybe even a *heroic* one.

Because many heroic followers will wish to become heroic leaders, the last chapter is devoted to an exploration of what it takes to ensure the good health of an organization. Here we examine the ten components of an organization that help determine its effectiveness. It is by identifying the strengths and weaknesses among these components, and correcting the weaknesses, that the heroic leader improves his or her organization and sustains its organizational good health.

To make this book as useful as possible to busy readers, at the end of each chapter is a handy diagnostic checklist of questions that should be helpful in quickly assessing the status of the six habits of the heroic follower in your own life. In addition, there is a comprehensive *Mind & Heart Smart Survey* at the end of this book that will be helpful in identifying the behaviors that are necessary to develop into a heroic follower.

1

BACK TO BASICS!

An effective theory is a possession for life.

—William Hazlitt

LAYING THE FOUNDATION

As a young high school basketball coach, I learned that whenever my team was playing poorly and becoming disorganized, it was always time to "go back to the basics." Invariably, when we spent the next few practices focusing exclusively on the basic skills of shooting, passing, dribbling, and defending, our overall play would improve. Similarly, in other life situations, I have found that laying a foundation or developing a philosophy of life and having that to fall back on in times of duress is very helpful indeed. The academics often refer to this concept as "theory informing practice." That is, in order for one's practice to be effective, it should be based on theory. And, if the practice is found to be faulty, one should refer back to the theory to correct this failed practice. In business circles, this idea is expressed in terms of "function preceding form." The structure of an effective organization should adapt to the function and not vice versa. Thus, we start our discussion about the heroic follower with the basics.

Dr. Scott Martin, an industrial psychologist and senior director of consulting at London House, a Chicago-based consulting firm, conducted an extensive study on the basic traits of successful people and pinpointed five specific abilities that they commonly share. The study was based on a battery of psychological tests called the System for Testing and Evaluation of Potential (STEP), developed at the University of Chicago. STEP takes three hours to complete and measures traits such as intelligence, education, communication skills, energy, leadership abilities, and social attitudes. Over the course of fifteen years, the test was taken by about four thousand individuals from entry-level positions up to the top leadership positions. Of the more than thirty traits tested for, Dr. Martin found five that distinguished the most highly successful people among those participating. Later, after forty validation studies, one could predict who would be the high achievers by their possession of these five basic traits.[1]

The first of these traits is the willingness and ability of these individuals to take responsibility. The second trait is creativity. Highly effective individuals are not necessarily more intelligent than those who are not as effective, but they are more creative. And their creative style differs from that of artists or musicians because their success hinges on being creative within many constraints. A highly successful person's creative solutions have to be legal, ethical, and acceptable to one's colleagues and to the public.

The third trait is stress tolerance. The study confirmed that highly successful people can accomplish their responsibilities without feeling stress as acutely as those who are less effective. The fourth trait is personal insight. Top achievers know their own strengths and limitations. The final trait is communication. The highly effective individuals, whether they be leaders or followers, possess the ability to communicate in all ways: talking, listening, and writing.

According to Martin, the first of these traits, responsibility, is the most basic. In order for an individual to grow to be highly successful, one must be able and willing to take on responsibility. In other words, before becoming a leader, one must be willing and able to be an effective follower.

In his book *Heroic Leadership*, Chris Lowney suggests leaders must possess four unique values in order for them to be effective: self-awareness, ingenuity, love, and heroism. According to Lowney, heroic leaders understand their strengths, weaknesses, values, and worldview. They also confidently innovate and adapt to embrace a changing world. In the process, they engage others with a positive, loving attitude and energize themselves and others through heroic ambitions. I would argue that many of these same values are requisites for heroic followers.[2]

MOVING FROM DEPENDENCE TO INDEPENDENCE

In 1976, Stephen Covey conducted an extensive review of the success literature of the first 200 years of the United States. He read biographies, autobiographies, and articles that were written on what it takes to become a successful person. During the first 150 years, virtually all of the success literature dealt with fundamental values and character traits: integrity, patience, trustworthiness, fidelity, temperance, and humility.

The success literature during the next 50 years shifted from the qualities of success to the trappings of success: superficial skills training marked by such slogans as "Swimming in the mainstream," learning how to influence other people, teaching people how to get what they want fairly quickly. We have strayed from character development to a personality ethic focused on skills and techniques that captivate and manipulate.

Covey's "habits" approach teaches us that we must first establish the qualities of character, and progress from a state of personal and professional dependence to independence. Early in an individual's development, Covey emphasizes the importance of self-mastery and self-esteem. Later he stresses the need to establish oneself in a more public way, thus moving from dependence to independence. Ultimately, one reaches a position of interdependence, but only to the degree that one has mastered the "basics" of self-mastery and self-esteem.[3]

Covey points out that the private victory of self-mastery and self-esteem must precede the public victory that is independence and interdependence. It is in these earlier traits that an individual's principles and values are defined. These values then become the touchstone by which a character is shaped, responses to circumstances are chosen, and decisions are made. It is only after this foundation is developed that we reach the point of a personal continuous improvement process where we are constantly working to maintain and improve ourselves physically, mentally, socially, and spiritually. It is only then that we view ourselves as lifelong learners, always seeking opportunities for personal and professional growth. Once again, the requisite for being a highly effective leader is to be a highly effective follower. One needs to understand, know, and value oneself before he or she can hope to positively affect and interact with others.

Lawrence Kohlberg suggests a similar path. In his stages of moral development, he details how one moves from the early stage of personal concordance to interpersonal concordance, and finally, to intrapersonal concordance in one's moral growth. According to Kohlberg, one grows more sophisticated in one's moral growth as the stages are achieved—the most highly developed being the intrapersonal stage.[4]

McCann and Ferry suggest that with the current emphasis on the open systems model of organizational structure, it is important that managers understand the nature of interacting groups or subsystems. They urge managers to recognize the importance of interdependence and to assess the nature and extent of interdependence in an organization; by doing this, they will better understand the potential for conflict and the impact one part of the organization will have on another part. Another important implication of open systems theory is the significance of the external environment to the organization. The effective leader needs to evolve from interdependence to *intradependence*. I would suggest that *followers* also need to recognize these implications.[5]

In this book, I suggest a path to leadership and interdependence that begins with developing the basics of becoming a heroic follower, progressing to the ultimate goal of becoming the heroic leader. A potential leader on this path moves through the stages of dependence and independence by nurturing what I call the habits of the *mind*, finally achieving intradependence by developing the habits of the *heart*.[6]

The foundation or basics of the highly effective follower include developing the traits or habits of the mind of purpose, responsibility, flexibility or adaptability, and the ability to communicate effectively. Once these traits or habits are mastered, the follower moves from dependence to independence, and after developing the habits of the heart of respect and sensitivity and practicing these habits in the workplace and in one's personal life, the follower moves onto the stage of intradependence, and at this point develops into the *heroic* follower. The heroic follower, then, is poised to become the heroic leader.

The first habit of the mind that effective followers must develop is purpose, that is, to have the end in mind before one begins. Just as an effective leader needs to develop a personal and professional mission and vision, so does the effective follower. Emanating from one's mission and vision should be a set of goals through which the mission is achieved. The development of measurable strategies is the next step in the process of becoming a follower with a purpose. Without such a "roadmap," the follower is destined to a professional and personal life of confusion and dysfunction.

The next important habit of the mind is for the effective follower to develop a sense of responsibility. Here the effective follower develops an internal locus of control whereby the follower feels in control of his or her own destiny. Too many individuals in our society have an external locus of control that prompts them to attribute blame to others for their own shortcomings. Developing an internal locus of control will allow effective followers to accept accountability for their own behavior and prompt them to be proactive rather than reactive in their personal lives and in the workplace.

Communication is the next important habit of the mind that needs to be developed in the effective follower. The effective follower needs first to understand before expecting to be understood. The ability to listen attentively and actively is an often forgotten component of effective communication. Making certain that one engages in two-way communication, with the opportunity for feedback, is also an important aspect of effective communication. Finally, communicating assertively, rather than nonassertively or aggressively, is a requisite for effective communication.

Flexibility or adaptability is another important habit of the mind that effective followers must master. Developing a high tolerance for change will help the follower become effective. Seeing the need for continuous improvement in one's personal and professional life is an attitude that will work to the effective follower's advantage. Of course, continuous improvement implies change. The two are intrinsically connected, and this connection is understood by the highly effective follower.

INTRADEPENDENCE AND THE HABITS OF THE HEART

The next step in our pilgrimage from dependence to independence to intradependence is for the highly effective follower to develop the habits of the heart, which include trust, respect, and sensitivity. In my earlier texts, *Educational Administration: Leading with Mind and Heart* and *The Human Touch in Educational Leadership,*[7] I suggest that possessing the knowledge and skills of leadership is only half the battle. To be a complete leader, one must also develop a value system, or philosophy, of leadership that guides the leader's actions and provides the leader with the "human touch." It is through the lens of these values that the "heart" of leadership is developed. In his recent book, *The Spirit of Leadership,* Robert Spitzer also acknowledges that the heart of a leader is as important as the mind in inspiring an organization toward greater change, growth, ethics, and team behavior.[8] In this book, I suggest that the same thing could be said of followers, that is, to be a truly heroic follower and one who has reached the stage of intradependence, one needs to follow with both mind and heart.

The habits of the heart begin with trust and respect, both self-respect and respect for others. The heroic follower needs to establish a covenantal relationship with the other followers and with the leader. This relationship is not built on a contractual or protocol relationship, but on a deeper, more personal relationship in which the follower truly respects and recognizes the gifts or charisms of every colleague.

A corollary to trust and respect is the habit of the heart that I call sensitivity. The highly effective follower is sensitive to the feelings and needs of others. The heroic follower needs to display an emotional dimension to his or her behavior. The ideal follower needs to possess a high degree of emotional intelligence whereby the follower has: (1) the ability to be aware of, to understand, and to express oneself; (2) the ability to be aware of, to understand and relate to others; (3) the ability to deal with strong emotions and control one's impulses; and (4) the ability to adapt to change and to solve problems of a personal, social, and professional nature.

Now that we have established the underlying theory or basics of what it means to be a heroic follower, we are now in a better position to explore these habits of the mind and heart in more detail.

Heroic Follower

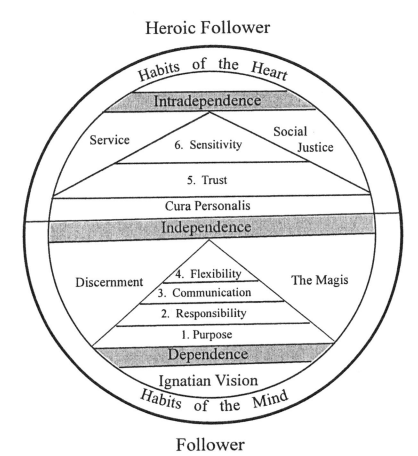

Follower

Figure 1.1.   Heroic Follower Wheel

NOTES

1. Scott Martin, Are you CEO material? Here are five clues, *Executive Strategies*, November 1996, 10.

2. Chris Lowney, *Heroic Leadership* (Chicago: Loyola Press, 2003).

3. Charles S. Farnsworth and Dennis I. Blender, It starts with trust: Building organizational effectiveness, *ASBO International*, January 1993, 10–16.

4. L. Kohlberg, *The Philosophy of Moral Development* (San Francisco: Harper & Rowe, 1969).

5. J. E. McCann and D. L. Ferry, An approach for assessing and managing interunit interdependence, *Academy of Management Review* 4 (1979): 113–119.

6. Robert H. Palestini, *Educational Administration: Leading with Mind and Heart* (Lanham, MD: Rowman and Littlefield Publishing, 2002).

7. Palestini, *Educational Administration*; Robert H. Palestini, *The Human Touch in Educational Leadership*, (Lanham, MD: Rowman and Littlefield, 2003).

8. Robert J. Spitzer, SJ, *The Spirit of Leadership: Optimizing Creativity and Change in Organizations* (Provo, UT: Executive Press Publishing, 2000).

2

START THE RACE KNOWING WHERE THE FINISH LINE IS!

Nothing contributes so much to tranquilize the mind as a steady purpose—a point on which the soul may fix its intellectual eye.

—Mary Wollstonecraft Shelley

A SENSE OF PURPOSE

To some people, the term *sense of purpose* conjures images of jobs requiring sweat and toil, characterized by hours in a high school electrical shop or apprenticeships with master craftspersons. But for many, this same term is defined as that particular goal, job, or skill for which a person is especially gifted or talented and for which one holds a special affinity or love, coupled with a sense that one was called or destined to follow that path. It is this definition, specifically directed toward one's work, which is being used here. A sense of purpose suggests having a calling, life project, or path to follow that defines who we are, as well as providing a framework that helps define our personal history. A sense of purpose has come to be conceptualized as a gracious discovery that strikes a balance between our deepest desires, hopes, and unique gifts that are called into action by the needs of others and realized in response to that call.[1]

Parenthetically, the lack of purpose in one's life is what ultimately led to the deadly duel between Alexander Hamilton and Aaron Burr at the beginning of our democracy. Hamilton believed that because Vice President Burr lacked a purpose in life or ideology and drifted from policy to policy depending on what was most expeditious at the time, he would never be an effective president. Hamilton ultimately lost his life after expressing this opinion, but history exonerated Hamilton in that it was widely recognized, even by George Washington, that Burr did in fact lack a consistent purpose or ideology in his life. As a result, Burr's integrity was constantly being questioned.

Once we, as individuals, have acknowledged our longing, how do we define a path or purpose in life? Psychotherapist Gregory Bogart has conceptualized a path to vocation that embodies aspects of contemporary thinking. Bogart described the process in finding one's sense of purpose from a Western psychological perspective and the perspective of Eastern spiritual practice. From following his own life and the lives of his clients, he asserts eight steps, not necessarily experienced in a linear journey, to find and follow one's sense of purpose.[1]

1. *Preparation to find a sense of purpose.* In this process, an individual liberates him- or herself from the expectations of family and society and comes to terms with his or her own expression of essential nature directed by spiritual guidance or inner voice.
2. *Experiencing illumination.* Once an individual has opened awareness to certain vocational and personal goals, illumination is the process of inner knowing that the path is the correct one to follow, and that it is in tune with the individual. Illumination may come in a flash or be experienced over time. Illumination may be the result of the responses and positive feedback of others who serve as confirmation that the path chosen is the correct one.
3. *Receiving confirmation of the sense of purpose.* Bogart suggests that confirmation of the purpose comes in three forms: continued inner peace with the choice, continued confirmation of the correct choice by others with whom we interact, and continued situations that present themselves that confirm our choice was the correct one.
4. *Developing our skill in attaining the purpose chosen.* As individuals pursue their chosen purpose, there is still a sense that it is an

evolving process. There is constant reevaluation, especially if we strive to make our outer work match our inner calling. The sense of purpose may be developed through continued academic work or further enhancement of natural gifts. Many individuals are fortunate to have the work that supports their livelihood also match their sense of purpose. If this is not the case, one spends a great deal of time developing a sense of purpose that must be expressed after work.

5. *Coping with interpersonal issues and searching for a sacred sense of purpose.* Bogart writes that though one's sense of purpose may be personalized, the means to express it usually is limited, defined, and even constrained by one's social condition and situation and the historical period in which one lives. A sense of purpose, in Bogart's view, is marked by the individual's response to social conditions. An individual with a sense of purpose usually delights in interacting with others who share similar convictions. He continues by saying that it is natural for people to want to share their purpose in life with others, receive positive responses, and be appreciated for what they are doing.

6. *Resolving problems and pitfalls.* Pursuing a purpose is not without its difficulties. Various vocations that fulfill one's sense of purpose may place individuals in dangerous and life-threatening situations or require difficult sacrifices. They may put a person at odds with family and friends and on paths that are outside the conventional norms. Bogart asserts that it is the constant reevaluation of our situation and the evolving nature of our purpose in life that eases any doubts and keeps us reaffirming our path.

7. *Building a sacred vessel so that vocation becomes a spiritual path.* Bogart states that having a sense of purpose is more than satisfying one's personal ambitions. For some, it is a way of transforming one's life into a vessel for spiritual growth and living in a way that is consistent with religious teachings, spiritual traditions, and humanitarian ideologies. He continues that a life that includes a sense of purpose also signifies that an individual is self-actualized, with energy derived from this awareness used in a meaningful manner. The sense of purpose may arise from connections with various forms of transcendence, contemplation, inner voice, or will

of a higher power, be it religious or spiritual in origin or not. But an individual still must follow the path and engage in activities that are focused and realized in a particular time and place.

8. *Defining the meaning of a sense of purpose.* Bogart concludes his steps to finding one's sense of purpose with the personal sense of satisfaction that one achieves when one realizes that life has a purpose. The individual can find contentment and joy, spiritual enlightenment, and a sense of a meaningful and purposeful life.

A SENSE OF PURPOSE AS SELF-FULFILLMENT AND SELF-ACTUALIZATION

Having a sense of purpose is central to how one defines one's personal identity. A sense of purpose can serve the needs of self-definition, self-justification, and identity through devotion to a higher ideal of service. Gregory Jones, former dean of Duke University's School of Divinity, stated that having a sense of purpose is a major ingredient in a life that is meaningful and flourishing, and it impacts the development of self. It is the impact on the self that Jones describes as helping the individual differentiate between simple work and a life's calling. It is the recognition of this differentiation between a job and a vocation that became the cornerstone of Maslow's observation on self-actualized people.[3]

Maslow described his interactions with two devoted teachers who were far different from the ordinary teachers with whom Maslow had previously interacted. His experience with these two teachers very much mirrored subsequent research in the area of self-fulfillment and self-actualization. Maslow routinely made notes about both of these teachers, concluding that they had similar characteristics, admitting though, that his observations were fraught with methods lacking scientific rigor. Knowing the criticism of work without scientific methods, Maslow humorously cites that the consistently observable patterns he noted with his experimental group of self-actualized subjects were juxtaposed to the rest of the world as a control group. One of the consistent patterns Maslow describes in these individuals, and most important for this discussion, is that these individuals were involved in causes outside their own skins, in something outside of themselves. "They are devoted, working at something which is very precious to them—some calling or vocation or purpose. . ." (1970, p. 42).

In describing individuals with purpose as self-actualized individuals, Maslow is indicating that these individuals have reached the apex in his basic needs hierarchy. The continuum of basic needs commences with physiological needs at the lowest level, and progresses through safety needs, belongingness and love needs, and esteem needs, with satisfaction of lower-level needs allowing the individual to progress to needs of a higher order. He hypothesizes that even after all basic needs are satisfied, there is still the need for individuals to continue further toward self-fulfillment, a striving for them to be all that they can be. Maslow refers to the needs of self-actualized people as *metaneeds*, and their motivations as *metamotivations*, differentiating them from those belonging to people motivated by lesser needs in the hierarchy.

Maslow continues that self-actualization does not occur automatically after all basic needs are met, but it becomes apparent to those individuals who, in addition to having their basic needs met, also are free of illness, use capabilities positively, are motivated by a set of values, and have a overriding purpose in life. As mentioned above, he characterizes self-actualized individuals as having a purpose, a calling, or a dedication to something bigger than themselves, beckoned by fate or destiny and fueled by selflessness and passion. Maslow states that self-actualized individuals describe being born to do their work or feeling the job was just the right fit, leading Maslow to hypothesize that there was a sense of some predestination, or preestablished condition, that was experienced by these individuals to their chosen fields.

In addition, Maslow asserts that for these self-actualized individuals, their sense of purpose transcends the division between work and play; he describes subjects who will spend their time off joyfully still engaged in work-related activities, making it difficult to distinguish their work from their hobbies. The work they do represents how they define themselves as individuals, making it difficult to separate their work lives from their lives outside of work. Called to their work, his subjects found it difficult to imagine themselves in any other kind of pursuit. Maslow observes, as many others have, that earnings are not the primary motivation for these individuals, noting that salary represents only a small part of the compensation received from a work defined by higher ideals. Maslow therefore contends that the role that money plays in the life of those whose basic needs are satisfied is far different from its role in the lives of those still functioning at lower levels of the basic needs continuum.

In concurrence with the observations of other researchers, Maslow notes that individuals who have a purpose in life and are called to their work describe fulfillment because the work satisfies their need to achieve some greater ends than just the work itself. The work is loved because of the values embedded in the work itself and because it satisfies the individual's ultimate goal or purpose. The rewards of the job are described in terms such as truth, beauty, justice, doing good, and other abstract values. The individuals' sense of themselves is transcended to incorporate who they are in relation to needs outside of themselves and greater than their own.

True to Maslow's description of the hierarchical nature of basic needs, he describes consequences for self-actualized individuals if their metaneeds are unsatisfied and they have not met their full life potential. Maslow does not place metaneeds on the same type of continuum, citing that "each individual seems to have his or her own priorities or hierarchy or prepotency, in accordance with his or her own talents, temperament, skills, capacities, etc." (1970, p. 313). Although he does not describe deficiencies of metaneeds in the strong language that he describes the lack of satisfaction of lower needs in the continuum, he cites behavioral consequences to unmet metaneeds as *metapathologies* resulting in individuals experiencing a variety of conditions, including alienation, meaninglessness, apathy, hopelessness, despair, and joylessness. Thus, there is distinct advantage to having a strong purpose in life, since it creates a path that could eventually lead to self-actualization. And, without a purpose in life, it is not only unlikely that self-actualization will be achieved but also likely that the individual will be haunted by conditions such as alienation, meaninglessness, and so forth.[4] One might now ask, how am I to formulate and articulate this sense of purpose in my life? Some suggestions follow.

THE IGNATIAN VISION

More than 450 years ago, Ignatius of Loyola, a young priest born to a Spanish aristocratic family, founded the Society of Jesus, the Jesuits, and wrote his seminal book, *The Spiritual Exercises*.[5] In this book, he suggested a "way of life" and a "way of looking at things" that has been propagated by his religious community and his other followers for almost five centuries. His principles have been utilized in a variety of ways. They have been used as an aid in developing the spiritual life of individuals; they have been used to formulate a way of learning that has become the curriculum and instructional method employed in the sixty Jesuit high schools and the twenty-eight Jesuit colleges and universities in the United States; and they have been used by people seeking to develop their own administrative style. Together, these principles comprise the *Ignatian vision*.

There are five Ignatian principles that we will explore here as a foundation for developing a philosophy of life or a sense of purpose in one's life: (1) Ignatius' concept of the *magis*, or the "more"; (2) the implications of his notion of *cura personalis*, or "care of the person"; (3) the process of *inquiry* or *discernment*; (4) the development of *men and women for others*; and (5) service to the *underserved* and marginalized, or his concept of *social justice*.

At the core of the Ignatian vision is the concept of the *magis*, or the "more." Ignatius spent the greater part of his life seeking perfection in all areas of his personal, spiritual, and professional life. He was never satisfied with the status quo. He was constantly seeking to improve his own spiritual life, as well as his secular life as leader of a growing religious community. He was an advocate of "continuous improvement" long before it became a corporate slogan, long before people like W. Edwards Deming used it to develop his Total Quality Management approach to management, and long before Japan used it to revolutionize its economy after World War II.

The idea of constantly seeking "the more" implies change. The *magis* is a movement away from the status quo, and moving away from the status quo defines change. The Ignatian vision requires individuals and institutions to embrace the process of change as a vehicle for personal and institutional improvement. For Ignatius' followers, frontiers and boundaries are not obstacles or ends, but new challenges to be faced, new opportunities to be welcomed. Thus, change needs to become a way of life. Ignatius further implores his followers to "be the change that you expect in others." In other words, we are called to model desired behavior—to live out our values, to be of ever-fuller service to our communities, and to aspire to the more universal good. Ignatius had no patience with mediocrity. He constantly strove for the greater good.

The *magis* principle, then, can be described as the main norm in the selection and interpretation of information. Every real alternative for choice must be conducive to the advancement toward perfection. When some aspect of a particular alternative is *more* conducive to reaching perfection than other alternatives, we have reason to choose that alternative. We all encounter certain "dilemmas" during every working day. The *magis* principle is a "way of seeing" that can help us in selecting the better alternative.

At first hearing, the *magis* principle may sound rigid and frightening. It is absolute, and Ignatius is unyielding in applying it, but not rigid. On the one hand, he sees it as the expression of our love of humanity, which inexorably seeks to fill all of us with a desire not to be content with what is less good for us. On the other hand, he sees that humanity not only has its particular gifts, but also has its limitations and different stages of growth. If a choice would be more humane in the abstract than in the concrete, that choice would not be seen as adhering to the *magis* principle. For example, tracking students according to ability in schools can be seen as humane in the abstract because the homogenous group can be taught more easily, but in the concrete it can be dehumanizing because it labels certain students as being "at risk." Ignatius would advise us to focus on the concrete in resolving this dilemma.

In every case, then, accepting and living by the *magis* principle is an expression of our love of humanity. So, whatever the object for choice, the measure of our love of neighbor will be the fundamental satisfaction we will find in choosing and acting by the *magis* principle. Whatever one chooses by this principle, no matter how undesirable in some other respect, will always be what one would most want as a moral and ethical member of the human race.

Closely related to the principle of the *magis* is the Ignatian principle of *inquiry* and *discernment*. In his writings, Ignatius urges us to challenge the status quo through the methods of inquiry and discernment. To Ignatius, the need to enter into inquiry and discernment is to determine God's will. However, this process is of value for the purely *secular* purpose of deciding on which "horn of a dilemma" one should come down. To aid us in utilizing inquiry and discernment as useful tools in challenging the status quo and determining the right choice to be made, Ignatius suggests that the ideal disposition for inquiry and discernment is humility. The disposition of humility is especially helpful when, despite one's best efforts, the evidence that one alternative is more conducive to the betterment of society is not compelling. When the discerner cannot find evidence to show that one alternative is more conducive to the common good, Ignatius calls for a judgment in favor of what more assimilates the discerner's life to the life of poverty and humiliation. Thus, when the *greatest* good cannot readily be determined, the *greater* good is more easily discerned in a position of humility. These are very demanding standards, but they are consistent with the *magis* principle and the tenets of critical humanism.

In addition to the *magis* principle norm, taking account of what has just been said and of what was said earlier about the norm of humility as a disposition for seeking the greater good, the relationship of the greater good norm to the greatest good norm can be clarified. The latter is absolute, overriding, always primary. The greater good norm is secondary; it can never, in any choice, have equal weight with the first *magis* principle. It can never justify a choice of actual poverty and humiliation over riches and honors if the latter are seen to be more for the service of humanity in a particular situation or choice. In other words, if being financially successful allows one to better serve the poor and underserved, financial success would be preferred to actual poverty.

Ignatius presents us with several other supplemental norms for facing our "dilemmas." In choices that directly affect individuals who are underserved or marginalized, especially the poor, Ignatius urges us to give preference to those in need. This brings us to his next guiding principle, *cura personalis*, or care of the person.

Another of Ignatius' important and enduring principles is his notion that, despite the primacy of the common good, the need to care for the individual person should never be lost. From the very beginning, the *cura personalis* principle has been included in the mission statement of virtually every high school and college founded by the Jesuits. It also influences the method of instruction suggested for all Jesuit schools in the *Ratio Studiorum,* the "course of study" in these institutions. All Jesuit educational institutions are to foster what we now refer to as a "constructivist" classroom, where the student is an active participant in the learning process. This contrasts with the "transmission" method of instruction where the teacher is paramount, and the student is a passive participant in the process. In the Ignatian vision, the care of the person is a requirement not only on a personal needs basis, but also on a "whole person" basis, which would, of course, include classroom education. Businesses would also do well to practice this principle. Many, in fact, do.

This principle also has implications for how we conduct ourselves as highly effective followers. Ignatius calls us to value the gifts and charisms of our colleagues and to address any deficiencies that they might have and turn them into strengths. For example, during the employee evaluation process, Ignatius would urge us to focus on the formative stage of the evaluation far more than on the summative stage. This would be one small way of applying *cura personalis* theory to practice.

The fourth principle that we wish to consider is the Ignatian concept of service. Once again, this principle has been propagated from the very outset. The expressed goal of virtually every Jesuit institution is "to develop men and women for others." Jesuit institutions are called on to create a culture of service as one way of ensuring that the students, faculty, and staffs of these institutions reflect the educational, civic, and spiritual values of the Ignatian vision.

Institutions following the Ignatian tradition of service to others have done so through community services programs, and more recently, through service learning. Service to the community provides students with a means of helping others, a way to put their value systems into action, and a tangible way to assist local communities. Although these are valuable benefits, until recently there was no formal integration of the service experience into the curriculum and no formal introspection concerning the impact of service on the individual. During the last ten years, there has been a movement toward creating a more intentional academic relationship. Service has evolved from a modest student activity into an exciting pedagogical opportunity. In the past, service was viewed as a cocurricular activity; today it plays an integral role in the learning process.

Since many institutions are situated in an urban setting, service gives them a chance to share resources with surrounding communities and allows reciprocal relationships to form between the organization and local residents. Immersion into different cultures—economic, racial, educational, social, and religious—is the vehicle by which people make connections. Working side-by-side with people of varying backgrounds significantly influences us, forcing us outside of our comfort zones and into the gritty reality of how others live. Through reflection, we have the opportunity to integrate these powerful experiences into our lives, opening our eyes and hearts to the larger questions of social justice. Peter-Hans Kolvenbach, the Superior General of the Jesuit order, in his address on justice in American Jesuit universities in October 2000, used the words of Pope John Paul II to challenge Jesuit educators to "educate the whole person of solidarity for the real world," not only through concepts learned in the classroom, but also by contact with real people.[6]

Upon assuming the position of Superior General in 1973 and echoing the words of Ignatius, Pedro Arrupe declared, "Our prime educational objective must be to form men and women for others; men and women who will live not for themselves but for others. . ." In the spirit of these words, the service learning movement has legitimized the educational benefit of all experiential activity. The term "service learning" means different things to different people, and debates on service learning have been around for decades, running the gamut from unstructured "programmatic opportunities" to structured "educational philosophies." At Ignatian institutions, service learning is a bridge that connects faculty, staff, and students with community partners and their agency needs. It connects academic and student life views about the educational value of experiential learning. It also connects students' textbooks with human reality, and their minds and hearts with values and action. The programs are built on key components of service learning including integration into the curriculum, a reciprocal relationship between the community agency and student, and structured time for reflection, which is very much related to the Ignatian principle of *discernment* discussed earlier.

Participation in service by high school and college students, whether as a cocurricular or a course-based experience, correlates to where they are in their developmental process. Service work allows students to explore their skills and limitations; to find what excites and energizes them; to put their values into action; and to use their talents to benefit others, to discover who they are, and who they want to become. By encouraging students to reflect on their service, these institutions assist in this self-discovery. The reflection can take many forms: an informal chat, a facilitated group discussion, written dialogue, journal entries, reaction papers, or in-class presentations on articles. By integrating the service experience through critical reflection, students develop self-knowledge of the communities in which they live and knowledge about the world that surrounds them. It is only after the unfolding of this service-based knowledge that the students are able to synthesize what they have learned into their lives. Through this reflection, the faculty members also have an opportunity to learn from and about their students. Teachers witness the change and growth of the students firsthand. In short, "service to others" changes lives.

The implications of "service to others" for heroic followers are clear. Followers can enhance their effectiveness, not only by including the idea of service to others in their personal mission statements, but also by modeling it in their personal and professional lives. The concept of heroic followers becoming the "servant of the servants" is what we have in mind here. Servant followers do not inflict pain, they bear pain, and they treat their peers as fellow "volunteers," a concept that we will explore more fully later.

The Ignatian concept of "service" leads into his notion of solidarity with the underserved (poor) and marginalized and his principle of *social justice*. We begin with an attempt to achieve some measure of clarity on the nature and role of social justice in the Ignatian vision. According to some, Ignatius defined justice in both a narrow and wide sense.[7] In the *narrow* sense, it is "justice among men and women." In this case, it is a matter of "clear obligations" among "members of the human family." The application of this kind of justice would include not only the rendering of material goods but also immaterial goods such as "reputation, dignity, the possibility of exercising freedom."

Many of Ignatius' followers also believe he defined justice in a *wider* sense "where situations are encountered which are humanly intolerable and demand a remedy." These situations may be a product of "explicitly unjust acts" caused by "clearly identified people" who cannot be obliged to correct the injustices even though the dignity of the human person requires that justice be restored, or they may be caused by nonidentifiable people. It is precisely within the structural forces of inequality in society where injustice of this second type is found, where injustice is "institutionalized." In other words, injustice is built into economic, social, and political structures both national and international, causing people to suffer from poverty and hunger; from the unjust distribution of wealth, resources, and power.

It is almost certain that Ignatius did not only concern himself with injustices that were purely economic. He often cites injustices about "threats to human life and its quality," "racial and political discrimination," and loss of respect for the "rights of individuals or groups."[8] When one adds to these the "vast range of injustices" enumerated in his writings, one sees that the Ignatian vision understands its mission of justice to include "the widest possible view of justice," involving every area where there is an attack on human rights. We can conclude, therefore, that although Ignatius was to some degree concerned about commutative justice (right relationships between private persons and groups) and distributive justice (the obligations of the state to render to the individual what is his or her due), he was most concerned about what is generally called social justice, or "justice of the common good." Such justice is comprehensive; it includes the above strict legal rights and duties, but it is more concerned about the natural rights and duties of individuals, families, communities, and the community of nations toward one another as members of the human family. Every form of justice is included in and presupposed by social justice, but with social justice, it is the social nature of the person that is emphasized, as well as the social significance of all earthly goods, the purpose of which is to aid all members of the human community to attain their dignity as human beings. Many of Ignatius' followers believe that this dignity is being undermined in our world today, and their main efforts are aimed toward restoring that dignity.

In the pursuit of social justice, Ignatius calls on his followers to be "in solidarity with the poor." The next logical question might then be, who are the poor? The poor are usually thought to be those who are economically deprived and politically oppressed. Thus, we can conclude that the promotion of justice means to work to overcome the oppressions or injustices that cause poverty. The fallacy here, however, is that the poor are not necessarily oppressed or suffering injustice, and so Ignatius argues that our obligation toward the poor must be understood to be concerned with "inhuman levels of poverty and injustice." It is not primarily concerned with the "lot of those possessing only modest resources," even though those of modest means are often poor and oppressed. So, we conclude that the poor include those "wrongfully" impoverished or dispossessed.[9]

An extended definition of the poor, one that Ignatius would espouse, would include any of these types of people:

First would be those who are economically deprived and socially marginalized and oppressed, especially those with whom one has immediate contact and who one is in a position to assist.

The second group would include the "poor in spirit," that is, those who lack a value system or an ethical and moral sense.

The third group would include the emotionally poor; those who have psychological and emotional shortcomings and are in need of comfort.

In defining the poor in the broadest way, Ignatius exhorts us to undertake social change in our roles as leaders and followers, to do what we can do to bring an end to inequality, oppression, and injustice.

IMPLICATIONS FOR THE HEROIC FOLLOWER

Each of the principles of the Ignatian vision noted above has a variety of implications for heroic followers. The *magis* principle has implications for followers in that it calls for us to continually seek perfection in all that we do. In effect, this means that we must seek to continually improve. And, since improvement implies change, we need to be champions of needed change in our personal and professional lives. This means that we have to model a tolerance for change and embrace not only our own change initiatives but also those in other parts of the organization. An in-depth application of the Ignatian vision to the process of change will be discussed later.

The principle of *cura personalis* has additional implications. To practice the Ignatian vision, one must treat people with dignity under all circumstances. *Cura personalis* also requires us to extend ourselves in offering individual attention and attending to the needs of all those with whom we come in contact. Being sensitive to each individual's unique needs is particularly required. Many times in our efforts to treat people equally, we fail to treat them fairly and equitably. Certain individuals have greater needs than do others, and many times these needs require exceptions to be made on their behalf. For example, if an employee does not report to work on time, but the tardiness is because he or she is going through some personal trauma, the principle of *cura personalis* calls on us to make an exception in this case. It is likely that many would consider such an exception to be unfair to those who made the effort to report to work on time, or they might say that we cannot possibly be sensitive to the special needs of all of our colleagues. However, as long as the exception is made for anyone in the same circumstances, Ignatius would not perceive this exception as being unfair. In fact, the exception would be expected if one is practicing the principle of "care of the person."

The Ignatian process of *discernment* requires highly effective followers to be reflective practitioners. This is helpful in discovering our *purpose* in life. It calls on us to be introspective regarding our personal and professional behavior. We are asked to reflect on the ramifications of our decisions, especially in light of their cumulative effect on the equitable sharing of power and on the marginalized individuals and groups in our communities. In effect, the principle of discernment galvanizes the other principles embodied in the Ignatian vision. During the discernment process, we are asked to reflect upon how our planned behavior will manifest the *magis* principle, *cura personalis,* and service to the community, especially the underserved, marginalized, and oppressed.

The development of men and women for others requires the heroic follower to have a sense of service toward those with whom he or she interacts as well as to develop this spirit of service in others. The concept of "servant followership" requires us to encourage others toward a life and career of service and to assume the position of being the "servant of the servants." Ignatius thinks about leadership in terms of what the gospel writer Luke calls the "one who serves." The follower owes something to the institution in which he or she works. The follower is seen in this context as steward rather than owner or proprietor.

The implications of Ignatius' notion of social justice are myriad for the heroic follower. Being concerned about the marginalized among our peers is required. We are called to be sensitive to those individuals and groups that do not share equitably in the distribution of power and influence. Inclusion, respect for diversity, and collaborative behavior are encouraged among followers imbued with the Ignatian tradition. Equitable representation of all segments of society should be sought whenever feasible. Behavior such as this will assure that the dominant culture is not perpetuated to the detriment of the minority culture, rendering the minorities powerless.

Chris Lowney, who has written on the success of the formal followers of the Ignatian vision, the Jesuits, addresses the question of why are they so successful. How have they succeeded when so many other companies and organizations have long since failed? Lowney indicates that their success is due primarily to the adherence to these very principles. He further contends that in addition to these principles, the Jesuits focus on engendering four unique values that make them effective: self-awareness, ingenuity, love, and heroism. In other words, they train their novices to understand their strengths, weaknesses, and values; to have a worldview (self-awareness); to confidently innovate and adapt to a changing world (ingenuity); to engage others with a positive, loving attitude (love); and to energize themselves and others through heroic ambitions (heroism).[10]

According to Lowney, self-awareness is at the foundation of the four pillars of what it takes to be a heroic follower. The person who knows what he or she wants can pursue it energetically. No one becomes an accomplished person by accident. Only those individuals who know their weaknesses can cope with them and possibly conquer them. Individuals who have reached a plateau in their personal and professional development can resume an upward movement only by identifying and addressing their weaknesses. Thus, knowing thyself is fundamental if one is to become a heroic follower.

The road to becoming a highly effective follower, then, involves appreciating oneself as talented; identifying personal and professional baggage that prevents the realization of one's full potential, especially weaknesses that manifest themselves in the form of habits; articulating personally motivating goals and ambitions in the form of a mission statement that includes one's personal sense of the *magis*; determining what one believes in and what impact one wants to make; developing a worldview that guides interaction with others; and acquiring the habit of updating oneself on all of the above on a frequent, even daily, basis.

The second pillar that leads to personal success is the characteristic of ingenuity. Ingenuity is the readiness to cross the world at a moment's notice, as the Jesuits did and still do. It is the willingness to dream up new and imaginative approaches to challenges that have puzzled others. And it is the creative embracing of new paradigms and cultures. What distinguishes Jesuit ingenuity is not so much its characteristic behaviors: imagination, adaptability, creativity, flexibility, and the ability to respond rapidly are not new. However, the defining aspect of Jesuit ingenuity is that these priests have been trained to adopt the demeanor, attitudes, and worldview that make adaptability and creativity possible.

There are two vital ingredients to Jesuit ingenuity that are taught through Ignatius' *Spiritual Exercises.* One is indifference that frees followers from the prejudices, attachments, fears, and narrow-mindedness that can block the energetic pursuit of new opportunities. Secondly, the *Exercises'* final meditation, "The Contemplation to Attain Love," imbues the young priests with an optimistic vision of a work thoroughly inspired by divine love. Ingenuity blossoms when the personal freedom to pursue opportunities is integrated with a profound trust and optimism that the world is filled with such opportunities. Imagination, creativity, adaptability, and rapid response become the keys for finding and unlocking those opportunities.

Love is the next of the four pillars on which is built the Ignatian way of proceeding. When I was a young man who had just entered the teaching profession, I was also the varsity basketball coach. Like other coaches, I attended coaching clinics as a means to professional development. One year, I attended a clinic where the main clinicians were Dean Smith, former coach of North Carolina University, and Bobby Knight, then coach of Indiana University. Both coaches were successful then, and almost three decades later their reputations remain intact.

In the morning session, Bobby Knight explained how fear was the most effective motivator in sports. If you want your athletes to listen to you and you want to be successful, you need to instill fear in them. In the afternoon session, Dean Smith explained how love is the most effective motivator in sports and in life. If you want to win and be successful, you must engender love in the athletes.

You can understand my sense of confusion by the end of that clinic. Here were two of the most successful men in sports history giving contradictory advice. As a young and impressionable coach, I was puzzled by these apparently mixed messages. Over the intervening years, I have often thought about that clinic and tried to make sense of what I had heard. After these many years, I have drawn two conclusions from this incident, both of which have had a significant impact of my philosophy of life.

The first conclusion has to do with the situational nature of leadership. Bobby Knight and Dean Smith impressed upon me the truism that no one leadership style is effective at all times and in all situations. The second conclusion is that despite both styles reaping short-term success, the better style for ensuring long-term success is one that inspires love, trust, and respect. Just as athletes become robotic and fearful of making mistakes when fear is the motivator, so do employees who are supervised by an autocratic manager. Initiative, creativity, and self-sufficiency are all stymied by the leader who instills fear in his or her followers. Thus, I arrived at my conclusion that highly effective people instill love, trust, and respect in their peers and colleagues. Ignatius of Loyola preached this message more than four hundred years ago.

Ignatius exhorted his followers to behave "with greater love than fear." Francis Xavier, one of Ignatius' original followers, explained that "Society of Jesus means to say 'a Society of love and conformity of minds,' and not 'of severity and servile fear.'"[11] Jesuit records brim with such expressions indicating that love is the cornerstone of the Jesuit way of proceeding.

The last of the four pillars on which the Jesuit way of proceeding is based is personal heroism. But what is it about the Jesuit way of proceeding that convinces its members that they are contributing to the greatest enterprise in the world today? This is an especially intriguing question in light of the skepticism and cynicism exhibited by many followers in other organizations. How many times have you run across a nasty salesclerk, taxi driver, food server, teacher, or even a physician with a poor bedside manner? Haven't we repeatedly asked ourselves why these people seem so bitter? What is it in their personal or professional lives that causes them to be so unheroic? The answer may be that they lack, in their organizations or in their personal lives, the experiences that Jesuits routinely acquire.

First, the Jesuits invite new recruits to turn a corporate aspiration into a personal mission. Thus, such concepts as the *magis, cura personalis,* discernment, service to others, and a concern for social justice become internalized. Second, the Jesuits create a company culture that stresses heroism, modeling the virtue themselves. Virtually all of them could easily be in another company that would provide them with greater material rewards. Third, the Jesuits leaders give each person an opportunity to enlarge himself by contributing meaningfully to an enterprise greater than his own interests. This includes opportunities to further their education and engage in apostolates that satisfy their self-actualization needs. They believe in the words of Frederick Herzberg, the famous behavioral psychologist, who observed that one cannot motivate anyone to do a good job unless he or she has a good job to do.

THE MISSION

Ordinarily, the way one states one's *purpose* in life is in the form of a mission or mission statement. The mission statement can serve as a roadmap, even an inspiration, to individuals to make choices that lead to excellence. Research studies indicate that there are several benefits to having a formal personal and professional mission. These benefits include having a sense of commitment, having a clear value framework for making consistent judgments and decisions, and providing a systematic way of living one's life.

Developiing a sense of mission may take years, but the benefits to any individual or organization will far outweigh the investment of time and energy expended in the initial process of defining the purpose of one's life. M. J. Wheatley indicates the significance of a sense of mission or purpose when she writes, "No person or organization can be an effective cocreator with its environment without clarity about who it is intending to become."[12] She elaborates on the importance of a purpose in life, indicating that without a clear mission individuals are tossed and turned with every shift in the environment. She equates creating a clear purpose or mission with creating a power in the individual. Congruency is important and messages matched by behavior must permeate though the individual as a vital influence. Wheatley insists that stability in an individual comes from a deepening center, a clarity about who he or she is. When the individual knows who he or she is, what one's strengths are, and what one is trying to accomplish, the person can respond intelligently to changes in the environment. Finally, she proposes that the individual with a clear purpose is one of integrity where words will be seen, not just heard.

The heroic follower of today and the future will be able to mobilize people around his or her mission, making it a powerful force in uncertain times. A clear mission will allow the individual to experience autonomy and significance in one's environment. The success or effectiveness of any individual can be measured against the specific statement of purpose in the form of goals and objectives. Through a consistent focus on mission, the followers gives their dispersed and diverse peers a clear sense of direction and the opportunity to find meaning in their lives.

Pfeffer goes a step further, emphasizing the importance of the maturation of the mission to implementation. Success comes from successfully implementing strategies, not just having them. Successful followers understand the importance of implementation, not just strategy; moreover, they recognize the crucial roles of others in the process. Implementation capability derives in large measure from how followers are treated, their skills and competencies, and their efforts in consciously adhering to their personal missions. Therefore, a people-centered strategy on the part of an organization will allow a climate of trust to develop that encourages individuals to implement both their own personal missions and that of the organization. Organizations with integrity are those where each person is trusted to work deeply with those principles it values, to interpret them, learn from them, talk about them, and, through many interactions, develop an emerging pattern of ethical behavior.[13]

It is important to note that many authors write of the essential component of establishing a climate of trust within the organization as a foundational requirement to implementing a shared mission. A personal mission statement can provide this same sense of integrity to the individual. There are at least three types of trust within an organization or an individual:

1. *Disclosure trust* is the belief that information shared between manager and employer or between individuals will not be used to hurt either party. This type of trust deals with values, beliefs, attitudes, and feelings.
2. *Contractual trust* is the belief that words, promises, and verbal or written agreements between a manager and employee (or between two individuals) can be depended upon. This type of trust can be described as reliability.
3. *Privacy trust* is the belief that neither the person nor the personal information of either an employee or manager will be violated.

These individuals will not invade the privacy of another or harm them in any way. This type of trust addresses honesty and respect for each other.[14]

THE ELEMENTS OF MISSION

Campbell and Tawadey propose that mission is comprised of four elements: purpose, strategy, values, and behavior standards. The organization or individual that defines a purpose is inspiring and worthy of the support of its stakeholders or peers. The stakeholders or peers then join the purpose by giving their loyalty to the organization or individual. In return, the peer needs to define what he or she expects to gain from the relationship. The description of the inspiring purpose avoids playing to the selfish interest of the stakeholders; it is for a high ideal, the good of society. With the higher ideal as the purpose, an organization or an individual is able to gain cooperation of all its peers to the same cause or purpose, and rivalry between peers is reduced because all individuals can more readily bond around a commonly understood sense of mission.

Campbell and Tawadey identify strategy as the commercial rationale for how the individual or organization is going to achieve its purpose or mission. The mission describes the central elements of the strategy explaining an environmental domain and why this purpose is attractive as well as identifying the advantage that it will provide.

These researchers describe the values as the beliefs of the individual or organization that have a moral base, the founding stones of the corporate or individual "religion." They are hard to articulate because they are assumptions that lie behind many of one's rules and behavior standards. The mission statement identifies values that link with the individual's purpose, act as beliefs that the individual can feel proud of, and reinforce the individual's strategies. Choosing values that have the highest priority is an essential part of developing a mission.

The fourth element of mission is behavior standards. Mission is only made real when it affects behavior or when it guides people's actions, helping them to decide what to do and what not to do. The mission should clearly describe important behavior standards that serve as reasons for the strategy and the values. These behavior standards should be described in such a way that enables individuals to judge whether they have behaved correctly.[15]

DEVELOPING A PERSONAL MISSION STATEMENT

The highly effective follower needs to begin with an end in mind. Thus, the heroic follower needs a sense of *purpose.* This notion requires one to create and apply a personal mission statement as a constitution for daily living. The heroic follower must envision the desired results and important values to guide her or his activities or endeavors. Many people gain a sense of who they are from the opinions, perceptions, and paradigms of the people around them. Through this type of social learning, they mold who they are and what they achieve. The most effective people, however, determine their own future. Instead of letting others determine their destinies, they plan and implement their own results. What they have in their mind shapes their future. These people develop their own personal mission statement and set of goals. They may do it informally, but they do it nonetheless.

In one's daily life, mission statements are invaluable. If you know what you want to accomplish in a meeting, for example, you can define the purpose of the meeting, enabling the participants to focus on the intended goals. Likewise, if you are preparing a speech, you may write down what you want the audience to do as a result of having listened to you and keep this goal in perspective as you develop your speech. In considering these examples, the need for a mission statement or having a purpose in mind is obvious.

A personal mission statement is a powerful document that expresses your personal sense of purpose and meaning in life. It acts as a governing constitution by which you evaluate decisions and choose behaviors. The process of writing a mission statement allows us to reevaluate our old paradigms and create new ones based on our values. Creating a personal mission statement involves as much discovery as it does creation. We envision and explore our future using the endowments of introspection, imagination, conscience, and free will.[16]

A personal mission statement encourages you to think deeply about your life and helps you examine your innermost thoughts and feelings.

It allows you to clearly articulate what is important to you. It expands your perspective and imprints self-determined values and purposes firmly in your mind. It provides direction and commitment to values and enables you to make daily progress toward long-term goals.

Beginning with a sense of purpose is a habit of mental creation, the plan, and the definition of who we want to be and what we want to do. By defining a purpose before we begin, we increase our quality of life as we determine our course and work toward our planned destination. With a purpose in mind, we are more likely to arrive at that destination.

As we develop our value system and set goals to operationalize it, we are constantly reinventing ourselves, replacing ineffective patterns of thought and behavior with effective ones. Reinventing is a habit of deliberate awareness and mental creation backed by clear intention. Some people center their decisions on work, pleasure, friends, enemies, spouse, self, church, or material things, but if we focus exclusively on any one of these courses, we empower circumstances to direct and control us.

Principles are part of human conscience. When people make decisions based on principles or values, the decisions are usually wise ones which increase their happiness and well-being. Principled people divorce themselves from the emotion of a situation and make proactive choices after discerning all of the alternatives. Therefore, every mission statement answers at least two questions: Why am I here? And upon what principles do I base my life?

The first question reveals some fundamental personal issues. It asks that we examine our public, private, and deep inner lives and define what character traits, contributions, and achievements we value. As part of the process, we should list desired results. The second question asks us to determine the principles and values whereby the mission can be accomplished. What lies behind every individual is not as important as what lies within and ahead of that person.

Writing a mission statement is a pilgrimage in self-discovery. It serves as a way to discover one's purpose, to uncover one's talents, interests, and desires. The personal traits of self-awareness, imagination, conscience, and free will can help in the process.

Another important consideration in developing a personal mission statement is the role(s) one plays in life (employee, parent, spouse, etc.). Within each role, goals define what we want to achieve. Goals are the basis for weekly and daily planning. These goals should be integrated into one's personal mission statement.

Writing a personal mission statement, then, involves addressing the things that are important to you. What are the things that you want that are really important—tangible, like a house, and intangible, like a happy family life? Ask yourself: What is the meaning of my life? What talents do I have and how do I want to use them? What are the ethical and moral characteristics that I want to exhibit? Who has served as a positive role model for me? What characteristics does this person have that I would like to emulate? What is the legacy that I want to leave? Think of the roles that you play in life (employee, mother, sister, grandparent, friend, etc.) and how you want to be perceived in each of these roles, By systematically addressing these questions, you can develop your own personal mission statement.

EXAMPLES OF MISSION STATEMENTS

A typical personal mission statement might read as follows:

Our Family Mission

The mission of our family is to create a nurturing place of order, love, happiness, and relaxation, and to provide opportunities for each person to become responsibly independent and effectively interdependent, in order to achieve worthwhile purposes.

Other examples are:

My Personal Mission

I will work to develop the courage to speak my mind and stand by my principles. Since I am approaching retirement age and will have more time available, I will inform, educate, and mentor those who have not had the experience in life and the careers that I have had. I will use my additional leisure time to return to a more creative life. I will devote more attention to the support and nurturing of my daughter and my grandchildren. I will become a catalyst for bringing together friends and family on a more regular basis. Although I will not be spending as much time in my professional life, I will seek to understand criticism instead of being defensive and try to engage in a win/win approach to resolving conflicts. I will continue to volunteer for charitable organizations and not thrive on any recognition but be very altruistic in my service. I will seek to learn more about my faith and be more in touch with my spirituality.

My Mission Statement

To live my life ever aware that who I am is as much what others see as it is what I believe.

To live my life without excessive indulgences, aware that my mind and my body are my true assets.

To love my family with many indulgences, aware that they are my only treasure.

To deal with others with honesty and integrity, tolerance and compassion, equity and consideration.

To dedicate my remaining years to helping others find purpose in their lives, ensuring that my influence on others is consistent with my values and principles.

To teach others that which I believe to be right in both the personal and professional arenas, yet never presume that my way in the only way.

To live my life on purpose and with purpose, and to use my full potential.

DEVELOPING A VISION STATEMENT

Many times, it is helpful to individuals to "summarize" their mission statements into a personal vision statement. Mission statements often contain so many concepts that one is hard-pressed to remember them all. And if one cannot remember all of the concepts in one's mission statement, the likelihood of integrating them into one's daily life is not high. This is why a shortened version of a mission statement in the form of a vision statement can be very helpful. One can develop a *personal* vision statement and/or a *professional* vision statement.

Suppose you were a principal of a school. How would you develop a professional vision statement? Although there seems to be a sense of mystery on the part of some regarding what a vision statement is, the process for developing one is not all that complex. The first step is to develop a list of broad goals or purposes. In the case of our school principal example, "All Children Achieving" is an example of such a goal or purpose. These goals should be developed in conjunction with representatives of each segment of the school community, who, along with you, have to achieve these goals. Developing them alone will not encourage "ownership" by the entire school community and will, therefore, endanger their successful implementation.

The next step in the process is to merge and prioritize the goals and to summarize them in the form of a short and concise vision statement, which might read like the following:

> Our vision for the Exeter School is that all of our graduating students, regardless of ability, will say, "I have received an excellent education that has prepared me to be an informed citizen and leader in my community." Our students will have a worldview and, as a result of their experience in the Exeter School, will be committed to a process of lifelong learning and the making of a better world by living the ideals of fairness and justice through service to others.

The key concepts in the above vision are: *all students achieving, excellence, leadership, multiculturalism, lifelong learning, values, and community service.* It is this limited number of concepts that all members of this school community need to have on their minds as they go about their daily activities. With this limited number of concepts, it is more likely that they will be constantly on their minds and truly guide their actions. This same process can be used in developing one's own *personal* vision.

THE IMPORTANCE OF GOALS AND OBJECTIVES

A flowery and nebulously worded mission statement is useless unless accompanied by clearly understood goals, objectives, and strategies. Thus, it is important to develop a list of goals, objectives, and strategies based on your personal and professional mission statement. This process can take the form of a strategic plan to operationalize your mission statement.

The strategic planning process should be understood as a dynamic ebb and flow of events in the life of an individual or institution. The so-called chaos theory tells us that life is a process, constantly changing and evolving. Therefore, it should not be surprising to see that some of the best-laid plans become obsolete before they see the light of day. Mirror Lake, for example, is slowly drying up and evolving into a meadow. If you were planning strategically, you would do well to buy your grandchild a kite rather than a boat if he or she lived near Mirror Lake.

The moral of the story, therefore, is to plan for the unexpected as well as the expected. Even though your quality of life may currently be prosperous and healthy, the only way to sustain this success is to plan for the possibility of difficult times. How do we know that the unexpected will eventually occur? One need only look at history.

What prevents us from planning accurately is our paradigm for how things are. We want to find order when the reality is chaos. We like to think that events occur in a linear way; this is how we have been trained. The positivistic view leads us to believe that we can accurately predict outcomes. The reality is that events occur in sporadic and unpredictable ways. Our charge, then, is to find order in this apparent chaos. Thus, we must see our plans as constantly evolving and changing. The process is ongoing. The plans themselves change so frequently that they are of limited value. Dwight Eisenhower aptly pointed out that: "planning is all, but plans are nothing." The primacy of the planning process over the plan itself is a notion that the astute follower will constantly keep in mind.

So let us look at the planning process. Strategic planning is a process that was first developed and refined in business and industry, but has been adopted by a variety of individuals and institutions throughout the nation. Strategic planning begins with the development of a mission or vision statement. Goals and objectives are derived from the mission, and strategies are developed for achieving them. It is common practice to create a task force composed of representatives from all levels of the organization to develop a strategic plan. For an individual, it is also a good idea to seek input in developing such a plan. The process must look forward into the future.

As we have seen, the process of developing a mission statement involves establishing a strong consensus about our unique purposes in life. Many times the mission needs to be revised to adapt to current realities before the process can continue.

The mission statement, then, must be developed through discussion among the various constituencies that make up the heroic follower's environment, be an outgrowth of a discussion of unique individual and peer purposes, and reflect the unique character of the individual. The vision statement of the individual is derived from the mission statement. It is often a concise summary of the mission.

The individual should next develop a set of goals and objectives that he or she deems appropriate in the context of the mission. Goals are more specific and give direction to the action that needs to take place to achieve them. The goals should be expressed in terms that promote easy assessment. It should be clear to an objective observer whether the goals have been achieved. Thus, the goals, objectives, and strategies should be increasingly more behavioral, that is, they should be measurable, make someone accountable for their attainment, and provide a timeline for their completion. It is hoped that the mission and goals of the highly effective follower will reflect his or her values and ideals.

The strategic planning process is completed by operationalizing or implementing the plan, evaluating its effectiveness, and institutionalizing it or making it part of the heroic follower's identity or character.

A PERSONAL/PROFESSIONAL STRATEGIC PLAN

Using some of the concepts contained in the mission statements mentioned earlier, the beginnings of a *professional* strategic plan might read as follows:

Goal: Being recognized as being competent at my job.

> *Objective I*: To be thoroughly prepared for each day's activities

>> *Strategy I*: I will set aside thirty minutes each night to review my activities of the day and prepare for tomorrow.

>> *Strategy II*: I will do so through the lens of the Ignatian vision:

     a. the *magis* (always seeking "the more")
     b. discernment
     c. *cura personalis* (care of the person)
     d. service to others
     e. social justice (service to the underserved and underrepresented)

The following is the beginning of a *personal* strategic plan:

Goal: Being of service to those in need

    Objective I: To dedicate as much of my spare time as reasonable to organizations that help those in need.

        Strategy I: To maintain membership in two charitable organizations (e.g., Red Cross, Breast Health Institute).

        Strategy II: To participate in organizing at least two fund-raisers in each of these organizations per year.

        Strategy III: To attend at least four fund-raising events each year.

        Strategy IV: To contribute 5% of my after-tax income to these and other charitable organizations.

    Objective II: To be available to attend to the needs of my immediate and extended family.

        Strategy I: To babysit for my grandchildren whenever possible.

        Strategy II: To act as power of attorney for my aging bachelor uncle.

        Strategy III: To devote as much time as is feasible to be a caregiver to my invalid mother-in-law.

Notice that each of the strategies above complies with the standards of measurability, accountability, and timelines. Also, these are only partial examples of goals, objectives, and strategies. A full-blown strategic plan would contain a number of objectives and as many as ten strategies under each objective. This may seem like a tedious task, but if one wishes to set him- or herself apart from other followers, it is this kind of attention to detail that will do so.

THE ACT OF SUB-MISSION

We have suggested that one way for the heroic follower to operational-ize a sense of purpose is to develop a professional and personal mission statement. At times, however, it is necessary to subjugate one's own mission to that of one's family or the workplace. In these instances, the heroic follower will be practicing submission or, for emphasis, *sub-mission*.

The word *submission* literally means to substitute another priority for one's own priority. Thus, sub-mission should occur when the common good is better served by subjugating one's own personal or professional mission to that of another. For example, if your personal mission includes continuing your education in order to be upwardly mobile and to prepare yourself to take advantage of any promotion opportunities that arise, but your wife is suddenly diagnosed with breast cancer, your personal mission may need to be compromised in order to provide time for you to be a caregiver for your wife. Similarly, if your professional mission statement has you advancing in your company at the local level, but the company needs your expertise at a plant in another geographical location, the heroic follower may choose sub-mission of his or her own goals in deference to those of the company.

CONCLUSION

The heroic follower needs to begin with an end in mind. To be highly effective, the follower should develop a sense of purpose. This sense of purpose is normally operationalized through a personal and professional mission statement. One's mission statement is further refined into a vision statement. The follower's mission and vision are best realized through one's personal and professional strategic plan. The strategic plan consists of goals, objectives, and strategies that are progressively more measurable and accountable, and that contain reasonable time-lines. The purpose (in the form of a mission statement) is the foundation on which the framework is built for a follower to develop into a heroic follower. However, a sense of purpose is just the beginning. Realizing one's purpose in life requires other habits or traits like commitment, adaptability, attention to detail, and communication in the form of building community.

At the heart of the heroic follower is the characteristic of commitment. Every generation has witnessed a core group of individuals who have shown remarkable determination to attain their goals and make a difference in the world. It started with the English colonists who struggled to sustain their small flocks of colonial settlers in the midst of overwhelming odds. And it continues today in the constant struggle to keep our dreams and aspirations alive in an often hostile and uninviting environment.

A second important habit or characteristic is adaptability. The success of individuals in reaching their goals has often been assured by the willingness of these folks to change their plans in accordance with and in response to an ever-changing environment. Successful followers realized early on that a rigid, doctrinaire ideology was a recipe for failure. By combining many of the effective elements of the old with the creative elements of the new, highly effective followers not only survive but, in fact, flourish.

A third important habit is attention: in particular, attention to detail. Heroic followers are known for seeking perfection in the form of the *magis* (the more) in everything that they do, both at the personal and professional levels. This attention to detail is emblematic of highly effective followers and is one reason that they tend to stand out among their peers. For example, if one is an administrative aid in a school, simple things like following up on absentees to make sure that they have parental or physician approval for the absence, and checking attendance every class period of the day to be sure that students are not truant even for one class, are examples of the attention to detail that is intrinsic to heroic followers. This kind of strict attention is often lacking in their less effective peers.

A fourth characteristic, and one that James Coleman's research indicates may be the most important one, is community. Coleman conducted his studies on community on public versus nonpublic schools. He found that nonpublic schools, for example, have always reflected the goals, aspirations, and even the prejudices and fears of the neighborhoods that supported them. The principals and teachers in these schools are often drawn from the very neighborhood in which the school resides. Public school teachers, on the contrary, often lived outside the neighborhoods where they taught, and a school superintendent or a school committee "downtown" established the curriculum and procedures. In addition, nonpublic school parents were in basic agreement as to what they wanted and expected from their schools, whereas the pluralistic nature of public schools often militates against commonly accepted goals. Thus, according to Coleman, a constant flow of communication creates a sense of community that, in turn, allows nonpublic school students to achieve at a higher level than their public school counterparts, even after income variables are taken into account. Similarly, highly effective followers are able to communicate in such a way as to build a community of other followers and increase their effectiveness. We will discuss these additional habits of highly effective followers in succeeding chapters. [17]

DIAGNOSTIC CHECKLIST

Here are a few questions you can address to assess your sense of *purpose*:

1. Have you developed your own personal and professional *mission statement*?
2. Have you further delineated it into a *vision statement*?
3. Have you developed a personal and professional *strategic plan* based on your mission statement?
4. Are the goals and objectives in your plan *measurable* and do they have *timelines*?

NOTES

1. G. Bogart, *Finding Your Life's Calling* (Berkeley, CA: Dawn Mountain Press, 1999).

2. Denise B. Wing, Educating as a vocation: Letting their lives speak (doctoral dissertation, Saint Joseph's University, October 2004), 36.

3. Gregory Jones, Vocation, *Christian Century* (1990): 716–718.

4. Abraham Maslow, *Motivation and Personality* (New York: Addison-Wesley, 1970).

5. Andre Ravier, SJ, *Ignatius of Loyola and the Founding of the Society of Jesus* (San Francisco: Ignatius Press, 1987).

6. Martin R. Tripole, SJ, *Faith Beyond Justice* (St. Louis: Institute of Jesuit Sources, 1994).

7. Jules J. Toner, SJ, *Discerning God's Will: Ignatius of Loyola's Teaching on Christian Decision Making* (St. Louis: The Institute of Jesuit Sources, 1991).

8. Christopher Chapple, *The Jesuit Tradition in Education and Missions* (Scranton, PA: University of Scranton Press, 1993).

9. *Documents of the 34th General Congregation of the Society of Jesus* (St. Louis: Institute of Jesuit Sources, 1995).

10. Chris Lowney, *Heroic Leadership* (Chicago: Loyola Press, 2003).

11. Chris Lowney, *Heroic Leadership*, p. 113.

12. M. J. Wheatley, *Leadership and the New Science: Discovering Order in a Chaotic World* (San Francisco: Berett-Koehler Publishers, 1999).

13. J. Pfeffer, *Managing with Power: Politics and Influence in Organizations* (Boston: Harvard Business Press, 1992).

14. Lynn Giambri, Administrator and staff perceptions of the leadership role in the effective operationalization of the mission of the 21st century Christian school (doctoral dissertation, Saint Joseph's University, 2003).

15. A. Campbell and K. Tawadey, *Mission and Business Philosophy: Winning Employee Commitment* (Oxford: Heinemann Professional Publishing, 1990).

16. Stephen Covey, *Seven Habits of Highly Effective People* (New York: Free Press, 1990).

17. James Coleman, Thomas Haffer, and S. Kilgore, *High School Achievement: Public, Catholic and Private Schools Compared* (New York: Basic Books, 1982).

3

IT'S NOT ALWAYS
THE TEACHER'S FAULT!

One's philosophy is not best expressed in words; it's expressed in the choices one makes. In the long run, we shape our lives and we shape ourselves. The process never ends until we die. And the choices we make are ultimately our responsibility.

—Eleanor Roosevelt

The second habit heroic followers need to develop is a sense of responsibility or accountability. Much of this development process involves developing an internal locus of control. If a teacher gives an examination at the end of a unit of study and a particular student scores very poorly in the test, the student can react in one of two ways. The student can blame it on the teacher, believing that if the teacher had delivered the lesson in a better way, the student would have done better in the test. This view, of course, would demonstrate an external locus of control—the most common locus in our society. Or, the student could react by believing that if he or she studied harder, the student would have done better on the examination. In this case, the student is holding him or herself accountable for the behavior and is displaying an internal locus of control. Heroic followers tend to display the latter, more responsible behavior.

ORGANIZATIONAL BEHAVIOR

In order to gain an insight into what it takes to develop the habit of being responsible or accountable for one's own behavior, we can look at how an internal locus of control is developed within the culture of an organization. I have visited schools where principals argue that the only things that tie their schools together are the marching band, the athletic program, and a common concern for parking. Employees of other organizations and institutions voice similar sentiments. The truth, however, is that the organizational behavior or *culture* of the organization is the tie that truly binds.

Organizational culture is composed of the shared beliefs, expectations, values, and norms of conduct of its members. In any organization, the informal culture interacts with the formal organizational structure and control system to produce a generally clear understanding of the "way things are done around here." Even more than the forces of bureaucracy, the organization's culture is the glue that binds people together. It is through this culture that our images of reality are shaped, often in an unconscious manner.

COMPONENTS OF CULTURE

In determining the nature of organizational culture, we can analyze its components: beliefs, expectations, and shared values; heroes and heroines; myths and stories; rituals and ceremonies and the physical arrangements in the organization. Basic organizational philosophy reflects the beliefs, expectations, and shared values of its leaders. Together these drive the organization toward its goals. Basic beliefs—which influence employee behavior and attitudes, define success for employees, and establish standards of achievement—may be a function of the requirements of the milieu in which the organization functions as well as of its national culture.

Heroes and heroines transmit culture by personifying its corporate values. Leaders viewed in this way reinforce the basic values of an organization's culture by providing role models, symbolizing their organization to the outside world, preserving the organization's special qualities, setting a standard of performance, motivating employees, and making success attainable and human. Managers who create heroes and heroines foster a set of corporate values that may stabilize the current organization or expedite change. We are all familiar with the long-time respected faculty member who fulfills this role in a school, the super salesperson in a car agency, or the founding CEO of a company.[1]

Myths, in this context, are stories about institutional heroes and heroines that facilitate the transmission and embedding of culture. What does the repeated telling of a story about the spectacular rise in standardized test scores under a certain principal tell you about a school's culture? Does a story about a school's success in sports under a certain principal give the same impression and reflect the same culture? The themes of such stories provide clues to an organization's culture.

Ceremonies such as retirement dinners or employee-of-the-month awards contribute to organizational culture by dramatizing the organization's basic values; for example, the award of a pin for twenty-five years of service reflects a company that values loyalty. Often linked with a corresponding organizational story, such events can provide an explanation of new behavior patterns. Such ceremonies can also act as rites of passage, delineating entry into an organization's inner circle. They can also expedite transitions in leadership, such as the inauguration of a new college president.

The selection and arrangement of offices and furnishings often reveal significant insight into an institution's culture. Compare the school, for example, that provides only a mail slot for its teachers to one that offers shared office space and telephones to its faculty. How might the cultures of these two schools differ? How could the physical arrangements in an organization cultivate teamwork? The way an institution addresses these issues helps define its culture.

THE PROCESSES OF ORGANIZATIONAL BEHAVIOR

We will now explore areas of organizational behavior that deal with the way we perceive events or other people; the way we understand the events and people we perceive; the way our past experiences and acquisition of knowledge and information influence this description and diagnosis; and the way we form attitudes based on our perceptions, understanding, and experience. These four processes are referred to as perception, attribution, learning, and attitude formation. Understanding them greatly enhances a highly effective follower's ability to assimilate into the organization's culture and develop a sense of responsibility in him- or herself and others.

Perception is the process by which each person senses reality and comes to a particular understanding or view. It is an active process that results in different people having somewhat different, even contradictory, views or understandings of the same event or person. Rarely do different observers describe events or persons in exactly the same way. Often administrators and their subordinates, coworkers, or supervisors see and describe the same situation differently.

Perceptions sometimes suffer from inaccuracies or distortions. Although such biases are normal and human, they can have significant consequences when administrators or other members of the institution base actions upon potentially invalid distortions. We will discuss stereotyping, the halo effect, projection, and the self-fulfilling prophecy as examples. Additional distortions include suppression, repression, denial, displacement, and rationalization.[2]

Stereotyping occurs when an individual attributes behaviors or attitudes to a person based on the group or category to which that person belongs. "Women teachers can't control a class" and "Administrators are all dictators" illustrate stereotyping. We frequently stereotype according to ethnicity, race, gender, and class.

Why does stereotyping occur? Often, individuals do not gather enough information about others to describe their behaviors or attitudes accurately. So these individuals may look for shortcuts to describe certain phenomenon without spending the time to analyze those phenomenon completely. Alternatively, some individuals have personal biases against certain groups. Historical attitudes toward certain cultural groups may result in stereotypes. Americans may have certain views of Europeans and different views of Japanese, based on their historical experiences with the two groups. Using stereotypes reduces the accuracy of our perceptions about these groups.

The halo effect refers to an individual's letting one salient feature of a person dominate the evaluation of that individual. For example, a supervisor might evaluate an employee who is willing to volunteer for extra projects as having the attitude necessary to be a leader. A neat personal appearance can cause a person to be judged as precise and very well-organized.

The halo effect frequently occurs in assessments of employee performance. Individuals may be judged on the basis of one trait, for example, promptness, neatness, or enthusiasm, rather than on a composite of traits and skills demonstrated over a period of time.[3]

Have you ever heard someone say, "My boss is prejudiced," "My supervisor doesn't like women," or "My father doesn't like minorities"? These observations about these individuals may be accurate, but they may also be a reflection of the observer's prejudices.

Projection refers to an individual's attributing his or her own attitudes or feelings to another person. Individuals use projection as a defense mechanism, to transfer blame to another person or to provide protection from their own unacceptable feelings. Individuals frequently attribute their own prejudices against minorities, supervisors, or employees, for example, to the other party. Hence, projection and its dysfunctional consequences can increase as the work force becomes more diverse; individuals who lack understanding or mistrust people who are different from themselves may project these insecurities onto others.

Projection involves an emotional biasing of perceptions. Fear, hatred, uncertainty, anger, love, deceit, or distrust may influence an individual's perceptions. In union-management relations, for example, each side attributes feelings of mistrust to the other side. Management might state that the union mistrusts them, when, in fact, it is management that mistrusts the union. They project their own feelings onto the other group, representing them as that other group's feelings.

In many situations, some participants expect certain behaviors from other participants. They then see these behaviors as occurring whether or not they actually do. Their expectations become self-fulfilling prophecies. They may expect workers to be lazy, bossy, or tardy; then they perceive they actually *are* lazy, bossy, or tardy. These expectations may be associated with stereotyping, the halo effect, or projection.

Our expectations influence and bias our perceptions of others, reducing their accuracy; they also have been shown to influence the performance of those of whom we have expectations. We are all familiar with the many studies that have linked teacher expectations and student achievement. If a teacher expects a minority student to fail, oftentimes the student does fail. In contrast, if a teacher expects all children to achieve, the children usually achieve.

DEALING WITH DISTORTIONS

How can we reduce dysfunctional perceptual distortions in organizations? First, individuals must gather sufficient information about other people's behavior and attitudes to encourage more realistic perceptions. Supervisors, for example, must judge an individual's performance on his or her observed behavior, rather than on the behavior of a group to which the person belongs. Second, highly effective followers must check conclusions they draw to ensure their validity. Third, they must differentiate between facts and assumptions in determining the basis of their perceptions. Fourth, they must distinguish among various aspects of an individual's behavior, rather than grouping even superficially related aspects. They must separate appearance from performance, productivity from attendance, personality from creativity. Fifth, to eliminate or reduce projection, individuals must first identify their own true feelings. Do they feel anger, uncertainty, and mistrust? After recognizing these feelings, administrators must repeatedly assess whether and how those feelings are influencing their perceptions of others.

PERCEPTION IN A MULTICULTURAL ENVIRONMENT

Cultural differences exist in how individuals process information. They affect the cognitive map, or the content and structure of the schemata used to understand the environment and influence behavior. They affect the stimuli we select to perceive, the way we organize them, and how we interpret them. Our cultural background may cause us to distort our perceptions in predictable or unpredictable ways.[4]

Cross-cultural misperceptions occur for at least four reasons. First, we have subconscious cultural blinders that cause us to interpret events in other countries and other cultures as if they were occurring in our own. Second, we lack a complete understanding of even our own culture and its influence on our behavior. Third, we assume people are more similar to us than they are. Finally, our parochialism and general lack of knowledge about other cultures contribute to our misperceptions. An awareness of these differences can help us consider and represent the perspectives of several different observers when we describe events or people. If we can incorporate many people's perceptions into an account of a person or event, our description should be more accurate than if we attend only to our own perceptions. To act responsibly is to understand the process of perception, to avoid perceptual distortions in oneself, and to expose them when they arise in others.

THE ATTRIBUTION PROCESS

The need to determine why events occur is a common one and is inherent in the diagnostic approach that individuals often take toward problem solving. Many of us, whether consciously or not, first ponder the reasons for many events and then decide why the events occurred. In this way, we attribute causes to the events. We move from description to diagnosis. As might be expected, different people often attribute a different cause to the same event.

Attribution theorists and researchers have studied the process of determining the causes of specific events, the responsibility for particular outcomes, and the personal qualities of individuals participating in the situation. One researcher has suggested that this process occurs in three stages. First, we observe, or are told about, another person's action. Second, having identified the action, we determine whether the observed behavior was intended or accidental. Did the change in performance occur on purpose, or did it just happen by accident? For example, if we assume that a decline in a company's stock prices occurred accidentally, we will attribute its causes to fate, luck, accident, or a similar uncontrollable phenomenon. If, however, we assume that the decline was intended or controllable, we then move to stage 3. We question whether situational causes or personal characteristics explain the behavior. We might consider, for example, that the new product line was the major explanation of the change in performance; if so, we will attribute the decline to situational factors. If, on the other hand, we feel that laziness or ineptitude influenced performance, then we are likely to conclude that personal dispositions motivated the change. Although both situational and personal factors may have influenced the change in performance, we often simplify our understanding and attend primarily to only one cause.

ACHIEVEMENT, ATTRIBUTIONS, AND AFFECT

According to Abraham Maslow and other motivational theorists, we are all born with a need to achieve. Heroic followers will have a greater need to achieve than their peers. Performance is the visible indicator of achievement motivation, but performance is supported by a complex system of not-so-visible thoughts and feelings. When we succeed or fail at a task, we naturally think about who or what was behind our success or failure. We look to assign responsibility, to understand the cause of our performance. That is, we make *attributions* about who or what was responsible for how we performed. These attributions are systematically related to feeling good, bad, or indifferent after we succeed or fail. That is, attributions have affective or emotional consequences. Because our attributions influence both our subsequent behavior and our feelings, we need to be aware and knowledgeable of them.

We can classify attributions along three dimensions: the source of control, stability, and controllability. The locus (source) of control can be internal or external. If you say you sold a used car because of your ability as a salesperson, you are attributing your success to an internal characteristic—your ability. If you believe that you sold the car because of its quality and style, you are attributing your success to an external factor—the car.

Stability, or the lack of it, is another characteristic of attributions. That is, some attributions refer to a temporary factor, relating only to a specific task; others refer to more lasting factors, relating to a series of tasks. Suppose you lose your job. An unstable attribution might refer to your lack of effort ("I didn't apply myself as well as I could have that particular day"); a stable attribution might refer to perceived discrimination on the part of the supervisor ("My supervisor is known to be tough on everybody").[5]

Attributions also vary along a dimension called controllability. If you feel, for example, that the difficulty of the task was responsible for your failure ("I didn't do well because I didn't have my own office to work out of"), you are describing a cause that is beyond your control. If you feel that you did not do well because you did not put in the proper amount of effort, you are attributing your failure to a factor that you can control.

How we classify attributions can affect our performance on future tasks, If you believe a failure is controllable (for example, the result of lack of effort), you may be spurred on by that failure to do better next time. If you believe, however, that you cannot control the cause of the failure, you may not even try to improve your performance. Failure itself, then, is not harmful, but attributing failure to causes over which you have no control is harmful and is not a characteristic or habit of the heroic follower. The heroic follower takes *responsibility* for his or her own behavior and performance.

CAUSAL ATTRIBUTION PATTERNS

The research on attributions reveals that only a small number of categories are regularly used by individuals to account for their successes and failures—effort, ability, mood, task difficulty, and luck. We also know from a metanalysis of dozens of studies that adults usually hold to an egotistic attribution system. That is, they ordinarily attribute success to internal factors and failure to external factors. But some individuals do not use this ego-maintaining strategy. These individuals who attribute failure to lack of ability come to expect failure regularly. Because they expect to fail because of lack of ability, these individuals shy away from challenging tasks. Obviously, this is not a productive characteristic for these individuals.

In addition to attributing failure to an internal characteristic like lack of ability, some individuals also attribute their success to external characteristics like good luck. With this kind of attribution for success, these individuals cannot find any sensible reasons to make a great effort to succeed in their work. Therefore, these attribution patterns can be considered maladaptive. Unfortunately, we find these maladaptive attribution patterns most prevalently among the marginalized in our society, for example, minority groups, the poor, the disabled, and women.

Those who most often attribute their success or failure to their own behavior are said to have an internal locus of control. Those who do the opposite are considered to have an external locus of control. These relatively stable patterns of behavior are associated with many other personal characteristics. Causal attributions often determine the by-products or consequences of success or failure. Pride and shame are maximized when achievement outcomes are ascribed to internal forces and are minimized when success and failure are attributed to external forces. Thus, success attributed to high ability or hard work produces more pride and external praise than success that is perceived as due to the ease of the task or good luck. In a similar manner, failure perceived as caused by low ability or a lack of effort results in greater shame and external punishment than failure attributed to the excessive difficulty of the task or bad luck. In conclusion, locus of causality influences the affective or emotional consequences of achievement outcomes.[6]

Learned helplessness is another phenomenon that is an outgrowth of attribution. While the person with an internal locus of control for success and an external locus of control for failure enters each task optimistically, the individual with an external locus of control for success and an internal locus of control for failure goes into each task with a feeling of helplessness. Learned helplessness, the extreme negative self-concept of a worker, can be debilitating. Their belief that they do not have the ability to succeed often means they do not even try. There is a method to this apparent madness, however. By not attempting difficult tasks, they attribute their poor performance to low effort, which is less shameful in our society than is low ability. Heroic followers need to be alert to these patterns in themselves and in their peers, because attribution patterns can be changed, as we will see next.

ATTRIBUTION TRAINING

There have been many training programs developed to foster achievement-oriented behavior in individuals. One kind of program, based on the achievement-motivation approach, emphasizes changes in behavior and rewards these changes. Slightly less emphasis is given to changed cognitions. Another kind of program, based on the attribution approach, emphasizes change in how people think about their behavior. Both programs show some evidence of success.

McClelland established a training program for owners and operators of small businesses in India. He gave short intensive courses for twenty-five to one hundred hours over a five- to ten-day period. The results showed that the businessmen became much more enterprising for several years after the training. In round numbers, about one-quarter to one-third of the small businessmen with whom he worked would become unusually active in any given two-year period if none of them underwent achievement motivation training. However, with such training, fully two-thirds of the men became active in the two years following it. Similar results were also obtained in Spain and among both black and white businessmen in the United States.[7]

Summarizing about twenty years of these kinds of motivation-change studies, it has been pointed out that these programs often result in more realistic goal setting, less fear of failing, increased hope for success, higher opinions of one's own competence, and less general anxiety and dislike for work. The point is that the motive to achieve is not fixed. It can be changed, perhaps not easily, nor in everyone, but under the proper conditions many who are not now motivated to achieve can be transformed by changing their attribution processes. In doing so, they will be fine-tuning their sense of responsibility or accountability.

MODELING INTERNALITY

As we have demonstrated, individuals tend to attach causes to their success and failure in systematic ways. The goal of attribution training programs is to alter these patterns so that *both* success and failure are attributed to internal forces and individuals reflect an internal locus of control. It now appears that some aspects of internality can be learned from others who systematically reinforce and model internal attributions.

What does this mean for heroic followers? When the follower, or a peer, seems resigned to failure and appears to lack a sense of personal responsibility, the heroic follower should set up a program of systematic reinforcement for him- or herself or the peer. The idea is to get individuals to attribute their problems to their own lack of effort and to reinforce that insight. Self-monitoring, self-instruction, and self-reinforcement strategies can be used to teach more appropriate attribution patterns. Thus, what heroic followers say and do can have an influence on themselves and others with regard to their attribution patterns. But, in order to address this question of attribution, one needs to know that it exists and is present in each of us. Once we recognize its presence, we can go about doing something about it. Simply put, what to do about it is to *be the change that we expect in others*. This modeling of desired behavior is a facet of social learning, which we will discuss more fully shortly.

ATTRIBUTIONAL BIASES

Attributions and attributional errors occur in predictable ways, based on a variety of factors. An individual can participate in a situation as an actor or an observer. Research about such attributions indicates that an actor in a situation emphasizes the situational causes of a behavior and deemphasizes the personal factors to protect his or her self-image and ego; the observer does the reverse. As mentioned earlier, a student who does poorly in a test might attribute his or her poor performance to the teacher's inability to get the subject across. Whereas the teacher, being the observer in this situation, might attribute the student's poor performance to poor study habits.

Research has suggested that in performance appraisals in general, subordinates attribute performance more to situational causes, while administrators attribute subordinate behavior to personal causes. In addition, actors are less likely to assume moral responsibility for an action because they attribute it to external causes. Recognizing this bias should alert heroic followers to possible inaccuracies in their attributions and diagnoses. These misattributions become particularly significant in the conduct of performance reviews.[8]

ATTRIBUTION AND LOCUS OF CONTROL

Attribution and locus of control are closely related. Locus of control is the feeling an individual has about whether he or she is in control of his or her own destiny. Whether one believes that internal or external factors affect future events determines whether one has an internal or external locus of control. Those with an internal locus of control believe that future events are determined by their own individual abilities and personal qualities, while those with an external locus of control attribute future outcomes to factors outside their control. Thus, the student who attributes a poor performance in a test to the teacher's inability to get the subject across can be said have an external locus of control, while the student who attributes the poor performance to his or her own lack of preparation would tend to have an internal locus of control. The objective, then, for heroic followers would be to develop a strong internal locus of control in both themselves and their peers.[9] For example, do you know of any of your coworkers whom you hesitate to approach because he or she is not able to accept even the most constructive criticism without going into some form of apoplexy? Defensive individuals such as these will not be capable of learning from their mistakes because, in their minds at least, they cannot accept making a mistake. If such a person is disorganized, for example, the individual will never overcome this deficiency because it will never be recognized. We often say that a person like this is in denial. These individuals represent classical cases of persons with an external locus of control. It is safe to say that an individual like this will never become a heroic follower, much less be selected as a leader.

THE LEARNING PROCESS

In addition to perception and attribution, learning—which refers to the acquisition of skills, knowledge, ability, or attitudes—influences both description and diagnoses of organizational behavior. In this section, we focus on the way individuals learn, beginning with three models of learning and concluding with the implications of learning.

Behaviorists emphasize external influences and the power of rewards in learning. They emphasize the link between a given stimulus and response. Recall Pavlov's groundbreaking work with dogs. He noted that, upon presentation of powdered meat blown through a tube (unconditioned stimulus) to a dog, the dog salivated (unconditioned response).

The ringing of a bell (neutral stimulus) yielded no salivation responses. After pairing the ringing bell with the meat several times, Pavlov then rang the bell without the meat, and the dog salivated (conditioned response). In classical conditioning, after repeated pairing of neutral and unconditioned stimuli, solitary presentation of the neutral stimulus led to a conditioned response.[10]

Operant conditioning extends classical conditioning to focus on the consequences of a behavior. While a stimulus can still cue a response behavior, the desired or undesired consequence that follows the behavior determines whether the behavior will recur. For example, an individual who receives a bonus (a positive consequence) after creative performance (behavior) on a work assignment (stimulus) is more likely to repeat the creative behavior than if his or her performance is ignored (a negative consequence).

In contrast to the behavior-reinforcement links that are central to behaviorist theories, cognitive theorists emphasize the internal mental processes involved in gaining new insights. They view learning as occurring from the joining of various cues in the environment into a mental map. In early cognitive experiments, rats learned to run through a maze to reach a goal of food. Repeated trials would cause a rat to develop and strengthen cognitive connections that identified the correct path to the goal.[11]

Employees, too, can develop a cognitive map that shows the path to a specific goal. In this case, the cognitive processes join the stimulus to result in a given behavior. On-the-job training, like a new teacher induction process, should result in a new cognitive map of job performance for junior teachers.

Extending beyond both behavioral and cognitive learning theories, social learning theory integrates the behaviorist and cognitive approaches with the idea of modeling or imitating behaviors. Learners first watch others who act as models, next develop a mental picture of the behavior and its consequences, and finally try the behavior. If positive consequences result, the learner repeats the behavior; if negative consequences occur, no repetition occurs. The learning impact occurs when the subject tries the behavior and experiences a favorable result, as in the behaviorist approach. At the same time, the learner's development of a cognitive image of the situation incorporates a basic aspect of cognitive learning. The existence of social learning makes it important that teachers take their responsibility of acting as exemplars for the students very seriously. In addition, leaders need to model the behavior that they expect of their followers.[12]

IMPLICATIONS OF LEARNING

How can heroic followers encourage their own and others' learning in the workplace? They can ensure that appropriate conditions for learning exist; providing appropriate stimuli (e.g., professional development materials) should facilitate acquisition of the skills or attitudes desired. They should reinforce desired learned behaviors. They should also provide environmental cues that encourage learning; structuring a context that supports learning is essential. In effect, just as we advise teachers to adapt their teaching styles to the variety of learning styles of their students, heroic followers must adapt their interpersonal relations styles to the variety of learning styles that are present in their personal and professional lives.

Followers can use the following modeling strategy, for example. First, the follower should identify the goal or target behaviors that will lead to improved performance. For example, a more extensive use of collaborative working activities will lead to improving a coworker's social skills. Second, he or she must select the appropriate model and determine whether to present the model through a live demonstration, videotape, other media, or a combination of all of these. Third, the follower must make sure the colleague is capable of meeting the technical skill requirements of the target behavior. For example, further training might be necessary. Fourth, the follower must structure a favorable and positive learning environment to increase the likelihood that the coworker will learn the new behavior and act in the desired way. Starting collaborative working activities with particularly skilled individuals will ensure success. Fifth, he or she must model the target behavior and carry out supporting activities such as role-playing. Conducting a group meeting using cooperative learning techniques would be an example of such a strategy. Sixth, the follower should positively reinforce reproduction of the target behaviors both in training and in the workplace. Praise for a colleague is typical of such a reward. Once the target behaviors are reproduced, heroic followers must maintain and strengthen them through a system of rewards until the behavior is institutionalized, that is, becomes part of the individual's nature or culture. One might suggest that this is someone else's job. That might be the response of an average follower, but not the response of a heroic follower. The heroic follower sees this as his or her responsibility in helping to make an organization a *learning organization*.

DEVELOPING PRODUCTIVE ATTITUDES

Another aspect of organizational behavior and culture is attitude formation. An attitude is a consistent predisposition to respond to various aspects of people, situations, or objects that we infer from a person's behavior or expressed attitude, as well as from other cognitive, affective, or connotative responses. Attitudes are pervasive and predict behavior toward their objects. We might, for example, determine an individual's job satisfaction by inferring it from his or her general demeanor on the job or by asking the person to describe his or her attitude. We often use attitude surveys or other collections of attitude scales to assess individuals' attitudes toward their jobs, coworkers, supervisors, or institutions at large.[13]

COMPONENTS OF ATTITUDES

Research has suggested that attitudes have three components: cognitive, affective, and behavioral. The cognitive component includes the beliefs an individual has about a certain person, object, or situation. These learned beliefs, such as "All students can learn," serve as antecedents to specific attitudes. Although we have many beliefs, only some are important enough to lead to significant attitudes. The affective component refers to the person's feeling that results from his or her beliefs about a person, object, or situation. A person who has worked hard but has not been recognized in some way may feel anger or frustration because he or she feels hard work deserves promotion and recognition. The affective component becomes stronger as an individual has more often and directly experienced a focal object, person, or situation and as the feeling is expressed more often. The behavioral component is the individual's behavior that occurs as a result of his or her feeling about the focal person, object, or situation. An employee may complain, request a transfer, or lower productivity because he or she feels dissatisfied with the work.[14]

A more recent way of looking at attitudes takes a sociocognitive approach. It considers an attitude as a representation of an individual's interaction with his or her social environment. The object of an attitude is represented as a member of a category in a person's memory. Then an individual uses the attitude to help evaluate an object, deciding, for example, whether it is good or bad, positive or negative, favored or not, and then determining the strategy to take toward it.

ATTITUDES IN A MULTICULTURAL WORKPLACE

The more diverse the work force, the more likely it is that individuals will have an array of attitudes. Their beliefs, formed in large part from their socioeconomic backgrounds and other experiences, could vary significantly. Recent research suggests significant changes in attitudes toward various national and racial groups, as well as toward various gender roles.

As the work force becomes multinational, diagnosing the basis of attitudes and predicting their consequent behaviors becomes more problematic. According to one researcher, national cultures have been described as differing on four dimensions, which he labels power distance, uncertainty avoidance, individualism, and masculinity. Power distance is the extent to which a society accepts the fact that power in institutions and organizations is distributed unequally. Uncertainty avoidance refers to the extent to which a society responds to the potential occurrence of uncertain and ambiguous situations by providing career stability, establishing formal rules, not tolerating deviant ideas and behaviors, and believing in absolute truths and the attainment of expertise. Individualism implies a loosely knit social framework in which people are supposed to take care of themselves and their immediate families only. The opposite, collectivism, is characterized by a tight social framework in which people distinguish between in-groups and out-groups. Masculinity is the ex-

tent to which the dominant values in society reflect traditionally mascu-
line behaviors, such as assertiveness and the acquisition of money and
things, and a lesser concern for relationships. As a result of variations on
these dimensions, interpersonal processes, group behavior, and organizational structure vary in different cultures.[15]

EMPLOYEE OWNERS

One of the ways of building a sense of responsibility in followers, but
which is in most cases out of control of followers, is to engender a sense
of ownership among the employees of an organization. If an organization is to be successful in improving employee morale and responsibility, everyone in it needs to feel that he or she "owns the place." They
have to believe that they are shareholders in the company even though,
technically, they may not be. Taking ownership is a sign of one's love for
an institution. In his book, *Servant Leadership*, Robert Greenleaf says,
"Love is an undefinable term, and its manifestations are both subtle and
infinite. It has only one absolute condition: unlimited liability!" Although it might run counter to our traditional notion of American capitalism, employees should be encouraged to act as if they own the place.
It is a sign of love, and its only condition is "unlimited liability" or having a sense of *responsibility* for the place.

So, esprit de corps can be put into continuous practice by developing
a culture of co-ownership. Stakeholders who believe that they have real
ownership in an organization will have a desire for the common good
leading to common cause and synergy. This, in turn, will open the way
for them feeling greater responsibility, more participation, open communication, openness to change, cross-functional teaming, and creativity. To the degree that we feel like co-owners, we begin to invest more
of our identity in the group. As this occurs, followers become co-
responsible and therefore free to act for the good of the organization.
This freedom to act for the good of the organization decreases defen-
siveness and opens the way to increased trust and a willingness to go
"beyond the call of duty."

The concept of employee owners can occur in many different settings. In addition to occurring in organizations, intimate co-ownership

occurs within a family or among good friends. Collegial co-ownership can occur in a community organization. Civil co-ownership can occur within political or cultural groups. As the individual invests himself or herself in more groups, he or she becomes more interpersonal in his or her identity. The individual becomes interested in the ultimate good among these groups, that is, the common good. These individuals create a social self that goes beyond their own self-interest. This attitude creates more responsibilities, but they are perceived as worthwhile because they contribute to the richness of one's inner world and are reflected in one's relations with the outer world. Their lives become effective, influential, and optimistic, and they become indispensable to those with whom they interact.

Robert J. Spitzer, SJ, says that co-ownership is achieved in four stages: (1) solicitation of ideas for upcoming decisions, (2) sharing relevant information with stakeholders about decisions, (3) proactive listening, and (4) feedback and response.[16]

Spitzer refers to minimalistic models and maximalistic models to allow us to discover an appropriate middle ground that will meet our own individual needs. The following are *minimalistic* approaches to co-ownership:

Step 1: Solicitation of ideas. Many organizations hold monthly forums where employees can share their ideas with management, and rewards are given to those with the best suggestions. Recognition and a reward system should be developed to motivate employees to make suggestions and assure that they are being listened to and taken seriously. It is important, however, that at the beginning of each session the ground rules are set on how the ideas will be used and what the reward system will be.

Organizations also respect the customers' need to be considered co-owners by holding listening sessions or developing customer advising groups to solicit ideas on how to better design products and deliver services.

Similar advising groups can be established for suppliers, vendors, and others who service the organization. Interacting groups should be fostered so that the suppliers can talk to the customers and the employees so that the outcome is a product that meets the customers' needs and can be developed in the most efficient way. For example, if I am administering a school, it is important that the product—education—be delivered in such a way as to satisfy both the knowledge or achievement needs of the students and parents and the physiological and psychological needs of the teachers. In other words, there needs to be something in it for everyone, so that each person feels he or she has a stake in the results.

Step 2: Sharing information. To foster a sense of co-ownership, certain critical information needs to be shared. The mission, vision, goals, and objectives of the organization need to be shared. Ideally, the various stakeholders have had input into the development of the mission, vision, and goals. Sharing this information shows the followers where they can be of help in attaining the goals and tends to foster full participation. Without this sense of being needed, the followers tend to give only a half-hearted effort because they do not see the work as being self-actualizing.

Step 3: Proactive listening. Proactive listening is also called active listening and is defined as listening where *both* parties in the communication are active, not just the communicator. Thus, proactive listening requires a sense of mutual concern on the part of both the speaker and the listener. This allows both parties to be empathetic to the needs of each.

When followers realize that they are being listened to proactively, they tend to communicate from the open self, and a trusting relationship develops between the parties. It promotes more creative results because both parties feel secure in the relationship. Thus, the follower acquires the sense of being a co-owner.

Both parties benefit from proactive listening, not just the speaker. Transformational learning has a tendency to take place in this kind of setting. That is, since there is a high level of trust, both parties are more prone to change their way of thinking in the process. The listener, for example, may transform his or her attitude toward the speaker because of the content of the communication and the compelling argument that the speaker may have made. If the listening is not proactive, this transformation is less likely to take place because the inactive listener may have preconceived views of the speaker that are never challenged.

Step 4: Feedback and response. In my view, feedback is the most important component of the communication process. Two-way communication is almost always preferable to one-way communication. If followers are to see themselves as employee-owners, they not only have to believe that their ideas are being heard and appreciated, they also have to have evidence that they are. This evidence is often provided by feedback in the form of public or private acknowledgement and/or reward. This process can also be helpful in determining exactly what type of acknowledgement would be most appropriate. Simply ask the followers what type of reward might be best received. This is a common-sense suggestion, but in my experience, most reward systems are devised by leadership teams without ever asking the followers for any feedback.

INITIATIVE AND CREATIVITY

Once the heroic follower develops a sense of responsibility, it is likely that initiative and creativity will follow. As an individual begins to think of him- or herself as a co-owner at work or in his or her personal life, the individual is motivated to improve his or her environment. Thus, the follower will tend to take the initiatives that he or she thinks will do so. In many cases, these initiatives will be innovative and, thus, manifest at least a modicum of creativity. Since the follower trusts and respects the environment and the individuals in it, the follower is more willing to take risks, knowing that failures will be tolerated.

Inasmuch as the feeling of being employee-owners provides followers the internal motivation that enhances their participation, initiative, creativity, and teamwork, it also enhances the morale of the organization. Instead of creating passive aggression, this environment frees followers to reflect good will toward management and peers alike. Their sense of empowerment and respect motivates them to reach their potential and maximize their performance. Even though these followers are taking more initiative and producing at a higher level, they feel far less overburdened and tired. They look forward to coming to the workplace each day and feel a sense of excitement and accomplishment about their duties. As long as this culture prevails, passive aggression and other negative attitudes will be replaced with initiative and creativity.

In the absence of fear and force, followers will feel free to innovate. This kind of creativity occurs when one grasps a connection among diverse realities. It is not simply an experience or an observation. It is an awareness of relationships. These relationships could be temporal, geographical, cause and effect, numeric, attitudinal, ethical, or interpersonal.

Some natural connections already exist and are there to be discovered. Other connections await a creative mind to invent them. Whether we are discovering connections or inventing them, we must have the capacity to see them.

Creativity may be provoked by necessity, by the love of knowledge, or by a sense of altruism. On the other hand, seeing a new connection may be impeded by fear and one's reluctance to move out of the current paradigm. These conditions cause blind spots that inhibit new perspectives by forcing old perspectives into one's inquiry process. In order to be creative, it is important to test the adequacy of old paradigms and to acknowledge that the old paradigm may be outdated. It is not necessarily that the old paradigm is wrong, but that it needs to be revised in order to deal with the challenges of today.

The willingness to consider new possibilities and alternatives reveals a second dimension of the human psyche that must be present if one is to be creative. A dimension that is present in all of us is a conventional dimension that patterns itself according to old paradigms. The second dimension, one of experimentation and curiosity, has little concern for old methods and connections and is open to new ways of looking at things. It prefers exploration and surprise. This dimension is not always present in individuals and is almost never present in an atmosphere of fear and force.

In order for creativity to take place, the psyche has to disengage from the status quo or current paradigm: it needs to feel free to take risks, it needs to be relaxed, and it needs to allow time for connections from past knowledge to new knowledge to take place. The famous story of Archimedes discovering the concept of displacement is a good example of creativity in action. Archimedes was charged with determining the volume of the king's crown. He could not do so using the conventional method of measuring volume by using the Pythagorean Theorem because the crown was not in the form of a circle or a cube. While taking a bath, Archimedes noticed that when he descended into the bathtub, the level of the water rose. "Eureka! I have found it!" was his famous response. His psyche had gone through the various phases that allowed him to make his discovery. He disengaged from the conventional wisdom, he felt free and relaxed, and consequently, he allowed the connections and clues to naturally emerge.

How can we condition ourselves to be open to innovation and creativity? We should start by being willing to yield to our inverse insights. When we run up against the proverbial brick wall, we need to be open to looking at new alternatives and also be willing to allow the time to do so. Routine is fast, and we are programmed to be time conscious. Creativity is not fast. We need to allow the time for new alternatives to surface and time for trial and error to take place. Once again, if the culture that we are in is fraught with fear, we will not feel that we have the liberty to take time to allow innovation to emerge.

Relaxation is another dimension of the psyche that fosters creativity. Insights frequently occur when we are taking a relaxing walk, sitting in a comfortable chair, or just plain daydreaming (or taking a bath, in Archimedes' case). On the other hand, when the psyche is in crisis management mode, it will default to the conventional way of doing things. So it is important for the heroic follower to carve out some time each day to relax and foster creative thoughts.

The problem with creativity is that the conditions for it are counterintuitive. In our culture of private enterprise and capitalism, efficiency is a valued trait. Getting things accomplished quickly and expeditiously is considered a priority, sometimes at the expense of quality. As we have seen, the helter-skelter world of big business is not exactly the environment in which creativity thrives. Furthermore, the fear and force intrinsic to competitive motivation compels the psyche to engage its conventional function to the exclusion of its creative one. The fear and blame environment leaves no room for risk-taking, relaxation, and deliberation. Thus, the psyche will confine itself to the current paradigm in an effort to comply with standard operating procedures, direct orders, hard deadlines, and the demands of the efficiency experts. So the heroic follower needs to develop a sense of responsibility, which in turn will motivate the heroic follower to think of creative initiatives that will better his or her professional and personal life.

IMPLICATIONS FOR HEROIC FOLLOWERS

To be a heroic follower with a sense of responsibility or accountability, one must become proactive rather than reactive. Reactive people allow moods, feelings, and circumstances to drive their responses. When the stimulus is positive, they feel good, but when the stimulus is negative, they feel bad. Because they let their circumstances control them, they feel victimized. They tend to blame and accuse others when things go wrong. They blame their attitude and behavior on things they cannot control. They respond to stimuli, often attributing behavior to genetic, psychic, and environmental determinants. An example of using a genetic determinant is, "I'm a morning person. Don't expect me to be able to function at nighttime meetings." A psychic determinant example is, "I am math phobic, so how do you expect me to balance my checkbook?" An example of an environmental determinant at work is, "My teacher is always grumpy. She always puts me in a bad mood."

Each of these elements of determinism can influence us; however, they do not have to determine us. It is up to us whether we allow them to do so. Despite genetics, the psyche, and our environment, we still have free will to make our choices. Responsible and proactive people use initiative and resourcefulness. In the space between stimulus and response, they use four human characteristics to make their choices:

- *Self-awareness*: the capacity to examine thoughts, moods, and behaviors
- *Imagination*: the mental ability to create things beyond experience and present reality
- *Conscience*: the inner awareness of right, wrong, and personal integrity
- *Free will*: the ability to act, independent of external influence[17]

Heroic leaders can expand their circle of influence by becoming more responsible and accountable. People who work within their circle of influence control their own attitudes and actions. In addition, they use values to choose strategies for influencing other people and things. As they work within their circle of influence, their trustworthiness increases, and others' confidence in their character and ability grows. As their confidence increases, their circle of influence also increases. Thus, one can readily see the value of developing a strong sense of responsibility. By using some of the suggestions made in this chapter, one can see *how* to develop a sense of responsibility.

DIAGNOSTIC CHECKLIST

Here are some questions you can use to assess your sense of *responsibility*:

1. Have you developed an *internal locus of control* whereby you are accountable for your actions?
2. Do you try to nurture a *learning environment* both at home and at work?
3. Do you foster an environment where *failure* is seen as a *learning experience* rather than looking to place blame?
4. Do you foster reasonable risk taking and *innovation* in your own life and with your colleagues?

NOTES

1. J. R. Gordan, *A Diagnostic Approach to Organizational Behavior* (Boston: Allyn & Bacon, 1991).

2. S. L. Brodsky, *The Psychology of Adjustment and Well-Being* (New York: Holt, Rinehart, and Winston, 1988).

3. M. E. Heilman and M. H. Stopeck, Being attractive, advantage or disadvantage? Performance evaluations and recommended personnel actions as a function of appearance, sex and job type, *Organizational Behavior and Human Decision Processes*, 35 (1985): 202–215.

4. S. G. Redding, Cognition as an aspect of culture and in relation to management processes: An exploratory view of the Chinese case, *Journal of Management Studies*, 17(2): 127–148; J.B. Shaw, A cognitive categorization model for the study of intercultural management, *Academy of Management Review*, 15(4) (1990): 626–645.

5. N. L. Gage and David Berliner, *Educational Psychology* (Boston: Houghton Mifflin, 1988).

6. D. Bar-Tal, *New Approaches to Social Problems: Applications of Attribution Theory* (San Francisco: Jossey-Bass, 1979).

7. D. C. McClelland, *The Achievement Motive* (New York: Appleton-Century-Crofts, 1953).

8. B. Weiner and J. Sierad, Misattribution for failure and the enhancement of achievement strivings, *Journal of Personality and Social Psychology* 31 (1995): 415–421.

9. H. H. Kelley, Attribution theory in social psychology, *Nebraska Symposium on Motivation* 14 (1967): 192–241.

10. I. Pavlov, *Conditioned Reflexes: An Investigation of the Physiological Activity of the Cerebral Cortex* (London: Oxford University Press, 1927).

11. E. C. Tolman, *Purposive Behavior in Animals and Men* (New York: Appleton-Century-Crofts, 1932).

12. A. Bandura, *Social Learning Theory* (Englewood, NJ: Prentice Hall, 1978).

13. G. Greenwald, Why are attitudes important? in *Attitude Structure and Function*, ed. A. R. Pratkanis, S. J. Beckler, and A. G. Greenwald (Hillsdale, NJ: Erlbaum, 1989), 1–10.

14. S. Oskamp, *Attitudes and Opinions*, 215 ed. (Englewood Cliffs, NJ: Prentice Hall, 1991).

15. G. Hofstede, Motivation, leadership, and organization: Do American theories apply abroad? *Organizational Dynamics* 9 (Summer 1980): 45–46.

16. Robert J. Spitzer, SJ, *The Spirit of Leadership* (Provo, UT: Executive Press Publishing, 2000).

17. Stephen Covey, *Seven Habits of Highly Effective People* (New York: Free Press, 1990).

4

DON'T CONTRIBUTE TO
THE COMMUNICATION GAP!

The one who listens does the most work, not the one who speaks.

—Stephen Covey

One of the perennial complaints in the workplace is a lack of communication between individuals and another segment of the working community. Often, the greatest perceived communications gap is between employees and management. When one is attempting to develop and/or sustain an environment or culture of employee ownership, the lack of effective communication can be debilitating. If the heroic follower is to be highly effective, then he or she must master the skill of effective communication so as to lessen any communication gaps that might exist.

The heroic follower needs to seek first to understand (listen) and then to be understood (speak). To properly understand a person's condition, state of mind, and problem, we need to first practice *active listening*. Before we communicate a suggestion, recommendation, or resolution, we should determine the cause and conditions surrounding the problem. A good physician first diagnoses the disease and then prescribes the cure. This same diagnostic and prescriptive process needs to occur for effective communication to take place between and among people. Therefore, listening is an important, though often neglected, step in the communication process. Unfortunately, most of our listening is perfunctory. We need to cultivate our listening so that it becomes what we call *active* listening. Active listening is most important when the communication has a strong emotional component, when there is a lack of trust, when there is a lack of understanding in the initial communication, and when the content is complex or unfamiliar.

In this chapter, we examine the nature of effective communication, a central organizational process that can occur at the intrapersonal, interpersonal, intragroup, intergroup, institutional, and public levels. As a linking mechanism among the various organizational subsystems, communication is a central feature of the structure of groups and organizations. It builds and reinforces interdependence between and among the various parts of the institution.

The chapter first describes the communication process and its five components: encoding, transmission, decoding, noise, and feedback. Next, it looks at downward, upward, and lateral communication. Then it discusses how interpersonal relations and attitudes affect the quality of communication, as well as issues of informal communication. It continues by presenting a set of strategies for improving communication accuracy. The chapter concludes with a discussion of an especially important aspect of communication, active listening.

WHY COMMUNICATION IS SO DIFFICULT

If you hear it once, you hear it a thousand times: "We just can't communicate." Kids mumble, "I can't talk to my parents. They don't understand me." Parents complain, "I can't talk to my kids. The only things they will communicate about are money and dirty laundry." A couple mutually agrees to separate after twenty years of marriage and three children. He tells a friend, "I don't think she ever really knew me. I was never able to tell her who I am." An employer learns a key manager is leaving and asks, "Why didn't you come talk to me if you were unhappy?" The employee responds, "I've tried in the past, but we have a communication problem." And the beat goes on.

The reality is that all of these people are communicating. You cannot "not communicate." Even silence says something. What they are not doing is connecting. It is ironic that in an era where we have discovered so much about human behavior and we continue to coin terms, we continue to communicate in the same ineffective ways. Like our predecessors, we tend to speak from positions of authority rather than equality, from distance rather than intimacy, from restraint rather than receptivity. Moreover, we unquestionably accept the truisms handed down from generation to generation that maintain the very barriers to communication that we need to topple, truisms like "familiarity breeds contempt," or "silence is golden," or "children should be seen and not heard."

What keeps us from communicating effectively? Much of what we say or do not say is governed by some kind of fear. Sometimes fears are grounded in reality and sometimes they are not. Irrational fears are called phobias, and many of us are unfortunately dominated by them. There are at least four basic fears that many of us have that have to be overcome in order for us to communicate effectively.[1]

First, many of us have the fear of speaking our minds. We often bite our tongues and swallow hard rather than causing hurt feelings or sounding less than bright. We are also afraid of being disliked for something that we say. We are afraid that if we are honest and forthright we will hurt people's feelings, insult them, or wound their pride. And we believe the myth that says when we hurt others, they will reject us and we will only end up hurting ourselves in the long run. So we keep silent.

The second fear is that of confrontation. Some people just do not like to fight with others in the form of debate. Thus, they avoid anything that may cause tension. As a result, effective communication never takes place and no transformational change ever happens in the relationship. Whether in their personal or professional lives, individuals need to overcome this fear in order to make their views known and to better participate in the communication process. Later, I will suggest that an assertive style of communication will overcome this fear.

Another fear that has to be overcome in the communication process is the fear of intimacy. Someone once described the beginning of true friendship as the moment two people reveal equally dangerous secrets about themselves. The willingness to lift the curtain and let somebody peek at the inner you is certainly an invitation to intimacy, and it is one that many people are very timid about offering. We tend to believe that our deep, dark secrets are unique, that no one else harbors desires or thoughts quite like our own. If we reveal our real selves and point out the location of the soft spots, we are afraid we will look foolish, mean, or even perverted, and we will lose the respect of others. We will make some recommendations later with regard to communicating from the open self that might be helpful in overcoming this fear.

The fear of commitment is also a barrier to effective communication. It is commonly believed that a verbal agreement to do something irrevocably locks us into meeting that commitment—a verbal contract is as binding as a written contract. Unfortunately, it is not always possible to fulfill a promise and, rather than risk the blame or criticism for failing to follow through, it becomes easier to say nothing. In an emotional moment at her father's funeral, Shannon told her brothers that since she was in a better financial situation than they were, she would take care of their mother's financial needs. A year later when her business suffered a decline, she went to her brothers and asked them to increase their support for their mother. They reacted with indignation. "You promised. If you didn't mean it, you should not have promised."

Conditions change. And reactions like those of Shannon's brothers are the very reason that most people are reluctant to make commitments. Commitments are especially risky with people who have witnessed your past performance and are likely to be around in the future to laud or criticize your performance. Fearing commitment is not a reason not to make them, but it would be prudent to make certain when one is communicating a commitment that it is qualified accordingly. For example, Shannon could have made the commitment but qualified it with the phrase, "as long as I am financially able."

Although these fears can interfere with one's potential to connect during the communication process, you can and must confront them. The main reason you may not be successful in confronting these fears is because you may not have been aware of them. Once they are realized, my experience is that most people are able to cope with them. These fears rarely, if ever, materialize when people communicate in a way that genuinely expresses their thoughts, feelings, and needs without blaming or demanding. Later in this chapter, I will make some suggestions along these lines that may be helpful.

THE COMMUNICATION PROCESS

Perception, attribution, motivation, individual personality and personal development, group characteristics, and organizational factors all affect the way individuals transmit information and receive information transmitted by another. We begin with a simple example of the communication process. A teacher recently asked the principal how long the new ecology unit would be. The principal responded by stating, "Ten weeks." When the teacher asked that simple question, and the principal replied, they both participated in a complex communication process.

In communication, an input is transformed by encoding and decoding, resulting in another meaning, or output, which is fed back to the sender. It is important that each of these steps follow three principles of ethical communication:

1. Organization members should not intentionally deceive one another.
2. Organization members' communication should not purposely harm any other organization member or members of the organization's relevant environment.
3. Organization members should be treated justly.[2]

ENCODING

Once a person has a meaning to convey, he or she needs to determine the means to convey that meaning, in other words, the way to encode it. The sender uses his or her own frame of reference as the background for encoding information. It included the individual's view of the organization or situation as a function of personal education, interpersonal relationships, attitudes, knowledge, and experience.

Going back to the teacher-principal example, the teacher had a meaning he wished to convey. The principal later learned that the teacher wanted to determine the content and comprehensiveness of the ecology curriculum. The teacher did not want to know its length but rather its scope. Notice that this meaning differs from the question he asked. Next, he had to decide how to encode this meaning. He had to decide, for example, an efficient way of getting the needed information. He considered, probably unconsciously, whom he should ask: the principal, a teacher colleague, the assistant principal? Should he ask the question by phone, in a letter, or directly? What specific question should he ask so that he would be understood? What nonverbal messages should accompany his question?

How else might the teacher have encoded the message to make it clearer? He might have asked what tasks would be included in the ecology curriculum development. Or he might have asked about the desired outcomes. In encoding the message, the teacher should have considered what was the most effective way to convey his desire for certain information. On the other hand, as we will see, the principal should have asked that the question be clarified so that she could respond accurately.

The choice of words or language in which a sender encodes a message will influence the quality of communication. Because language is a symbolic representation of a phenomenon, room for interpretation and distortion of meaning exists. Consider the instructor who decides to present an introductory class entirely in a language that few or none of the students understand. Think about the CEO whose directions are so ambiguous that the executive team cannot determine the most appropriate way of acting. In each of these cases, the inappropriate use of language can limit the quality of effective communication. People can use the same words but attribute different meanings to them; such bypassing more often occurs in cross-cultural situations or in stressful situations.

A sender can create misunderstandings by using language in a number of ways. The sender may use words that are too abstract and have many mental images associated with them. Or the sender may overgeneralize messages and fail to recognize subtleties. The use of jargon frequently creates misunderstandings, as does the use of slang or colloquialisms in speech. Some senders consciously use messages to confuse the issue. Some politicians have been accused of this, not to mention CEOs, supervisors, and other executives.

Misuses of language are especially common between leaders and their followers. A follower can create misunderstandings by distorting information upward, for example, telling the supervisor only good news, paying the supervisor compliments whenever possible, always agreeing with the supervisor and the other executives, insulating them from information detrimental to the follower, and so on. The supervisor, in turn, can create misunderstandings by withholding information or not conveying what he or she really thinks about the follower.

The use of gestures, movements, material things, time, and space can clarify or confuse the meaning of verbal communication. For example, the kind of facial expressions that accompany a request for time off may indicate its importance or triviality. Nonverbal cues serve five functions. They repeat the message the individual is making verbally; an individual who nods after he or she answers affirmatively confirms the verbal message with the nonverbal gesture. They can contradict a message the individual is trying to convey; a CEO who pounds the desk while stating that he or she does not care about the situation being discussed is using verbal and nonverbal communication that disagree. Nonverbal communication may, in some cases, be more powerful or accurate than the verbal communication. Nonverbal cues may also substitute for a verbal message; an individual with "fire in his eyes" conveys information without using verbal messages. Nonverbal cues may add to or complement a verbal message; a college dean who beams while giving praise increases the impact of the compliment to the colleague. Nonverbal communication may accent or underline a verbal message; for example, speaking very softly or stamping your feet shows the importance you attach to a message. Senders must recognize, therefore, the significance of nonverbal communication and use it to increase the impact of their verbal communication.

The actual transmission of the message follows the encoding; the sender must convey the message to the receiver. In this example, the teacher went to the principal's office. He walked in and asked how long the ecology curriculum would be. Thus, the transmission of his message took place primarily by verbal channels. In determining the appropriateness of this medium, the teacher should consider among other factors the medium's richness, which is determined by its speed of feedback, variety of communication channels, extent of personal interactions, and richness of language. As tasks become more ambiguous, leaders and followers alike should increase the richness of the media they use; for example, they should send nonroutine and difficult communications through a rich medium such as face-to-face communication, and routine simple communications through a lean medium such as a memorandum. They should also use rich media to increase personal visibility and implement institutional strategies.

USING ELECTRONIC MEDIA

The widespread availability of electronic media for communication, including the Internet, messaging, and conferencing systems, has had a significant impact on the accessibility of information and the speed of transmission.

Management information systems, now using computer-based software programs, also facilitate communication by making large quantities of information available and assisting in its analysis. Most organizations have information specialists who make relevant information available to the various parts of the community. Some organizations integrate the use of management information systems technologies into the regular performance of positions at all levels of the system.

The advent of the various communications technologies has influenced the amount of information transmitted in organizations. E-mail, for example, has revolutionized the process of communication. It makes new demands on individuals' writing skills.

DECODING AND LISTENING

Not only does the sender influence the effectiveness of communication, but the quality of listening by the receiver also helps determine communication quality. The principal in our example performed the next step of the communication process. She needed to decode the message she had received to attach some meaning to it. An individual's decoding of a message, like encoding, depends on his or her frame of reference. She might have interpreted the teacher's question in several different ways, again based on her frame of reference. She might, for example, have viewed the teacher's question as a plea for an easy workload; or she might have felt that the teacher literally wanted the information he requested, the number of weeks the curriculum project would require. If there had been conflict between the teacher and the principal, the principal might

Table 4.1. Features of Various Electronic Media

Type of Media	Brief Description	Type of Communication Supported	Timing and Geography	Typical Features
(1) Voice messaging	Augmentation for telephone communication Ability to leave and retrieve voice or synthesized voice messages	One-to-one One-to-many	Asynchronous Time independent Geographic distribution	Message forwarding Distribution lists Message storage and retrieval
(2) Electronic Messaging (EMC)	Substitution for telephone or face-to-face User creates a written document using a computer terminal or the equivalent	One-to-one One-to-many	Asynchronous Time independent Geographic distribution	Message editing Message creating and editing User receives messages in an electronic in-basket; messages may be answered, filed and/or discarded Message storage and retrieval Distribution list Message forwarding
Conferencing Systems (1) Audio and audiographic	Similar to telephone conference call Participants cannot see each other May have visual aids Substitution for face-to-face meeting, travel	Group	Synchronous Geographic distribution	Ability to transmit graphic materials accompanying a meeting
Conferencing Systems (2) Video	Substitution for face-to-face meeting, travel	Group	Synchronous Geographic distribution One-way in multiple locations Two-way in two locations only	Images of speaker and images of other participants displayed simultaneously Graphical materials also displayed

	Description	Mode	Timing / Distribution	Features
(3) Computer	Transmits voice and images of participants Can be one-way or two-way Substitution for face-to-face meeting, travel Meetings conducted using text (no audio, no video)	Group One-on-one	Synchronous or asynchronous Time independent Geographic distribution	Text editing, storage, and retrieval Transcript of proceedings maintained Ability for private communication among participants Ability to poll conference participants and collect results of a vote Bulletin boards Preparation and editing of shared documents
(4) Integrated Systems	Substitution for telephone or face-to-face Augmentation of traditional written communication Provides support for messaging, word processing, data processing, and administrative activities using a single interface	One-to-one One-to-many	Asynchronous Time independent Geographic distribution	Same features as electronic messaging Ability to create, edit, store, retrieve, and transmit formal documents Electronic calendars and scheduling Ability to retrieve shared documents. Support for traditional data processing

have interpreted the question as something meant to annoy her or distract her from her work, or as something that would support the principal's view of the teacher as incompetent. If her usual perception was that the teacher was a hard worker, then she might have interpreted the question as another indication of his concern and industriousness.

The misunderstanding between the principal and the teacher in our example emphasized the importance of listening. Collecting data is the first step in quality communication. Receivers can listen in directing, judgmental, probing, smoothing, or active ways. In effective listening, the receiver practices active listening by trying to understand both the facts and the feelings being conveyed. It requires determining what the speaker is trying to say from his or her own viewpoint. Consider the example of the principal and the teacher. If the principal acknowledged the feelings and body language of the teacher, she might have asked a probing question that would have clarified the situation and brought about an accurate response. Listeners, then, must recognize the importance of nonverbal communication and look for nonverbal cues that support or contradict verbal information. We will discuss active listening in detail later in this chapter.

NOISE

Many decodings reflect some noise or interference in the communication process. They suggest factors such as conflict between the principal and the teacher, or the principal's understanding of the messages in such a way that she did not "hear" what the teacher intended. Noise can include physical noise that interferes with transmission, such as static on a telephone line or the noise created by office machinery. But noise may be inaudible. The presence of a silent third party during a conversation may act as noise that distracts the receiver from hearing what the speaker is saying. Or the frame of reference of the receiver may cause that person to hear the message in a way other than the one in which it was intended. Noise can also include characteristics of senders or receivers, such as their socioeconomic background, experience, education, or value system.

What types of noise likely exist in communications described in the opening example? Differences in roles in the organization may create noise. Biases in their attributions for poor performance may create noise. So, too, may various perceptual predispositions, such as different personal and organizational goals, attitudes, and orientations.

FEEDBACK

Feedback refers to an acknowledgement by the receiver that the message has been received; it provides the sender with information about the receiver's understanding of the message being sent. The principal's feedback to the teacher, in which she provided only the length of the project, indicated an inaccurate understanding. If the principal had told the teacher that the project will involve a detailed feasibility study and cost analysis, the principal would have conveyed a different understanding.

Often, one-way communication occurs between administrators and their colleagues. Because of inherent power differences in their positions, administrators may give large quantities of information and directions to their staffs without providing the opportunity for the faculty and staff to show their understanding or receipt of the information. These managers often experience conflict between their role as authorities and a desire to be liked by their colleagues. Other administrators have relied on the use of written memoranda as a way of communicating with the staff. In addition to the inherent lack of feedback involved in this format, the use of a single channel of communication also limits the effectiveness of communication. The proliferation of the use of e-mail has alleviated this problem somewhat by providing a relatively facile feedback mechanism.

Why do administrators sometimes not involve their staffs in two-way communication? In some instances, administrators do not trust their colleagues to contribute effectively. In other situations, lack of self-confidence by the administrator makes him or her appear uninterested in or unconcerned about others' opinions. Or administrators assume that their staff has the same goals as they do, and thus they feel that input from colleagues is not required or would not add anything of significance to the process. Encouraging feedback from others helps show them that you are concerned about them as individuals, in ways that go beyond merely ensuring that they produce.

Followers also have responsibility for encouraging two-way communication. While managers may attempt to protect their power positions, followers attempt to protect the image their supervisor holds of them. For example, administrative assistants may withhold negative information about themselves or their activities. Or they may fail to inform their supervisor about their needs and values. Other followers mistrust their leaders and so withhold any information from them. Why do these situations arise? Some followers may assume that they and their bosses have different goals. Others mistrust their bosses. Still others lack persistence in seeking responses from their supervisors. Impression of management, therefore, plays a key role in whether individuals send feedback. They may assess in what way asking for feedback will be interpreted and how the resulting information will affect each person's public image. In order for effective communication to take place, then, followers must show that they, too, are willing to build relationships with their leaders.

THE DIRECTION OF COMMUNICATION

The individual's ability to successfully communicate is a function of his or her capability to encourage others to participate actively in the communication process. They must understand the significance of the direction of communication. Although structural factors facilitate and direct communication to a high degree in organizations, these hierarchical arrangements contribute to communication difficulties in organizations as well. Centralization of authority at the higher levels of the organization restricts the dissemination of information. Some organizational members may have access to more information than others. Some subsystems may have more access than other subsystems. Since some people either know much more or possess different information, centralization, which discourages shared information, increases the potential for misunderstandings among the various subsystems. The extent to which organizations have specialized workgroups also influences the quality of communication. Where differences exist among departments in their goals and expertise, communication among peers may be limited.

DOWNWARD COMMUNICATION

Executives often use this type of communication to disseminate information and directives to subordinates. Using downward communication to share both good news and bad news with followers should be followed by an opportunity for feedback. Encouraging face-to-face communication between all levels of employees and administrators through worksite visits or management/staff discussion groups, publishing staff newsletters, and even introducing a communication hot line, can facilitate accurate downward communication.

Too often, however, downward communication becomes one-way, with no provision for feedback. Although most administrators may intend to communicate accurately to their colleagues, some may consciously or unconsciously distort downward communication. Administrators can withhold, screen, or manipulate information. What results from this type of communication? Followers can become very distrustful of their managers and circumvent them to obtain accurate information. They may rely instead on rumors, obtaining equally distorted and potentially harmful information. In some organizations, downward communication between supervisors and immediate subordinates is relatively accurate, but information from top management fails to pass accurately through the hierarchy and reach the lower-level employees; managers may adjust or delay it along the way so it better fits their objectives. In addition, managers and followers may differ in their perceptions of the quality of downward communication. For example, if a superintendent delays the communication of poor standardized test scores for the school district until his or her contract is renewed, he or she would be thwarting the communication process and distorting downward communication, not to mention the ethical implications involved.

Although open communication has been considered a panacea for many organizational problems, some researchers have argued that characteristics of the individuals involved, their relationships, and the organization and environment in which they function should influence how open communication should be. Disclosure and directness can backfire if, for example, the CEO indicates prematurely to the workforce that a certain plant may be closing in a downsizing of the company. Letting out such information prematurely can have the effect of a self-fulfilling prophesy.

UPWARD COMMUNICATION

Encouraging ongoing upward communication as part of the organization's culture can minimize such dysfunctional consequences. Primarily a feedback vehicle, upward communication refers to messages sent from followers to their supervisors. Top and middle management must create a culture that promotes honest upward communication as a way of counteracting employees' tendencies to hide potentially damaging information. Such a culture encourages employee participation in decision making, rewards openness, and limits inflexible policies and arbitrary procedures. It also promotes creativity and innovation. Acting constructively on information communicated upward reinforces its future occurrence and limits administrative isolation. If a culture of open communication and trust is established in the workplace, followers will be more likely to be very frank and bring new ideas to the administration; whereas in a culture of coercion and vindictiveness, followers will withhold information and become defensive.

LATERAL COMMUNICATION

Sharing information, engaging in problem solving, and coordinating the workflow with employees at their same level in the organization complement both downward and upward communication. While some messages need to go through formal channels, many can be handled through informal channels, or laterally. Teachers sharing classroom management techniques with each other, car salespersons forming a support group with other car sales professionals, and custodians purchasing cleaning materials in conjunction with custodians in other institutions to save money on bulk purchases are examples of lateral communication. Communication directly between colleagues and counterparts typically has great speed and accuracy, although distortions can still occur in encoding, transmission, and decoding. Although employees in different or distant departments may have historical problems communicating directly, the advent of electronic communication devices should remove some obstacles. Still, in some cases, managers may insist that workers rely on the hierarchy for an exchange of information. This is especially true when communicating with the public. It is often necessary when communicating with the media, for example, that a uniform message be communicated. In these cases, the hierarchical approach is more appropriate.

Special roles in the organization can facilitate accurate lateral communication. Gatekeepers screen information and access to a group or individual. Situated at the crossroads of communication channels, these positions act as nerve centers where information among people and groups is exchanged. Human resource professionals and external relations personnel are examples of individuals who can serve the gatekeeper role. Mid-level administrators can also serve this role.

INTERPERSONAL RELATIONS AND COMMUNICATION

The relationship between the individuals or groups communicating, as well as the type of climate they create during their communication, affects the accuracy with which messages are given and received. The sender's and receiver's trust of and influence over each other, the sender's aspirations regarding upward mobility in the organization, and the norms and sanctions of the group to which the sender and receiver belong influence the quality of communication. When people trust each other, their communication tends to be more accurate and open; on the contrary, when they distrust each other, they are more likely to be secretive or hesitant to speak openly. This is why it is imperative for followers to engender trust in their colleagues if they expect to be effective. Suppose, for example, a working group leader establishes an elaborate induction program for those new to the group. In a culture of trust, group members will perceive the induction program as an appropriate way of assimilating new members into the group culture. In a culture of distrust, however, it is just as likely that such an elaborate induction program will be perceived as an attempt by the group leaders to co-opt the new members' loyalty to the detriment of the senior members of the group.

MULTICULTURAL COMMUNICATION ISSUES

Cross-cultural issues may affect the quality of communication. For example, differences in norms for the appropriate amount of interpersonal space exist in different cultures. Effective communication requires deciphering basic values, motives, aspirations, and assumptions across geographical, functional, or social class lines. It also means seeing one's own culture as different, but not necessarily better, than others. Cross-cultural miscommunication occurs when a receiver misunderstands the message transmitted by a sender of another culture. For example, if an African-American employee describes the company's CEO as an "operator" to a foreign-born Hispanic employee, the Hispanic will most likely not understand the implication.

The compatibility or incompatibility of the verbal and nonverbal styles used to communicate can also influence the effectiveness of intercultural communication. Verbal styles differ along a variety of dimensions. The Japanese camouflage the speaker's true intent in an indirect style, use role-centered or contextual language, and are receiver-oriented. The Arabs use an elaborate style or very expressive language in everyday communication. In contrast, North American communication can be described as direct, personal, instrumental, and succinct. Nonverbal communication also varies in cultures because individuals attach different meanings to interpersonal space, touch, and time. For example, interpersonal distance is low among South Americans, Southern and Eastern Europeans, and Arabs, and high among Asians, Northern Europeans, and North Americans.

To ensure quality communication, communicators should first assume that cultural differences exist, and they should try to view the situation from the perspective of their foreign colleagues. They can then adjust their encoding or decoding, as well as their use of language or listening skills, to respond to likely differences. Knowledge of the characteristics of diverse cultures facilitates such an adjustment. A cultural integrator, a person who understands differences in a society from the home country and the ways the organization can adapt to them, can also reduce the barrier of inadequate cross-cultural sensitivity. Until all individuals have cross-cultural sensitivity, such special arrangements may be necessary for quality multicultural communication. Multicultural considerations such as these are becoming increasingly important in educational institutions, especially those in higher education. It is not uncommon to have significant numbers of today's workforce and future workforces who are from cultures other than that of the majority.

IMPROVING COMMUNICATION

What can individuals do to improve their communication in both formal and informal settings? In this section, we examine three ways of increasing communication effectiveness: creating a supportive communication climate, using an assertive communication style, and using active listening techniques.

In communicating with their followers, leaders know they must create a trusting and supportive environment (leading with heart). Creating such a climate has the objective of shifting from evaluation to problem solving and formation in communication. They must avoid making employees feel defensive, that is, threatened by the communication. Effective leaders create such an atmosphere in at least six ways:

1. They use descriptive rather than evaluative speech and do not imply that the receiver needs to change. An administrator may describe employee traits in terms of strengths and areas in need of further development, rather than as strengths and weaknesses.

2. They take a problem-solving orientation, which implies a desire to collaborate in exploring a mutual problem, rather than trying to control or change the listener. A leader can ask the follower what he or she hopes to achieve in the near term, or for the fiscal year, rather than setting out a list of goals for the follower.

3. They are spontaneous and honest, and reveal their goals, rather than appearing to use "strategy" that involves ambiguous and multiple motivations. A CEO might share with the work community the need for restructuring and possible areas of downsizing rather than doing so surreptitiously.

4. They convey empathy for the feelings of their listener, rather than appearing unconcerned or neutral about the listener's welfare. They give reassurance that they are identifying with the listener's problems, rather than denying the legitimacy of the problems. When reviewing a union grievance with an employee, the manager may indicate sensitivity to the employee's position even though the decision may ultimately go against the employee.

5. They indicate that they feel equal rather than superior to the listener. Thus, they suggest that they will enter a shared relationship,

not simply dominate the interaction. A college dean may come out from behind the desk and sit next to a colleague to indicate a relationship of equality.

6. Finally, they communicate that they will experiment with their own behavior and ideas, rather than be dogmatic about them. They do not give the impression that they know all the answers and do not need help from anyone. An administrator can concede that he or she does not know if his or her suggestion will work, but ask that the employee in question "try it."[3]

In addition, supportive communication emphasizes congruence between thoughts, feelings, and communication. An individual who feels unappreciated by a supervisor, for example, must communicate that feeling to the supervisor, rather than deny it or communicate it inaccurately. Communication must also validate an individual's importance, uniqueness, and worth. Nondefensive communication recognizes the other person's existence; recognizes the person's uniqueness as an individual, rather than treating him or her as a role or a job; acknowledges the worth of the other person; acknowledges the validity of the other person's perception of the world; and expresses willingness to be involved with the other person during the communication.

THE ASSERTIVE COMMUNICATION STYLE

An assertive style, which is honest, direct, and firm, also improves communication. With this style, a person expresses needs, opinions, and feelings in honest and direct ways and stands up for his or her rights without violating the other person's rights. Assertive behavior is reflected in the content and the nonverbal style of the message. The assertive delegator, for example, "is clear and direct when explaining work to subordinates, doesn't hover, [and] . . . criticizes fairly, objectively, and constructively."[4]

Consider the situation of a superintendent of schools whose assistant has missed two important deadlines in the past month. How would she respond assertively? She might say to her assistant, "I know you missed the last two deadlines. Is there an explanation I should know? It is important that you meet the next deadlines. You should have let me know the problems you were facing and explained the situation to me, rather than saying nothing." Note that an assertive response can include the expression of anger, frustration, or disappointment, but it is expressed in terms that would allow the employee to explain the behavior. This distinguishes it from an aggressive style, which is inappropriate behavior.

We can further contrast the assertive approach to nonassertive and aggressive styles. Nonassertive communication describes behavior where the sender does not stand up for personal rights and indicates that his or her feelings are unimportant; the person may be hesitant, apologetic, or fearful. In the situation of a missed deadline, nonassertive behavior might involve saying nothing to your assistant, hoping the situation would not recur. Individuals might act nonassertively because they mistake assertion for aggression, mistake nonassertion for politeness or being helpful, refuse to accept their personal rights, experience anxiety about negative consequences of assertiveness, or lack assertiveness skills.

Aggressive communication stands up for an individual's rights without respecting the rights of the other person. Aggressive behavior attempts to dominate and control others by sounding accusing or superior. In the situation of the missed deadlines, an aggressive response might be "You always miss deadlines. You're taking advantage of me and the situation. If you miss another deadline, disciplinary action will be taken." While such a response may result in the desired behavior in the short run, its long-term consequences likely will be dysfunctional, resulting in distrust between the individuals involved. Ultimately, such behavior will reduce productivity, and will especially affect the submission of creative and innovative solutions offered to management by the employee.

COMMUNICATING ASSERTIVELY

The following exercise is valuable in helping the heroic follower to recognize the usefulness of an assertive communication style. It may also help improve your communication style if it is too aggressive or too nonassertive.[5]

Select the statement indicating your most likely response to each situation below:

1. When there's an unpleasant job that has to be done, I. . .
    a. Do it myself.
    b. Give it as punishment to someone who's been goofing off.
    c. Hesitate to ask a subordinate to do it.
    d. Ask someone to do it just the same.

Nonassertive communicators hate to ask people to do unpleasant work, and they often wind up doing it themselves (answers a and c). The aggressive communicators might give such difficult tasks as punishments (answer b). The assertive communicator might hesitate to ask the subordinate, but for the sake of efficiency would ask just the same (answer d).

2. When the boss criticizes me, I. . .
    a. Feel bad.
    b. Show her where she's wrong.
    c. Try to learn from it.
    d. Apologize for being stupid.

The aggressive communicator argues with the boss when criticized (answer b). Feeling bad or guilty, though a common reaction, is a nonassertive response (answer a). But apologizing for being stupid is the epitome of nonassertiveness (answer d). The assertive response, assuming the criticism is valid, is to try to learn from the remark (answer c).

3. When my salary increase isn't as large as I think it should be, I. . .
    a. Tell the boss in no uncertain terms what to do with it.
    b. Keep quiet about it.
    c. Say nothing, but take it out on the boss in other ways.
    d. Feel bad.

When people don't like a situation, but they say nothing about it, resentment builds up in them. This resentment often leads to forms of passive aggression; they "get back" in other ways. Answers (b), (c), and (d) are compliant reactions. Answer (a) is an aggressive reaction. No assertive choice was given here. Perhaps, politely addressing the issue with the supervisor may be the assertive way of communicating your dismay.

4. When the boss rejects a good idea of mine, I. . .
   a. Ask why.
   b. Walk away and feel bad.
   c. Try it again later.
   d. Think about joining the competition.

Planning to join the competition is passive aggression. Choices (a) and (c) are assertive responses.

USING ACTIVE LISTENING TECHNIQUES

The man who listens to the voice of a friend, or his wife, or his child, but does not catch the message in the tone of voice: "Notice me. Help me. Care about me," hears—but does not really listen.

The person who attends a concert with her mind on business, hears—but does not really listen. The person who walks among the songs of birds and thinks only of what's for supper, hears—but does not really listen.

The person who does not pay attention to his conscience, who turns away and thinks he has done enough already, hears—but does not really listen.

May we learn to listen to the music of the world, the infant's cry, the sighs of love.

May we listen to the call for help from the lonely.

May we listen for the sound of a heart breaking.

May we listen not only to the words of those we love, but for those things they don't say out loud.

May we begin to listen to the things inside ourselves that we did not have words for and find the words to say them.[6]

Our world is woefully lacking is good listeners. Listening is as much a part of effective communication as is talking. While most of us are born with the capacity to hear, we must learn how to listen. The person who merely hears is a passive receiver who accepts and stores information much like a tape recorder. But a good listener is an involved participant in an exchange.

Unfortunately, most people do not listen; they just wait for their turn to talk. Have you ever noticed that when you are listening to someone you unconsciously begin to compare how you would feel in a similar circumstance or what you would do if you found yourself in the same situation? Gradually, as they talk, your thoughts drift away from what they are saying and focus on your reactions to it. You agree or disagree; you proffer advice; you pronounce judgments. While these are perfectly natural responses, they are sure signs that you are not what we call an active listener. Active listeners engage in the following four steps: they observe, acknowledge, encourage, and interpret.

Active listeners observe by listening for sense data. They take special note of nonverbal cues and *observe* the speaker's facial expression. Do body movements tell you anything? How about posture or breathing rate? All of these signs convey messages that influence the interpretations that the active listener makes. Looking and listening for sense data can be particularly helpful when what you see does not concur with what you hear. Suppose you meet a friend on the street and casually ask, "How are you?" She replies, "Oh, fine. Great." But her voice is flat, her lips grim. You may be confused because her words do not reflect her demeanor. An active listener would probe for meaning by saying something like, "You don't look like you're doing well. Is there anything I can do?"

Active listeners often *acknowledge* what they hear in the form of paraphrasing. Obviously, this technique is only appropriate in certain situations; otherwise, it might sound like parroting and be insulting to the speaker. But you can also reflect your interest nonverbally, Nods, smiles, looks of concern, or comments like "that makes sense" or "that's interesting" can let the speaker know that you are actively listening. Also, try to establish eye contact when you listen. If you are looking away or skyward, it is a sign to the speaker that you are bored and not listening attentively.

Active listeners *encourage* those with whom they are communicating. They invite speakers to tell them more with short encouraging remarks like "I'd like to hear more about that," or "Can you fill me in on what your were feeling then?" Encouraging words can be far more potent than they seem. They can make the speaker feel that what he or she is saying is important and it can lead to further elucidation by the speaker. Encouraging the speaker is often most difficult for people in power positions. Many times, they want to control the conversation, thinking that they have the expertise to solve the problem, and if the speaker will just listen to them, all will be well. Even if this is the case, prudence should be practiced in these cases. The speaker is much more likely to benefit from the listener's advice if the speaker believes that the listener is truly listening, rather than simply waiting for a chance to interrupt with some sage advice.

Finally, active listeners *interpret* what the speaker is trying to communicate. Speakers often have difficulty making direct statements. They sometimes talk in circles, make deliberate omissions, or simply cannot find the correct words to accurately express their thoughts. Thus, it is up to the active listener to probe so that the ultimate message is clearly communicated. For example, suppose your little daughter says that she feels ill today and does not want to go to school. "Besides, I can always take the test some other day." An active listener parent would probably interpret the message to read, "I am not prepared to take the test today, so I'll think of a way of staying home from school until I am prepared."

Active listening, which requires understanding both the content and the intent of a message, can be facilitated by paraphrasing, perception checking, and behavior description. The receiver can paraphrase the message conveyed by the sender by stating in his or her own way what the other person's remarks convey. For example, if the sender states, "I don't like the work I am doing," the receiver might paraphrase it in a number of ways: "Are you saying that you are dissatisfied with the profession?" "Are you dissatisfied with this company?" "Are you dissatisfied with the specific job that you have?" Or "Do you wish to be reassigned to another plant or location?" Note that these ways of paraphrasing the original message suggest very different understandings of the original statement. The sender, upon receiving this feedback from the receiver, can then clarify his or her meaning.[7]

Alternatively, the receiver may perception-check, that is, describe what he or she perceives as the sender's inner state at the time of communication to check his or her understanding of the message. For example, if the sender states, "I don't like the work I am doing," the receiver might check his or her perception of the statement by asking, "Are you dissatisfied by the way you are being treated?" or, "Are you dissatisfied with me as a supervisor?" Note that answers to these two questions will identify different feelings.

A third way of checking communication is through behavior description. Here, the individual reports specific, observable actions of others without making accusations or generalizations about their motives, personality, or characteristics. Similarly, description of feelings, where the individual specifies or identifies feelings by name, analogy, or some other verbal representation, can increase active listening. For example, to help others understand you as a person, you should describe what others did that affects you personally or as a group member. Then you can let others know as clearly and unambiguously as possible what you are feeling.

ACTIVE LISTENING EXERCISE

Below are some statements that were made by employees to their manager. Read each statement and select the response that best represents active listening.[8]

1. Each day brings new problems. You solve one and here comes another. . . What's the use?
   a. I'm surprised to hear you say that.
   b. That's the way it is. There's no use getting upset over it.
   c. I know it's frustrating and sometimes discouraging to run into problem after problem.
   d. Give me an example so I know what you're referring to.

Answer (c) is the best response. This calls feeling to the employee's attention. The others cut off employee opinions or seek a facts review, which calls into question the employee's credibility.

2. At our meeting yesterday, I was counting on you for some support. All you did was sit there and you never said anything!
   a. I was expecting you to ask for my opinion.
   b. You're evidently upset with the way I handled things at the meeting.

c. Hey, I said some things on your behalf. You must not have heard me.

d. I had my reasons for being quiet.

Answer (b) is the best response. This directly encourages the employee to consider the personal feelings message that is being communicated and does not question the employee's perceptions.

3. I don't know when I'm going to get that report done. I'm already swamped with work.
   a. See if you can get someone to help you.
   b. All of us have been in that situation, believe me.
   c. What do you mean swamped?
   d. You sound concerned about your workload.

Answer (d) is the best response. This encourages the employee to determine if the intent is to send a message about overall workload and feelings about it.

4. I'm tired. That last sale really wore me out. I don't think I can handle another customer.
   a. Sure you can. Just rest a few minutes and you'll be fine.
   b. What have you been doing that's gotten you so tired?
   c. You sound like you're exhausted.
   d. We all get feeling that way; don't worry about it.

Answer (c) is the best response. This answer encourages the employee to consider a full message about personal perceptions and feelings and is not judgmental.

EXTERNAL COMMUNICATION

The open-systems model of organizational structure highlights the vulnerability and interdependence of organizations and their environments. External environments are important because they affect the internal structures and processes of organizations; hence, one is forced to look both inside and outside the organization to explain behavior within organizations. However, the growing necessity to interact with the outside environment places added responsibilities and demands on the organization's communications processes. The need to communicate with customers, government officials, advocacy groups, and the mass media cannot be denied. This necessity, however, is a relatively recent phenomenon and presents difficulties to administrators whose training does not normally include communicating with the public through the mass media.

Although the principles of effective communication still prevail when dealing with the outside community, some nuances need to be stressed. Perhaps the most important aspect of communication to consider when dealing with the public is the uniformity of the message. The message must be clear and consistent and must emanate from a single source. In these cases, the "chain of command" and "channels of communication" need to be well defined and structured along the lines of the classical model. It is imperative that the organization "speak with one voice." Someone in the organization should be designated as the clearinghouse for all external communication. This individual, or office, should review all external communication for clarity and accuracy and school personnel should be keenly aware of the organization's policy with regard to external communication. Thus, although a more loosely structured communication system is very appropriate for internal communications, a more tightly structured one is necessary for effective external communications.

MATRIX DESIGN

To overcome some of the problems of the classical structure of most organizations, matrix or mixed designs have evolved to improve mechanisms of lateral communication and information flow across the organization.

The matrix organization, originally developed in the aerospace industry, is characterized by a dual-authority system. There are usually functional and program or product line managers, both reporting to a common superior and both exercising authority over workers within the matrix. Typically, a matrix organization is particularly useful in highly specialized technological areas that focus on innovation. The matrix design allows program managers to interact directly with the environment vis-à-vis new developments. Usually each program requires a multidisciplinary team approach; the matrix structure facilitates the coordination of the team and allows team members to contribute their special expertise.[9]

The matrix design has some disadvantages that stem from the dual authority lines. Individual workers may find having two supervisors to be untenable since it can create conflicting expectations and ambiguity. The matrix design may also be expensive in that both functional and program managers may spend a considerable amount of time in meetings attempting to keep everyone informed of program activities.

The use of matrix design is not very common, but it is a viable way of organizing when communication needs to occur outside the "proper channels." The popularity of interdisciplinary and multicultural courses and programs in education has caused an increased interest in matrix design in that field. Many companies are informally organized in a matrix design. It would most likely serve these institutions well to consider it as a formal organizational structure, especially in cases when communication problems are evident.

INTERVIEWS

Communication problems are most acute when administrators conduct some type of employee evaluation such as an employment appraisal or an employment interview. In employment interviews, the communicators transmit information that allows them to make decisions about the fit between a job applicant and an available position. In performance appraisal, the administrator and employee share information about the employee's performance to date and future development.

The interviewer or assessor can ask open-ended questions or closed-ended questions. Open-ended questions allow the interviewee to structure the response to the question and present information that he or she feels is important

Closed-ended questions, such as "Tell me the first thing that you would do upon meeting a client for the first time," "Who was the person who was most influential in your career choice?" " Why do you want to work here?" and "How can you make a contribution to the mission of the organization?" allow the interviewer to focus a response more precisely. An interview can move from open-ended questions to closed-ended questions, alternate the two types of questions, or begin with closed-ended questions and end with open-ended ones.

The types of questions asked must also be geared to the nature of the position to be filled. In most interviews, the interviewer tries to make the interviewee feel at ease by beginning with questions that are relatively easy to answer and then moving on to questions that the interviewee may find more difficult.

Increasing the effectiveness of communication and the reliability of appraisals requires supervisors to obtain more complete descriptions of the employee's behavior. When we rely on a single source of information, persistent biases occur. One study indicated that raters who had a positive impression of ratees were most lenient and those with a negative impression were least lenient. Another suggested that the raters who thought workers did well in one area, such as dependability, tended to think the employee did well in several areas (halo effect).

Interviews can be conducted using a variety of different formats. Here is an interview agenda that can be effective:

1. Establish the atmosphere. Open the interview slowly and try to create a warm, pleasant, relaxed atmosphere that will reduce the candidate's anxiety.
2. Ask focused questions. Such questions will elicit the knowledge and information you need about the candidate. You want to learn the candidate's perceptions of personal strengths and weaknesses, understanding of the mission of the organization, philosophy of life, verbal fluency, and enthusiasm. The use of "what if" questions often works well to get the candidate indirectly to share these beliefs and attitudes with you.
3. Be an active listener. Ask open-ended questions rather than yes/no questions. Support the candidate verbally with body language and "tell me mores." He or she should be contributing about 70 percent of the conversation to your 30 percent during the interview.
4. Share organizational information with the candidate. Remember the candidate also has a decision to make (Do I want to come to work for you?). Talk about the specific job vacancy; the people with

whom he or she may be working, particularly if those individuals met the candidate; the kinds of products produced by the company; particular programs that the company may have; and information about the community if the candidate is not from the area.

5. Close the interview. Thank the individual for his or her time and openness. Share the next steps in the selection process including when he or she might expect to hear from you or how he or she might keep up with the decision process.

6. Write out your notes. Gather information from the others who participated in the interview process. Often a team discussion works well. If several candidates are to be interviewed before a decision is made, the use of a checklist or some formatted method of recording your perceptions is wise so that later comparison can be more objective.

The interviewing process is particularly important; if you make prudent and wise hiring decisions, they will preclude employee relations problems in the future. Many a problematic staff member could have been screened out during the recruitment and selection process by a particularly astute interviewer.

CONCLUSION

There is the story of a foreign-born plumber in New York who once wrote to the Bureau of Standards that he found hydrochloric acid fine for cleaning drains, and he asked if they agreed. Washington replied, "The efficacy of hydrochloric acid is indisputable, but the chlorine residue is incompatible with metallic permanence." The plumber wrote back that he was mighty glad the Bureau agreed with him.

Considerably alarmed, the Bureau replied a second time: "We cannot assume responsibility for the production of toxic and noxious residues with hydrochloric acid, and suggest that you use an alternative procedure." The plumber was happy to learn that the Bureau still agreed with him. Whereupon Washington wrote, "Don't use hydrochloric acid; it eats the hell out of pipes."

Communication with ease and clarity is no simple task. Because of the complexity of the process, communication gaps will almost certainly occur.

The heroic follower should do all in his or her power not to contribute to the communication gap. To help the follower, there are various orientations toward how communication can be most effectively carried out. Classical theory, social system theory, and open system theory all incorporate a perspective toward the communication process; in other words, who should say what through which channel to whom and toward what effect. Classical theory stresses that the communication process exists to facilitate the manager's command and control over the employees in a formal, hierarchical, and downwardly directed manner. The purpose is to increase efficiency and productivity.

The social system orientation suggests that to be effective, communication has to be two-way and that the meaning of the message is as much to be found in the psychological makeup of the receiver as of the sender. The channels can be informal as well as formal and include anyone who has an interest in a particular subject.

The open system orientation emphasizes the communication process working toward drawing the various subsystems of an organization into a collaborating whole. In addition, drawing the organization's actions into a close fit with the needs of its environment is an essential outcome of the process. This orientation emphasizes that between senders and receivers, the communication process must penetrate social class differences, cultural values, time orientations, and ethnocentrism of all types.

None of the conceptual frameworks, by itself, escapes the barriers to communication. The story of the plumber illustrates the problems of message coding, decoding, and transmission. We have suggested that in order for communication to be effective, we should adapt the process to the situation. We have suggested that when communicating with the outside community, a more structured process may be appropriate, while when communicating with the inside community, a less structured process might be more appropriate. Nevertheless, the heroic follower is more likely to flourish in the social or open systems environment than in a classical one.

DIAGNOSTIC CHECKLIST

Here are some questions that can be addressed to assess your *communication* skills:

1. How *effective* is your communication process?
2. What *barriers* to communication exist?
3. Are you communicating from the *open self* as much a possible?
4. Does communication include *feedback* where appropriate?
5. Is there a climate of mutual *trust and respect* to facilitate the communication process?
6. Are *active listening* and other techniques that improve communication being used?

NOTES

1. Sherod Miller, Daniel Wackman, Elam Nunnally, and Carol Saline, *Straight Talk* (New York: Rawson, 1984).

2. K. J. Krone, F. M. Jablin, and L. L. Putnam, Communication theory and organizational communication: Multiple perspectives, in *Handbook of Organizational Communication: An Interdisciplinary Perspective*, ed. F. Joblin, L. Putnam, K. Roberts, and L. Porter (Newbury Park, CA: Sage, 1987).

3. G. L. Kreps, *Organizational Communication*, 2nd ed. (New York: Langman, 1990).

4. A. J. Lange and P. Jokubowski, *Responsible Assertive Behavior* (Champaign, IL: Research Press, 1976).

5. Alberti and Emmons, The Communicating Assertively Activity, in *Your Perfect Right: A Guide to Assertive Listening*, 6th ed. (San Luis Obispo, CA: Impact Publishers).

6. S. Miller, D. Wackman, E. Nunnally, and C. Saline, *Straight Talk*.

7. R C Huseman and E. W. Miles, Organizational communication in the information age, *Journal of Management* 14 (2) (1988): 181–204.

8. Bruce Kemelgor, The Active Listening Exercise, in *Organizational Behavior: Learning Guide/Experimental Exercises* (Dryden Press, a Division of Holt, Rinehart, and Winston, Inc.)

9. D. B. Rogers and R. E. Farson, Active listening, in *Organizational Psychology: Readings on Human Behavior in Organizations*, ed. D. Kolb, E. Rubin, and J. McIntire (Englewood Cliffs, NJ: Prentice Hall, 1984).

5

BE THE CHANGE THAT YOU SEEK IN OTHERS!

To live is to change, and to be perfect is to have changed often.

—John Henry Newman

The next important habit for the heroic follower to master on the path from dependence to independence is flexibility or adaptability. Whichever term you prefer, both flexibility and adaptability imply *change*. Thus, in order to become a highly effective follower, one needs to develop a high tolerance for and willingness to change.

Human instinct seems to prefer the status quo. Intellectually, however, we all seem to realize that in order to progress, we need to experience change. Collectively, we have bought into W. Edwards Deming's notion that for any individual or institution to thrive, "continuous improvement" is an absolute necessity. And continuous improvement implies change. But none of this rationalizing makes it any easier to accept. When dealing with the process of change, we seem to operate on a visceral level. Our security need seems to militate against any sort of significant change. Nevertheless, if our institutions and our society are to progress, we need to overcome our instincts and implement the changes that will enable us to evolve as individuals and as a society.

In an earlier work, *The Ten-Minute Guide to Educational Leadership*, I suggest that if the educational leader systematically focuses on ten aspects of his or her institution each day, the administrator will be effective. These ten components include the school's organizational structure; its organizational climate; its leadership; its motivation, communication, planning, decision making, and conflict management processes; its power distribution; and its attitude toward change. Of these essential elements, I believe that an institution's tolerance of and ability to change is the most important element for success. I also believe that mastering the ability to successfully effect change to transform an institution is the culminating activity of the effective leader. However, this tolerance for change is an evolving habit that begins in one's role as a follower.

Developing a tolerance for change requires the heroic follower to have mastered all of the other elements necessary for developing effectiveness. In order to develop a high tolerance for change, the heroic follower must have a *purpose* in life, the follower must have a sense of *responsibility* or accountability, and the follower must have mastered the *communication* process. This is a daunting task—so daunting that the average follower is not able to cope with it. As a result, the individual who is flexible and tolerant of change remains the exception rather than the rule, and highly effective followers remain the exception rather than the rule.

AN INTEGRATED APPROACH TO CHANGE

The literature is replete with various suggested change processes, more or less based on functionalist/structuralist theory. Many of them contain elements that are helpful in leading to successful transformation, but few contain all of the necessary elements. As a result, through the process of trial and error, I have developed my own process for change. I call it an *integrated change* process because although there are distinct steps in the process, the key to their successful implementation is that many of them are implemented simultaneously rather than sequentially.

In an earlier work, *Ten Steps to Educational Reform: Making Change Happen*,[1] I suggest the following steps in the process:

1. Establishing a climate for change
2. Assessing the need for change
3. Creating a sense of urgency

4. Assessing favorable and opposing forces
5. Selecting among alternatives
6. Promoting ownership
7. Providing professional development
8. Operationalizing the change
9. Evaluating the change
10. Institutionalizing the change

Most attempts at effecting change fail because individuals have no plan at all or do not engage in all the steps in the process. Other failures occur when administrators try to implement the reform by following the change process steps sequentially rather than simultaneously; they get bogged down in one or another of the steps and are unable to bring the process to closure.

STEP 1: ESTABLISHING A CLIMATE FOR CHANGE

E. Mark Hanson, in his text entitled *Educational Administration and Organizational Behavior*, describes an incident regarding the process of change. Always interested in the processes of school improvement, he once asked the superintendent of a large, urban school district, "How does change come about around here?" She thought for a moment. "Well," she replied, "there is the normal way and the miraculous way. The normal way," she continued, "is where the heavens part and the angels come down and do the change for us. The miraculous way is when we do it ourselves."[2]

If a climate of change has been established in your institution and in your personal life, change will come to be expected. It will be perceived as something positive and routine. The need for change in the context of continuous improvement should be articulated constantly by heroic followers. Heroic followers should set the tone for change by taking every opportunity to articulate its necessity and model it in their own lives. For example, company staff meetings can be occasions for articulating the notion that if the institution is to progress, outcome-wise and operationally, it must be open to change. At the initial meeting, the possible changes that are anticipated during the upcoming fiscal year can be shared. At subsequent meetings, the need for change can be rein-forced. Establishing a climate for change is the first step in a systematic method of effecting change. Articulating the need for change, modeling change, and establishing trust and respect are behaviors that will help establish a climate for change.

In addition to articulating the need for change, to promote a positive school climate the follower must model a tolerance for change. Even if it is something simple, such as rearranging your office furniture every two or three years or changing the format of staff meetings to incorpo-rate innovative concepts like cooperative learning and shared decision making, the follower needs to lead by example. The follower must be perceived as being open to new ideas and providing a climate in which creativity is fostered. In other words, heroic followers should reflect the behaviors suggested in the title of this chapter: Be the change that you seek in others.

While fostering a climate for change, the follower must be careful not be perceived as being in favor of change for its own sake, or for his or her own sake. If this occurs, it can have a counterproductive or dys-functional effect. One way of precluding such a perception is to mutu-ally establish the basics or essentials of your institution—the things that are relatively constant and not subject to change—and those that must change for your institution to remain healthy. Such fundamentals as product excellence, individual attention, community involvement in de-cision making, and an emphasis on quality control might be identified as remaining constant, while production methods, processing methods, and organizational structure are subject to change. In other words, the *mission* and *goals* can remain constant for a while, while the *methods* of achieving them may be frequently changing. In establishing both the goals and the methods, however, remember to examine them under the lens of your personal and professional mission statement or purpose.

Another way to avoid being perceived as in favor of change for change's sake is to be certain that when a change is implemented, all of the steps in the process are followed. If this is done, it is more likely that the change will be implemented successfully in the first place, and if the change is not effective, the evaluation stage of the process provides an opportunity to move away from it gracefully. In addition, success breeds success. If the follower has a record of implementing change successfully, it paves the way for future change. If one also has a reputation for objectively evaluating the effectiveness of change and abandoning it if it is unsuccessful, this will foster a climate with a high tolerance for change.

If a positive climate for change is to be established, another requisite is an environment of trust and respect. Institutions do not amount to anything without the people who make them what they are. The individuals most influential in shaping institutions are essentially *volunteers*. Our very best employees and managers can work anywhere they please. So, in a sense, they volunteer to work where they do. As heroic followers, we would do far better if we looked on and treated our colleagues as volunteers. To engender trust and respect, we should treat our colleagues as if we had a *covenantal* rather than contractual relationship with them. We will speak more on covenantal relationships later.

If an institution is to be a place where change is not only tolerated, but also embraced, it must be successful in creating a culture of trust and respect so that everyone in it feels as if he or she "owns the place." We often hear educators refer to where they work as "school," such as "I will be staying at *school* late tonight, dear." On the other hand, beware of the teacher who says simply, "I will be staying at *work* late tonight." That teacher has likely not taken "ownership" in the place.

Taking ownership is a sign of one's love for an institution. In his book, *Servant Leadership*, Robert Greenleaf says, "Love is an undefinable term, and its manifestations are both subtle and infinite. It has only one absolute condition: unlimited liability!"[3] Although it might run counter to our traditional notion of American capitalism, employees should be encouraged to act as if they own the place; it is a sign of love, and it is a prerequisite for establishing a positive climate for change.

Diagnostic Checklist

Here are a few questions that you can address in assessing whether a *climate for change* has been established:

1. Is the need for change being *articulated* constantly?
2. Is the institution's staff *modeling* change?
3. Is a climate of *trust and respect* being nurtured?
4. Are the employees engaging in effective *change behavior*?

STEP 2: ASSESSING THE NEED FOR CHANGE

The next step in the integrated change process is the needs assessment. Unfortunately, this step is often ignored. Many leaders become enamored of one reform or another and try to implement it whether or not there is an identified and agreed-upon need. In the field of education, for example, reforms such as the whole language approach to reading, cooperative learning, block scheduling, interdisciplinary curricula, distance learning, and even site-based management have been adopted arbitrarily by misguided educational administrators. Unfortunately, this ill-advised fascination with the "fad du jour" takes place all too often not only in education but in all segments of business and industry. When implemented without a needs assessment, or at least an after-the-fact needs assessment, these changes are destined to failure.

Ordinarily, a needs assessment calls for a review of existing data and may require some surveying of clients and other appropriate reference groups. There is always a certain risk in a needs assessment. In the process of uncovering needs, one may also raise expectations that all of the respondents' concerns will be addressed. Fundamental to effecting change is priority setting and focus; thus, not all needs can be met immediately. Resources are in short supply, and difficult, sometimes painful, decisions have to be made about which from an array of critical needs requires attention. Three reference groups are especially important to the needs assessment and the change process: customers and employees, professional staff, and educational policy makers. Often, it is the employees who are left out of the process. Leaving them out, of course, has distribution of power implications and is not likely to foster a climate for change or ownership in the change process.

Consumer data are readily available in the records a typical company generates and maintains. Employee attendance records, analyses of employees with disabilities, transportation reports, and a host of other official and unofficial sources serve as basic data sources when it comes time to develop a profile of the organization and determine areas in need of reform or change. Informal discussions with colleagues, other professionals, and the customers themselves are another source of information. Employee and customer focus groups and systematic observation by both followers and leaders are still other ways of assessing whether there is a need for change in the organization.

Use of community and customer surveys can be very helpful to both the leader and the follower, as can various advisory groups. Such surveys are invaluable in determining customer and community expectations and attitudes and perceptions of the product needs of the customer base. The diverse nature of most communities requires that, for any survey, care needs to be taken that the necessary degree of randomness exists. Concern for complete information and diversity of opinion should also be reflected in the composition of advisory groups.

Another source of information regarding the needs of the organization is the professional staff. They can be helpful with regard to institutional needs and can offer specific observations about the nature of these needs. Staff surveys or any of a number of rational problem-solving processes is useful in needs assessments. Using some of these methods in combination can be effective. For example, a staff meeting may be used to brainstorm the strengths and weaknesses of the institution. The information could then be summarized and items generated for a survey to determine the perceived intensity and importance of the issues identified. A SWOT analysis, the Nominal Group Technique, or the Delphi Technique can then be used. These techniques will be discussed in detail later.

Central office personnel; corporate board members; local, state, and federal legislators; federal agencies; various advocacy groups; accrediting groups; and other such entities are examples of educational policy makers. They also should be consulted to identify the needs of the institution. The reports of accrediting associations, such as the Middle States Association, Phi Beta Kappa, the American Association of Colleges and Schools of Business (AACSB), the American Stock Exchange, the American Association of Manufacturers, and the Census Bureau Report can be valuable tools for assessing the needs of an institution.

Diagnostic Checklist

Here are a few questions you can address in assessing whether a *need for change* has been identified:

1. Have *data* been collected that indicate a need for change in your institution?

2. Has a formal or informal *needs assessment* taken place?
3. Did the needs assessment survey reflect the *mission and beliefs* of the institution?
4. Has the needs assessment corroborated the *anecdotal data*?
5. Has the need for the identified change been *promulgated* to the work community?

STEP 3: CREATING A SENSE OF URGENCY

Since our natural instinct is to resist change, to effect a needed change, a sense of alarm or urgency often must be created. To overcome our innate sense of inertia, the dire consequences of remaining in the status quo need to be articulated. There are a number of ways to create a sense of urgency, including citing comparable data and projected profit declines. But in creating a sense of urgency, the change agent must be aware that individuals and groups are often moved by dissimilar forces. In other words, what may cause a sense of urgency in one person may not do so in another.

Creating a sense of urgency or stress can have both functional and dysfunctional outcomes. Whether stress takes a constructive or destructive course in influenced by the sociocultural context in which the stress occurs, because differences tend to exaggerate barriers and reduce the likelihood of conflict resolution. The issues involved also will affect the likely outcomes. Whether the individuals or groups have cooperative, individualistic, or competitive orientations toward stress will affect the outcomes as well.

Effective change agent administrators learn how to create functional conflict and manage dysfunctional conflict. They develop and practice techniques for diagnosing the causes and nature of stress and transform it into a productive force that fosters needed change in the institution. Many universities, for example, have healthy competition among their schools (Business College, College of Arts and Sciences, College of Education, etc.) for recruitment of the most qualified students. This is an example of functional sense of urgency or stress.

One can see, then, that some stress is beneficial. It can encourage organizational innovation, creativity, and adaptation. By its very nature, capitalism and a market economy often spawn innovation and change in marketing techniques and, more importantly, in product improvement and quality control. In this case, creating a sense of urgency can result in more employee enthusiasm and better decision making. The challenge is to be able to create a sense of urgency without allowing it to become dysfunctional. This means that the change agent must know the stages of stress and when to intervene.

Diagnostic Checklist

Here are a few questions you can address in assessing whether a *sense of urgency* has been created:

1. Has the work community been taken to the *perceived stress stage* of development?
2. Have *compelling arguments* been developed for the change?
3. Have they been applied to the appropriate *constituencies?*
4. Has a *position paper* on the change been developed and distributed?

STEP 4: ASSESSING FAVORABLE AND OPPOSING FORCES

Accurate assessment of the forces that affect proposed reform is possibly the most important step in the integrated change process. Correctly identifying the forces that favor the reform and those that oppose it is crucial to effective implementation of the change. Further, the interventions chosen to neutralize the forces against change and enhance the forces in favor of it are instrumental to its eventual success.

The forces resistant to change can be considerable. These forces range from the simple ignorance of an individual to the complex vested interests of our own institutions' members. As the comic strip character Pogo phrased it, "We have met the enemy and he is us."

The forces resistant to change are an important part of the organization's environment or climate. They must be diagnosed, understood, and taken into account in the targeting process and in selecting a change strategy. The environment harboring the forces of resistance is typically not social or technical but sociotechnical. A sociotechnical interpretation of environment refers to the behavior of individuals as it is shaped by the interaction of technical characteristics such as instructional equipment, physical layout of the plant, activity schedules, and social characteristics such as norms, informal groups, power centers, and the like. As Chin and Benne point out, "the problem-solving structures and processes of a human system must be developed to deal with a range of sociotechnical difficulties, converting them into problems and organizing the relevant processes of data collection, planning, invention, and tryout of solutions, evaluation and feedback of results, replanning, and so forth, which are required for the solution of the problem."[4]

These resistances are particularly prominent in not-for-profit organizations, especially when a virtual monopoly exists. For example, according to Richard Carlson, a major organizational feature that contributes to resistance to change is the domestication of public schools and other educational institutions. A domesticated organization has many properties of the monopoly: it does not have to compete for resources, except in a very limited area; it has a steady flow of clients; and its survival is guaranteed.[5]

Although private schools and colleges do not possess all of these characteristics in the way that public schools do, many of the teachers view their institutions in this way. One often hears the college professor or the private school teacher proclaim in the light of declining enrollments, "That's the administration's problem."

Because these institutions are domesticated organizations, they do not face the problems of private organizations that make it necessary to build major change mechanisms into their structures. Change capability permits private organizations to make the necessary modification in production and product continually to hold their share of the market and expand it if possible. The domestication of the school builds in a layer of protective insulation that cannot be penetrated easily. Thus, to effect change in a domesticated organization becomes a greater challenge.

An interesting example of this type of organizational behavior was part of California's omnibus educational reform bill of 1983, which was intended to increase instructional time in the classroom. A comparative study had shown that California's students received 2.5 weeks' less instructional time than the national average. The bill offered financial incentives to districts to meet the target of 180 days a year and 240 minutes a day at a cost of $250 million annually for the first three years. The average high school needed to add four days to its school year and six minutes each day to qualify for the incentive award of $75 per pupil. The average elementary school needed to add four days for a $55-per-pupil-per-day bonus.

In light of a potential contract violation and teachers' resistance to increased instructional time without increased compensation, districts found creative ways to lengthen the school day and year without increasing instructional time. Some districts added one minute to each passing period between classes, which could add up to 900 minutes or about eighteen fifty-minute classes. Other schools extended homeroom periods by five minutes each day, totaling 900 minutes per year. Others added an extra recess to the school day. Some schools did add one or two minutes of instructional time to each class. When considering educational change in a domesticated organization, therefore, the result is not always the desired outcome. This phenomenon also occurs in other monolithic organizations like utility companies and in local, state, and federal agencies.

Goodwin Watson points out that during the process of effecting change, perceived resistance moves through a four-stage cycle. He describes the arrival of a reform in these terms: "In the early stage, when only a few pioneer thinkers take the reform seriously, resistance appears massive and undifferentiated. 'Everyone' knows better; 'No one in his right mind' could advocate the change. Proponents are labeled crack-pots or visionaries."

In the second stage, some support becomes evident, the pro and con forces become visible, and the lines of battle are drawn.

In the third stage, the battle is engaged "as resistance becomes mobilized to crush the upstart proposal." The supporters of the change are often surprised and frequently overwhelmed by the opposition's tenacity. Survival of the innovation depends on developing a base of power to overcome the opposition.

If the supporters of change are victorious in the third stage, the fourth stage is characterized by support flowing to the newly arrived reform. "The persisting resistance is, at this stage, seen as a stubborn, hidebound, cantankerous nuisance. For a time, the danger of a counterswing of the pendulum remains real." The cycle begins anew when another effort toward change occurs.[6]

Force Field Analysis

To understand the changing forces that affect a change, we can use an analytical technique called *force field analysis*, which views a problem as a product of forces working in different, often opposite, directions. An organization, or any of its subsystems, maintains the status quo when the sum of opposing forces is zero. When forces in one direction exceed forces in the opposite direction, the organization or subsystem moves in the direction of the greater forces. For example, if forces for change exceed forces against change, then change is likely to occur.

To move the educational institution toward a different desired state requires increasing the forces for change in that direction, decreasing the forces against change in the other direction, or both. Generally, reducing resistance forces creates less tension in the system and fewer unanticipated consequences than increasing forces for change. Suppose your organization is moving from analog to digital technology. Reducing the resistances to the changes created by the introduction of digital technology increases the likelihood of the changeover. When the employees and managers no longer resist change, the present state moves closer to the desired state.

Consider again our example of new technology. Moving from analog to digital is bound to encounter resistance. What are the opposing forces that one can anticipate? Certainly some of the staff will be against the change because it will entail new learning, and therefore, more work. On the contrary, what are the forces in favor of change? Once again, one can anticipate that certain members of the staff, especially those more creative and forward-looking employees, will favor the more innovative approach that is embodied in digital technology. A savvy heroic follower will be able to apply interventions that would neutralize the opposition and mobilize the forces in favor of

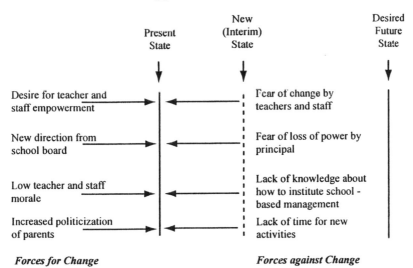

Forces for Change   Forces against Change

Figure 5.1.   Identifying Target Forces

this change. Using *Force Field Analysis* in a systematic way can be very helpful in bringing about desired change.

Changes in the organization's environment, such as new laws or regulations, rapidly increasing competition, or an unpredictable rate of inflation, may require the organization to implement new structures or reward systems. New programs resulting from the availability of improved technology; changes in competition in education; or unusual requirements of the new laws regarding individuals with disabilities, such as accessibility, inclusion, and/or mainstreaming may also affect the institution.

Finally, reduced productivity and effectiveness, product quality, satisfaction, commitment, or increased turnover or absenteeism may call for changes in intra- or international relations. One or two specific events external to the institution frequently precipitate the change. For example, the events of 9/11 generated a flurry of reforms that continue to this day. The events at Columbine High School are another example of how an external event can effect change in your own institution.

Forces known as *resistance forces* counteract the forces for change. Administrators might resist changes to their routines and supervisory activities; they may also be unwilling to relinquish their decision-making authority. Leaders may be unwilling to allocate the resources required to change the culture. Identifying and then reducing resistance forces may be essential to making an individual or group receptive to change.

Forces against a change often reside within the institution and stem from rigid organizational structures and individual thinking. Specific forces against change include employees' distrust of the change agent, fear of change, desire to maintain power, and complacency; lack of resources to support the change; conflicts between individual and organizational goals; and organizational inertia against changing the status quo. These forces frequently combine into significant resistance to change.

Resistance results from a variety of factors. First, it occurs when a change ignores the needs, attitudes, and beliefs on an organization's members. If employees, for example, have high security needs, they may see as threatening the decreasing influence of unions. Second, individuals resist change when they lack specific information about the change; they may not know when, how, or why it is occurring. Third, individuals may not perceive a need for change; they may feel that their organization is operating effectively and efficiently. In these cases, change often is neither voluntary nor requested by organization members. Fourth, organization members frequently have a we-they mentality that causes them to view the change agent as their enemy, particularly when change is imposed by representatives outside of the immediate work site. Fifth, members may view change as a threat to the prestige and security of the institution. They may perceive the change in procedures or policies as a commentary that their performance is inadequate. Sixth, employees may perceive the change as a threat to their expertise, status, or security. Introduction of a new computer-aided instructional system, for example, may cause teachers to feel that they lack sufficient knowledge to perform their jobs. Revision of an organization's structure may challenge their relative status in the organization. Introduction of a new reward system may threaten their feelings of job security. For effective change to occur, the change agent must confront each of these factors and overcome the resulting resistance. It helps a great deal if the change agent has engendered a sense of *mutual trust and respect* among his or her colleagues before the effort to effect change begins.

As we discussed earlier, many administrators might fight opposing forces with equal force. Human nature provokes many of us "to fight fire with fire." As sensitive heroic followers, however, we concern ourselves with sharing power and influence, not with eliminating it. Thus, in the process of applying Force Field Analysis, we must be careful to use compelling argument rather than coercion to neutralize opposing forces. Likewise, when we are developing and selecting alternatives, we must be careful to make the process inclusionary rather than exclusionary. Participative decision making needs to be employed, and group decision making should be the rule rather than the exception.

The heroic follower is careful to *inspire* his or her colleagues, but not *manipulate* them. Not only do our overall goals have to be laudable, but also the *means* by which we reach those goals must be laudable. So in utilizing the strategies suggested here, we must continually be concerned with the equitable distribution of power, the need to be other-centered rather than self-centered, the care of the person, and solidarity with the underrepresented. If we view our behavior under these lenses, we argue that a culture of mutual trust and respect will be developed and needed change will be more readily accepted.

Diagnostic Checklist

Here are a few questions you can address about your *assessment of forces:*

1. Is a *force field analysis* being performed?
2. Is it adequately identifying *favorable and opposing forces*?
3. Is there a systematic plan to *affirm and strengthen* the favorable forces?
4. Is there a systematic plan to *neutralize* the opposing forces?

STEP 5: SELECTING AMONG ALTERNATIVES

While the previously mentioned steps in the integrated change process are being addressed, the change agent should establish a committee or task force of "believers" to begin developing alternatives that would address the perceived need for change. Ideally, a deliberative consideration of the various alternatives should be undertaken, and the most cost-efficient and effective alternative should be chosen. All too often, however, "the powers that be" have chosen the alternative already and the change agent is expected simply to implement it. Of course, "the powers that be" in this instance would certainly not have been utilizing the principles espoused here if they determined the change by fiat. In these instances, however, the change agent should at least be free to adapt the reform to meet local needs.

Another phenomenon that sometimes occurs during this phase of the change process is the tendency to *satisfice,* or choose the alternative that offends the fewest individuals and/or groups, rather than choosing the best alternative. *Satisficing* is a term coined by Herbert Simon, a Nobel Prize winner in economics, who was critical of the so-called rational model of decision making, which indicates that decision makers develop and analyze all of the possible alternatives and select the best one available.

According to Simon, at a certain point in the decision making process, rather than the best possible alternative being chosen, in the interest of efficiency the decision maker will *satisfice,* or sacrifice the optimal for a solution or alternative that is satisfactory or good enough. For example, if a school is trying to decide between the traditional phonics approach versus the whole language approach to teaching reading, the change agent(s) may satisfice and choose an *integrated* model that combines the best aspects of both the phonics and whole language approaches. Thus, the change agent may sacrifice the optimal solution for one that satisfies the greatest number of constituencies.

In a similar approach to selecting an alternative, the model known as *decision making by objection* prompts decision makers not to seek an optimal solution to a problem, but to choose a course of action that does not have a high probability of making matters worse. The decision makers first produce a rough description of an acceptable resolution of the situation. Then they propose a course of action, accompanied by a description of the positive outcomes of the action. Objections to the action are raised, further delimiting the problem and defining an acceptable resolution. The decision makers repeat this process, creating a series of courses of action, each one having fewer objections than the previous one. Finally, the most acceptable alternative evolves. On the surface, this approach seems to violate the *magis* principle, but Ignatius tells us that where the greatest good is not attainable, the greater good is sometimes acceptable.

Once the force field analysis described earlier has been completed, it is time to generate alternatives that could be implemented to address the identified need effectively. Generally, a small committee representing as many of the institution's constituencies as appropriate should be established. The members of the committee should be those who are advocates of change with possibly a naysayer or two included as devil's advocates. In preparation for their work, committee members should be provided with the latest research findings regarding the reform being considered and be encouraged to make themselves aware of successful uses of the alternatives being considered. The so-called *best practices approach* can be effective in identifying possible alternatives and convincing staff members of the reform's efficacy. The alternative that is finally chosen should be the one that best fits the local needs and should be selected according to its (a) rationale, (b) proven effectiveness, (c) resource requirements, (d) distinctive qualities, (e) mission appropriateness, and (f) cost/benefits.

The next logical question that one might ask is how can change agents overcome barriers, reduce biases, and make more effective decisions regarding the selection of the appropriate reform alternative. There are at least three techniques that can improve the alternative development and selection process: (a) brainstorming, (b) the Nominal Group Technique, and (c) the Delphi Technique.

Groups of individuals use brainstorming to generate many alternatives for consideration in the selection process. In brainstorming, the group lists as many alternatives as possible without evaluating the feasibility of any alternative. For example, if a cost reduction program is needed in a company to offset continuing budget deficits, the change agent might be charged with listing all of the ways of reducing costs in a department. The absence of evaluation encourages group members to generate rather than defend ideas. Then, after ideas have been generated, they are evaluated, and selections are made. Although brainstorming can result in many shallow and useless ideas, it can also motivate members to offer new and innovative ideas. It works best when individuals have a common view of what constitutes a good idea, but it is more difficult to use when specialized knowledge or complex implementation is required. Since most reforms are complex in nature, brainstorming can only be used effectively in a limited number of cases and as part of the alternative generation process rather than as the alternative selection process.

The Nominal Group Technique is a structured group meeting that helps resolve differences in group opinion by having individuals generate and then rank in order a series of ideas in the problem solving, alternative generation, or decision-making stage of a planning process. A group of individuals is presented with a stated problem. Each person individually offers alternative solutions in writing. The group then shares the solutions and lists them on a chart, as in brainstorming. Group members discuss and clarify the ideas, then they rank and vote their preference for the various ideas. If the group has not reached an agreement, they repeat the ranking and voting procedure until the group reaches some agreement.

The size of the group and the diverse expertise of its members increase the usefulness of the Nominal Group Technique. It encourages each group member to think individually and offer ideas about the content of a proposal, and then directs group discussion. It moves the group toward problem resolution by systematically focusing on top ranked ideas and eliminating less valued ones. The Nominal Group Technique also encourages continued exploration of the issues, provides a forum for the expression of minority viewpoints, gives individuals some time to think about the issues before offering solutions, and provides a mechanism for reaching a decision expediently through the ranking-voting procedure. It fosters creativity by allowing extensive individual input into the process. Strong personality types dominate the group less often because of the opportunity for systematic input by all group members. It encourages innovation, limits conflict, emphasizes equal participation by all members, helps generate consensus, and incorporates the preferences of individuals in decision-making choices. However, unless the change agent is trained in the use of this technique, it is more prudent to use an organizational consultant trained in these techniques to act as a facilitator.

The Delphi Technique structures group communication by dealing with a complex problem in four phases: (a) exploration of the subject by individuals, (b) reaching understanding of the group's view of the issues, (c) sharing and evaluating any reasons for differences, and (d) final evaluation of all information. In the conventional Delphi, a small group designs a questionnaire, which is completed by a larger respondent group;

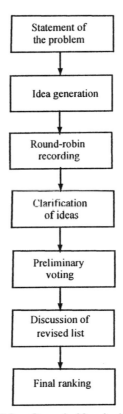

Figure 5.2.   Steps in Nominal Group

the results are then tabulated and used in developing a revised questionnaire, which is again completed by the larger group. Thus, the results of the original polling are fed back to the respondent group to use in subsequent responses. This procedure is repeated until the issues are narrowed, responses are focused, or consensus is reached. In another format, a computer summarizes the results, thus replacing the small group. Such group decision support systems have increased the focus on the task or problem; the depth of analysis; communication about the task, clarifying information, and conclusions; effort expended by the group; widespread participation of group members; and consensus reaching.

Delphi is very helpful in a variety of circumstances. First, if the decision makers cannot apply precise analytical techniques to solving the problem, but prefer to use subjective judgments on a collective basis, Delphi can provide input from a large number of respondents. Second, if the individuals involved have failed to communicate effectively in the past, the Delphi procedures offer a systematic method for ensuring that their opinions are presented. Third, the Delphi does not require face-to-face interaction, so it succeeds when the group is too large for such a direct exchange. Fourth, when time and cost prevent frequent group meetings or when additional premeeting communication between group members increases the efficiency of the meeting held, the Delphi technique offers significant value for decision making. Fifth, the Delphi can overcome situations where individuals disagree strongly or where anonymity of views must be maintained to protect group members. Finally, the Delphi technique reduces the likelihood of groupthink; it prevents one or more members from dominating by their numbers or strength of personality.

Another effective method of generating alternatives is the SWOT analysis whereby the strengths, weaknesses, opportunities, and threats affecting the organization are delineated. During the process, the opportunities identified can lead to a variety of possible alternatives.

On another issue related to developing alternatives, we often hear about the alleged virtue of bottom-up versus top-down strategies for generating changes and reforms. Applying the principles of empowerment prompts us to believe that the bottom-up approach would be more effective. Today, it is the minority view that top-down strategies are more effective. The fact of the matter is that neither of these strategies is maximally effective in isolation. Rather, integrating both top-down and bottom-up strategies for reform is most effective.

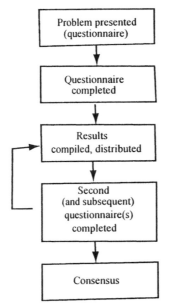

Figure 5.3.   Steps in the Delphi Technique

Small- and large-scale studies of top-down strategies have demonstrated consistently that local implementation fails in the vast majority of cases. The best-known study of voluntary adoption of top-down movements is the Rand Change Agent study conducted by Berman and McLaughlin and associates. They investigated federally sponsored educational programs adopted in 293 sites and found that, even though adoption was voluntary, districts often took on change projects for opportunistic rather than substantial reasons.[7]

On a more sweeping scale, Sarason argues that billions of dollars have been spent on top-down reforms with little to show for it. Sarason observes that such reform efforts do have an implicit theory of change: Change can come about by proclaiming new policies, or by legislation, or by new performance standards, or by creating a shape-up-or-ship-out ambiance, or all of the preceding. It is a conception that in principle is similar to how you go about creating and improving an assembly line—that is, what it means to those who work on the assembly line is of secondary significance, if it has any significance at all. The workers will change.[8]

In short, centralized reform mandates have a poor track record as instruments for change. This failure has led some to conclude that only decentralized, locally driven reform can succeed. Site-based management, or giving more decision-making power to the local level, is currently the most prominent manifestation of this focus. So far, however, the claim of superiority of grassroots initiatives is primarily theoretical. In reviewing evidence on site-based management in *The New Meaning of Educational Change*, one can conclude that restructuring reforms that involved decision making by schools may have altered governance procedures, but they do not affect the teaching-learning process in any significant way.

The evidence that bottom-up strategies are no more effective than top-down ones continues to mount. Taylor and Teddlie draw similar conclusions in their study of the extent of classroom change in "a district widely acclaimed as a model of restructuring." They examined classrooms in thirty-three schools (sixteen from pilot schools that had established site-based management programs and seventeen from nonpilot schools in the same district). They did find that teachers in the pilot schools reported higher levels of participation in decision making, but they found no differences in teaching strategies (teacher-directed instruction and low student involvement dominated in both sets of cases). Further, there was little evidence of teacher-teacher collaboration. Extensive collaboration was reported in only two of the thirty-three schools, and both were nonpilot schools. Taylor and Teddlie observe: "Teachers in this study did not alter their practice. . . Increasing their participation in decision making did not overcome norms of autonomy so that teachers would feel empowered to collaborate with their colleagues."[10] In sum, then, decentralized initiatives do not fare any better than centralized reforms.

A number of researchers have concluded that organizations, in general, that underwent successful revitalization followed a particular sequence in which individual, small-group, and informal behavior began to change first (bottom-up, if you will). This, in turn, was reinforced and further propelled by changes in formal design and procedures (structures, personnel practices, compensation systems, etc.) in the organization (top-down). Both local and central levels can be active and influential at all phases. These studies and my own experience have led me to promote an integrated change process that involves both top-down and bottom-up strategies that operate simultaneously in effectively implemented reform.

Top-down strategies result in conflict, or superficial compliance, or both. Expecting local units to flourish through laissez-faire decentralization leads to drift, narrowness, or inertia. Combined strategies that capitalize on the central office's strengths (to provide direction, incentives, networking, and monitoring) and the local institution's capacities (to learn, create, respond, and contribute) are more likely to achieve greater overall effectiveness. Such systems also have greater accountability, given that the need to obtain political support for ideas is built into their pattern of interaction.

Simultaneous top-down/bottom-up strategies are essential because dynamically complex societies are full of surprises. Only the negotiated capacity and strengths of the entire workplace community are capable of promoting organizational improvement while retaining the capacity to learn from new patterns, whether anticipated or not. Finally, one level cannot wait for the other level to act. Systems do not change by themselves; individuals and groups change systems. Breakthroughs occur when productive connections amass, creating growing pressure for systems to change. The more that top-down and bottom-up forces are coordinated, the more likely it is that complex systems will move toward greater effectiveness. Hence, *both* leaders and followers are needed to initiate and implement effective change.

Diagnostic Checklist

Here are a few questions you can address in assessing your success in *creating and selecting alternatives:*

1. Is *creative thinking* being used in developing possible alternatives?
2. Are representatives of *all segments* of the community involved in the selection process?
3. Does the alternative selected relate to *local* needs?
4. Are both *top-down and bottom-up* strategies being employed?

STEP 6: PROMOTING OWNERSHIP

It is a truism in business, and in other fields as well, that if a change or reform is to be implemented successfully, it must have the support of the workforce. Consequently, we often hear managers suggest that a new program does not have a chance of succeeding unless the employees take ownership of it. Most of us agree with the common sense of this assertion. But how is employee ownership fostered? Let me suggest four steps:

- *Respect people.* As we have indicated earlier, this starts with appreciating the diverse gifts that individuals bring to your organization. The key is to dwell on the strengths of your coworkers rather than on their weaknesses. This does not mean that disciplinary action, or even dismissal, will never become necessary. It does mean, however, that we should focus on the formative aspect of the employee evaluation process before we engage in the summative part. Leaders are obligated to develop colleagues' skills and place them in situations that will maximize their potential for success. For their part, followers need to take advantage of the opportunities available for professional development.
- *Let belief guide policy and practice.* We spoke earlier of developing a culture of civility in an institution. If there is an environment of mutual respect and trust, the institution will flourish. Leaders and followers need to let their belief or value systems guide their behavior. Style is merely a consequence of what we believe and what is in our hearts.
- *Recognize the need for covenants.* Contractual agreements cover such things as salary, fringe benefits, and working conditions. They are part of organization life, and there is a legitimate need for them. But in today's businesses, where the best people working in our institutions are similar to volunteers, we need covenantal relationships. Our best workers may choose their employers. They usually choose the institution where they work based on reasons less tangible than salaries and fringe benefits. They do not need contracts; they need covenants. Covenantal relationships enable educational institutions to be civil and hospitable, and they are understanding of individuals' differences and unique natures. They allow supervisors to recognize that treating everyone equally is not necessarily treating everyone fairly. Sometimes exceptions need to be made, and certain individuals need to be treated in special ways.
- *Understand that culture counts more than structure.* A small business recently went through a particularly traumatic time when the credibility of the administration was questioned by the staff. Various organizational consultants were interviewed to facilitate a heal-

ing process. Most of the consultants spoke of making the necessary structural changes to create better channels of communication. The consultant who was hired, however, began with the attitude that organizational structure has nothing to do with trust. Interpersonal relations based on mutual respect and an atmosphere of goodwill are what create a culture of trust. Would you rather work as part of a company with an outstanding reputation or work as part of a group of outstanding individuals who get along with one another? Many times these two characteristics are found in the same institution, but if one had to make a choice, my suspicion is that most people would opt to work with outstanding individuals.

So it all starts with trust. These are exciting times in American business. Revolutionary work processes and an increased use of technology are transforming the efficiency and productivity of many organizations. Empowerment, total quality management, the use of technology, and improved strategic planning are becoming the norm in American business. However, while these reforms have the potential to influence our business practices in significantly positive ways, they must be based on a strong foundation to achieve their full potential.

Achieving business effectiveness is an incremental, sequential improvement process. This process begins by building a sense of security within each individual so that he or she can be flexible in adapting to changes within the workplace. Addressing only skills or techniques, such as communication, motivation, negotiation, or empowerment, is ineffective when individuals in an organization do not trust its systems, themselves, or each other. An institution's resources are wasted when invested only in training programs that assist administrators in mastering quick-fix techniques that at best attempt to manipulate and at worst reinforce mistrust.

The challenge is to transform relationships from ones based on insecurity, adversarialism, and politics to those based on mutual trust. Trust is the beginning of effectiveness and forms the foundation of a principle-centered learning environment that emphasizes strengths and devises innovative methods to minimize weaknesses. The transformation process requires an internal locus of control that emphasizes individual responsibility and accountability for change and for promoting effectiveness.

If one is expected to create a sense of trust and to engender employee ownership of a change or reform, the change agent needs to be seen as making effective *decisions*. The administrative and organizational theory literature is in agreement about the two most important factors to be considered in determining the decision style that will produce the most effective decisions. While Vroom and Yetton's model includes the additional dimension of shared goals and conflict possibility, the two key elements are the *quality* and the *acceptance* of the decision.[11]

The two decision-making elements are quality, or the likelihood of one decision being more rational than another, and acceptance, or the extent to which acceptance or commitment on the part of subordinates is crucial to effective implementation of the decision. For example, if a new law is passed regarding handicapped accessibility in the workplace, and the quality of the decision (to promulgate it and make the physical accommodations) is more important than the acceptance, a unilateral decision is appropriate. Therefore, the appropriate decision style is *command*. That is, the administrator alone decides to promulgate it and make the structural arrangement necessary. In this case, there is no need for participative decision making. On the other hand, if acceptance is more important than quality, or if the quality and acceptance are both important, as in the development of a new employee evaluation instrument, the proper decision style is *consensus*. Finally, if neither the quality nor the acceptance is important, such as deciding what color to paint the rest rooms, *convenience* is the applicable style.

In addition to evaluating the quality and acceptance of a decision, one can assess how well it meets the criterion of ethical fairness and justice. Consider, for example, a dangerous defect in the braking system in a certain car model. Top executives are faced with the dilemma of whether to risk public outrage and the possible loss of sales by acknowledging the defect or to gloss over the situation.

Executives and staff can assess whether the decisions they make are ethical by applying personal moral codes or society's codes of values, they can apply philosophical views of ethical behavior, or they can assess the potential harmful consequences of behaviors to certain constituencies. One way of thinking about ethical decision making suggests that a person who makes a moral decision must first, recognize the moral issue of whether the person's actions can hurt or help others; second, make a moral judgment; third, decide to attach greater priority to moral concerns than financial or other concerns, or establish their moral intent; and finally, act on the moral concerns of the situation by engaging in moral behavior.[12] In conclusion, therefore, by combining the components of effective decision making with the characteristics of an ethical decision, the change agent can accomplish two important objectives: increasing employee ownership of change and building a culture of trust and respect.

Another issue that is important in developing ownership in the change process is the idea of empowerment. Empowering employees can have a motivating and energizing effect on their performance. According to Thomas Sergiovanni and John Moore, empowerment is not the same as acknowledging the de facto discretion that already exists in the workplace. It is a deliberate effort to provide employees and managers with the room, right, responsibility, and resources to make sensible decisions and informed professional judgments that reflect their circumstances.[13]

This effort calls for enhancing the professional status of employees by providing them with more autonomy, training, trust, and collegial opportunities to carry out their tasks—that is, not to treat them like assembly line workers who are told what to do, how to do it, and when to do it. The effectiveness of this task-oriented approach is being questioned in American industry even for assembly lines. The concept of empowerment has become a force in industry. Every individual should be given the freedom and flexibility to respond creatively to the vagaries of the workplace and, above all, to meet the needs of customers and clients. This approach engenders employee ownership and helps bring about change more effectively.

Diagnostic Checklist

Here are a few questions you can address in assessing whether you have created a sense of *employee ownership*:

1. Are efforts made to establish a sense of *trust and respect*?
2. Are the aspects of *quality and acceptance* being considered in the decision-making process?
3. Is the appropriate *decision-making style* being used in a given situation?
4. Is a sense of employee *empowerment* being established and fostered?

STEP 7: PROVIDING PROFESSIONAL DEVELOPMENT

Very often professional development, an essential part of the change process, is neglected or overlooked completely. Many reforms have failed because of an enthusiastic but ill-advised leader who has tried to implement a change before engaging in staff development. Sometimes even when staff development is provided, it has been ineffective. Negative responses to organized efforts in the name of staff development are the result of a history of poor experiences with activities that have taken place in the name of training and development. However well-intended such activities may have been, too frequently they have not addressed the needs of the individual or the institution, the nature of adult learners, the time and effort required, and the importance of staff development to the ultimate success of any change or reform.

Staff development is a form of human resource development: a process that uses developmental practices to bring about higher quality, greater productivity, and more satisfaction among employees as organization members. It is a function of an individual's knowledge, skills, and attitudes, as well as the policies, structure, and management practices that make up the system in which the employee works.

The most important resource in an institution is its staff. When the staff's thinking is congruent with organizational needs, and when the staff is well-trained, adaptive, and motivated, effective companies result. To achieve this goal requires attention to the various ways in which human potential can be realized and to the variety of needs that any particular person and group may have at any particular stage of development.

Diagnostic Checklist

Here are a few questions you can address in assessing the effectiveness of the *staff development plan*:

1. Is a staff *assessment and appraisal plan* in effect?
2. Is it used to develop a *staff development plan*?
3. Are both *group and individual* development plans in effect?
4. Is a *mentoring* system in effect?
5. Is *staff development* part of the process of change at your institution?

STEP 8: OPERATIONALIZING THE CHANGE

Action follows identification of target forces for and against change; development of, selection of, and implementation of intervention strategies; and the determination of a staff development plan. It is at this point that we operationalize the change, or give form to our vision. Although careful preparation for change increases the chances of success, it does not guarantee effective action. Placing the plan in operation requires establishment of the organizational structure that will best suit the change, and development of an assessment process to determine if the change is remaining on course. Briefing sessions, special seminars, or other means of information dissemination must permeate the change effort. Operationalizing the change must include procedures for keeping all participants informed about the change activities and its effects.

The use of a broad-based steering committee to oversee the change may increase its likelihood of success This group, composed of representatives of all areas of the institution (external and internal), can advise on program budget and organizational policies and priorities. It is helpful if the same task force is active throughout the change process in that it guarantees needed continuity.

Further, the dynamic nature of organizational systems calls for flexibility in action. All efforts must include contingency plans for unanticipated costs, consequences, or resistance. A strong commitment to the change by top leaders can buffer change efforts from these difficulties and ensure the transfer of needed resources to the action plan.

Managing large-scale organizational change might require a more elaborate approach. The process includes at least four components: (1) pattern breaking, (2) experimenting, (3) visioning, and (4) bonding and attunement.[14]

Pattern breaking involves freeing the system from structures, processes, and functions that are no longer useful. An organization can be open to new options if it can relinquish approaches that no longer work, or experiences a *paradigm shift.*

Experimenting by generating new patterns encourages flexibility and yields new options. Training small groups of administrators to institute teamwork illustrates this element. To experiment, organizations must have a philosophy and mechanisms in place that encourage innovation and creativity, and discourage coercion and fear of failure.

Visioning activities, such as building shared meaning throughout the institution and using the current mission statement, generate support for and commitment to the planned changes.

In the last component, *bonding and attunement*, management attempts to integrate all facets of the institutional change to move members toward the new way of action by focusing them on important tasks and generating constructive interpersonal relationships.

To operationalize a reform properly, the change agent needs to be keenly aware of the existing culture and the structure of the institution, and what form of organizational structure will best facilitate successful implementation of the change. For ease of operation, the various schools of thought regarding organizational structure can be grouped into three types of organizational theory: *classical organization theory, social systems theory,* and *open system theory*.

Classical Theory

The classical theorists believe that an application of bureaucratic structure and processes or organizational control will promote rational, efficient, and disciplined behavior, making achievement of well-defined goals possible. Efficiency, then, is achieved by arranging positions within an organization according to hierarchy and jurisdiction, and by placing power at the top of a clear chain of command. Scientific procedures also are used to determine the best way of performing a task, and then rules are formulated that require workers to perform in a prescribed manner. Experts are hired for defined roles and are grouped according to task specialization. Using rationally defined structures and processes such as these, a scientifically ordered flow of work can be carried out with maximum efficiency.

The conceptual model distilled from classical theory had a great impact on the practice and study of organizational life. It quickly spilled over the boundaries of industry and was incorporated into management practice in all sectors of society. In fact, it is currently the dominant structural theory utilized in most organizations. Thus, the tendency is to operationalize a change within the context of a classical structure. The obvious question is whether the classical structure lends itself effectively to all of the current change movements.

Social Systems Theory

Within the classical theory framework, the individual worker was conceived of as an object, a part of the bureaucratic machine. Preparing the work environment for maximizing labor efficiency was not unlike applying precepts from the physical sciences to the human domain of work. As Elton Mayo found in the Hawthorne Works studies, the impact of social-psychological variables within a worker group was significant. The discovery that workers could control the production process to a considerable degree, independent of the demands of management, shattered many of the precepts central to classical theory. A new era of organization theory, and one more in tune with a humanistic approach to the workplace, had arrived. This domain of thought is sometimes referred to as *social systems theory*.[15]

Classical management theory taught that the needs of the organization and the needs of the worker coincided—if the company prospered, the worker would prosper, as well. However, as an awareness of the basic differences between the needs of the individual and the needs of the organization grew, and as worker groups became more sophisticated in manipulating the production process, management technology gave birth to social systems theory and its approaches as a means of reducing conflict. The argument went that by being considerate, using democratic procedures whenever possible, and maintaining open lines of communication, management and workers could talk over their respective problems and resolve them in a friendly, congenial way.

Not unlike the classical theory of the previous generation, the human relations orientation to the problems of managerial control quickly spread to other sectors of society, including education. The social upheaval caused by the Depression and the turmoil of World War II created a receptive climate for this new administrative theory, Enthusiasm for the human relations orientation dampened considerable after the 1950s, however, because many worker organizations came to view it as just another management tactic designed to exploit workers.

Yet the study of behavior in social system settings intensified and a greater sophistication developed about how and why group members behave as they do under given conditions. In time, a natural social systems orientation to the analysis of behavior evolved in the literature as an alternative to the rational systems approach. The natural social systems orientation attempts to take into account how people do behave in organizations rather than how they should behave.

The conceptual perspective of the natural social systems model suggests that an organization consists of a collection of groups (social systems) that collaborate to achieve system goals on some occasions and that, on other occasions, cooperate to accomplish the goals of their own groups. Coalitions among subgroups within an organization form to provide bases on which action can be taken. Within the social systems framework, the study of formal and informal power is one of several critical variables used to identify and analyze the processes of organizational governance.

Open System Theory

During the 1960s, another strand of thought developed that originated in the new technostructure of society. The earlier two traditions of classical and social systems theory tend to view organizational life as a closed system—that is, as isolated from the surrounding environment. *Open system theory* sees an organization as a set of interrelated parts that interact with the environment. It receives inputs such as human and material resources, values, community expectations, and societal demands; transforms them through a production process; and exports the product into the environment with value added. The organization receives a return for its efforts so it can survive, prosper, and begin the cycle over again.

Within the systems theory context, the organization is perceived as consisting of cycles of events that interlock through exporting and importing with other organizations, which also are made up of cycles of events. Management is very complex because leadership has almost no control over the shifting conditions in the environment (e.g., new laws, demographic shifts, political climate, markets for products) on the input or the output side of the equation. Control of the production process is also complex because the various subsystems of the organization also are shaped by event cycles that are programmed by values, expectations, traditions, and vested interests. Changing these internal subgroups and their event cycles is difficult. The administrator attempts to stream the cycles together so that minimum conflict and inefficiency is generated.

Through the perspective of open system theory, a new logic on issues of organizational governance has emerged. It emphasizes the relationship of the organization with its surrounding environment, and thus places a premium on planning and programming events that cannot be controlled directly. The key to making an open system work effectively and efficiently is its ability to gather, process, and use information. In business, the ease with which a need is discovered, a goal is established, and resources are coalesced to meet that need determines the effectiveness and efficiency of that organization. This characteristic of the institution is particularly important if change is to take place effectively.

Contingency Theory

In recent years, a view of organization development has surfaced that treats each organization, and even entities within the organization, as unique. For centuries, this orientation has been at the core of practitioner behavior but has been seen as an anomaly, reflective of inefficiency or unpreparedness (managing by the seat of your pants), and thus was overlooked by management scientists. Currently, the changing situational character of management is now coming to be understood as a key to the management process itself.

Many management scholars and practitioners would now agree with the observation that *contingency theory* is perhaps the most powerful current and future trend in organization development. At this stage of development, however, contingency theory is not really a theory. Rather, it is a conceptual tool that facilitates our understanding of the situational flow of events and alternate organizational and individual responses to that flow. Thus, as a conceptual tool, contingency theory does not possess the holistic character of the three major models discussed earlier. In many ways, contingency theory can be thought of as a subset of open system theory because it is through open system theory that we come to understand the dynamic flows of events, personnel, and resources that take place in organizations. It is also helpful for understanding the process of change and the need for the institution undergoing change to have facets of all three mainstream organizational structures. It is equally important that the change agent be aware of the organizational structure impact on whether the reform is ultimately successfully implemented.

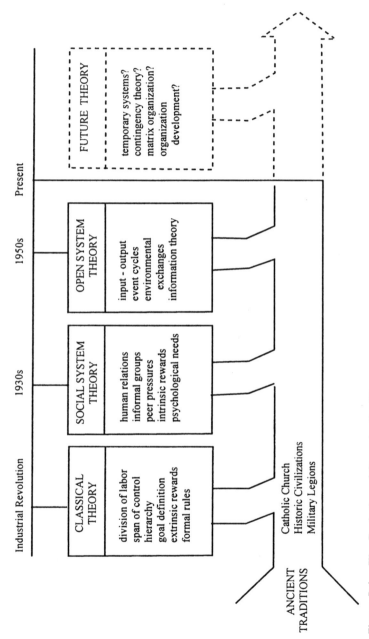

Figure 5.4. The Evolution of Organization Theory

Implementing the Plan

Once the organizational structure is in place, the next step in operationalizing the change is to devise and implement a plan of action. The reform project should be separated into a series of activities, with the complex activities being subdivided into elements or events, the completion of which will conclude the activity. Clearly defined responsibilities should be assigned and accepted. Before proceeding, there is need to establish realistic target dates, develop the project calendar, and put into place a monitoring and evaluation process. Project-planning computer software is of great assistance in organizing and managing large projects.

Diagnostic Checklist

Here are a few questions you can address in assessing your readiness to *operationalize* a change:

1. Has the organizational structure of your institution been *analyzed*?
2. Is an appropriate organizational *structure* in place?
3. If not, can one be *developed*?
4. Are the *best aspects* of the various organizational models being utilized?
5. Are characteristics of the *open system* and the *contingency* models of organizational structure present?

STEP 9: EVALUATING THE CHANGE

The next step in the integrated change process is the evaluation of the change. Authentic assessment is a topical issue in education these days. Many are questioning exactly how to assess performance most accurately, effectively, and fairly. After generations of focusing on program inputs, stressing program outcomes as an authentic measure of a program's effectiveness is gaining in popularity. The emphasis on outcomes should be applied to evaluation of a change or reform.

The change agent(s) should collect data about the nature and effectiveness of the change. The results of the evaluation indicate whether the change process is complete, or a return to an earlier stage should occur. The criteria for success should be specified in advance of a change effort. These criteria may be culturally linked and varied; they also should be closely related to the goals of the reform. If ineffective outcomes result from the introduction of site-based management, for example, the process should return to an earlier stage such as assessment to determine if the institution is really in need of it and whether the school community has been properly prepared.

One process for evaluating the effectiveness of a change or reform is to consider participants' affective reactions, learning, behavior changes, and performance changes.[16] Affective reactions are the participants' attitudes or disposition toward the reform. Questionnaires and interviews can be used to collect this information. Obviously, the change agent(s) is looking for development of a positive attitude toward the change. If it has been operationalized successfully, positive attitudes should prevail.

Learning refers to the participants' understanding of the change and the acquisition of new knowledge and skills as a result of its successful implementation. In the case of introducing cooperative learning techniques in the classroom, for example, did the participants develop an understanding of the principles of cooperative learning, and do they demonstrate the skills needed to implement it properly in the classroom? Classroom observations are one way of assessing whether appropriate learning has taken place. If the staff development phase of the integrated change process has been implemented properly, appropriate learning should be apparent.

Behavioral changes include *followers'* actions in the workplace. Do they interact appropriately with colleagues and others? The following behavioral changes might occur as a result of an effectively implemented change:

- *Communicating openly.* Sharing intentions, motives, needs, feelings, and observations. Asking for and giving feedback that is descriptive rather than judgmental, and specific rather than general. Using active listening techniques, including paraphrasing, summarizing, asking for clarification, and checking out the observation of one's external behavior and attitude. Using assertive communication techniques, rather than being nonassertive or aggressive.

- *Collaborating.* Discussing, planning, and revising the goals of the reform jointly and cooperatively. Using participative decision-making techniques, while avoiding arbitrary and unilateral decisions. Expanding influence skills so that compelling arguments for one's point of view can be made, rather than making decisions by fiat.
- *Taking responsibility.* Being a self-starter and not depending on constant direction. Taking the initiative to develop innovative and creative ways of performing one's duties. Streamlining the organization or department activities to promote operating efficiency.
- *Maintaining a shared vision.* Developing and communicating a clear philosophy, along with goals and objectives. Having and telling a story, a shared history that gives meaning to the institution's activities. Creating rituals and ceremonies to reestablish and remember values.
- *Solving problems effectively.* Defining problems in a nonadversarial way so that they may be resolved from a win/win perspective. Perceiving and projecting problems as challenges rather than obstacles. Using group problem-solving techniques where applicable.
- *Respecting/supporting.* Using the various motivational theories to generate enthusiasm and give affirmation to and support for desired behavior. Dwelling on an individual's strengths, rather than on his or her weaknesses. Giving individuals the benefit of the doubt, and not being judgmental. Exhibiting ethical behavior and treating everyone fairly. In other words, displaying the outcomes of practicing the Ignatian vision.
- *Processing/facilitating interactions.* Clarifying meeting goals and purposes. Reserving time at the end of meeting to critique what was done well/poorly, as well as what facilitated making the decision or performing the task. (A colleague of mine ends every meeting by asking each individual, "What did you learn today?" While this can be annoying if overdone, it is an effective example of processing/facilitating interactive behavior.)
- *Inquiring and experimenting.* Using an analytical approach to problem solving. In the process, looking for new and creative ways of addressing an issue. Frequently examining and questioning the existing structure and culture to be certain they maximize the institution's goals.

The following are common behavior changes that educational *leaders* exhibit when a change or reform has been operationalized properly:

- *Generating participation.* Involving other people when they have the necessary expertise, when the decision must be high quality, and when it requires high acceptance. Relaxing traditional lines of command and empowering others to make decisions. Assuming a delegating, coaching style rather than a directive, task-oriented style.
- *Leading with vision.* Continually articulating the institution's mission, goals, and objectives. Providing feedback mechanisms whereby faculty and staff own the institution's goals. Revising the institution's mission and the leader's personal vision when necessary.
- *Functioning strategically.* Articulating underlying causes, interdependencies, and long-range consequences and acting accordingly. Acting in an institutional mode, rather than a territorial one. Developing strategies and tactics to operationalize the institution's mission and goals. Developing among the faculty and staff the knowledge and skills required to meet future objectives.
- *Promoting information flow.* Communicating clearly the elements necessary to make the change effective. Being clear about expectations, commitments, and needs. Establishing multiple channels of communication and using the appropriate one under existing circumstances. Establishing the proper chain of command for the various types of communication. (For example, external communication ordinarily should follow a formal chain of command, while internal communication may follow a less formal, matrix line.) Enhancing mechanisms for feedback.
- *Developing others.* Teaching needed skills and preparing others within the institution to replace those who may leave. Rewarding desired behavior and delegating to those who prove ready and capable of increased responsibility. Providing opportunities for and building on employees' successes. Adapting one's leadership style to the readiness level of the follower(s).

Evaluating Institutional Change

In evaluating the effectiveness of an institutional reform and the process leading to the change, an institution may address the following questions:[17]

- How did the institution determine the knowledge and skills necessary to implement the reform, and what type of staff development program was used to bring about the desired results?
- What were the conditions—economic, political, and demographic—of the external environment at the time of the reform?
- Did the conditions in the external environment have an effect on the success of the reform?
- How much has the institution's internal environment changed, and has it had an effect on the effectiveness of the reform?
- What are the primary technologies necessary to implement the reform?
- Is the division of labor appropriate to implement the change?
- What is the prevailing norm of the institution regarding improvement efforts?
- How comprehensive and consistent with current organization theory were the guiding assumptions and models used in implementing the reform?
- Were the purposes and need to implement the reform clear and accepted?
- Was a change process established, and were all of the steps used and integrated?
- Were the appropriate change agents identified and empowered?
- How explicit and detailed were the plans?
- What were the intended outcomes of the program, and what were the actual outcomes?
- How were the outcomes assessed?

The answers to these questions will enable the evaluator to assess whether the reform attained its objectives and, if it did not, determine the possible reasons.

Diagnostic Checklist

Here are a few questions you can address in assessing the *evaluation* process:

1. Is an *evaluation process* an integral part of the change process?
2. Does the evaluation process use *authentic assessment* devices?

3. Is the evaluation process *outcome-based*?
4. Are the outcomes related to the reform's *goals*?
5. Is there a mechanism for *revising* the reform if the evaluation outcomes indicate that revision is appropriate?

STEP 10: INSTITUTIONALIZING THE CHANGE

If the evaluation process shows that the reform has been effective, the change then should become institutionalized—that is, the changed processes should be established as permanent ways of operating. Otherwise, when the current change agent leaves, the change may not be perpetuated. Ideally, the reform should become part of the organizational culture. It is in this way that a legacy is created from which future generations of employees, managers, and customers can benefit. The results of a failure to institutionalize a reform are often seen at the state and federal levels. How many times have we seen a governor or president set an agenda for change, only to have it scuttled and replaced with a different agenda by the subsequent administration? If a successful change is to prevail over time, it must be institutionalized.

Thus, action must extend beyond short-term changes for real organizational improvement to take place. Enculturating the change must be a significant goal of the integrated change process. How, for example, does a reform like site-based management become a permanent part of the governance structure of a school? Certainly, the way the activities are performed in moving from the first to the last step in the integrated change process will influence the permanency of the change. Accurate targeting of forces influencing change, followed by careful selection of change agents and intervention strategies, and concluding with effective action, contribute to long-range improvement.

In addition, mechanisms for continual monitoring of the changes must be developed and instituted. Permanent committees or task forces to observe ongoing implementation and outcomes can serve the monitoring functions. Formulation of new institutional policies and procedures based on the reform can encourage its continuation. Most important, however, is a commitment to the reform by the great majority of the workplace community. This community's commitment will expedite the reform's institutionalization.

Both leaders and followers, therefore, must build learning communities, ones that emphasize ongoing adaptability and self-generation, thereby emphasizing coping and looking at the world creatively. Peter Senge says, "Leaders in learning organizations are responsible for building organizations where people are continually expanding their capabilities to shape their future—that is, leaders are responsible for learning."[18]

Another way of institutionalizing a reform is by encouraging development of *heroes* who embody the institution's vision and *tribal storytellers* who promulgate it. We often hear individuals in various organizations describe a colleague as "an institution around here." Heroes such as these do more to establish the organizational culture of an institution than any manual or policies and procedures handbook ever written. The senior sales rep who is recognized and respected for his or her knowledge and fair treatment of customers and coworkers is an invaluable asset to an institution. This person is a symbol of the institution's character. The presence of these heroes sustains the reputation of the institution and allows the workforce to feel good about themselves and about the place where they work. The deeds and accomplishments of these heroes need to be promulgated to become part of the institution's folklore.

The deeds of these heroes usually are perpetuated by an organization's tribal storytellers—individuals who know the history of the institution and relate it through stories of its former and current heroes. An effective organization encourages the tribal storytellers, knowing that they are serving an invaluable service. They work at the process of institutional renewal, they allow the institution to improve continuously, they preserve and revitalize the values of the institution, and they mitigate the tendency of institutions to become bureaucratic. Every institution has its heroes and storytellers. It is the heroic leaders, and followers' function to see to it that things like manuals and handbooks do not replace the heroes and storytellers.

One caveat regarding these heroes and storytellers, however, is that they can also perpetuate the status quo and thus be a force against change. The key is to let them know first of a contemplated change. If informed at the outset and convinced of the reform's efficacy, the heroes and storytellers can be among the change agent's most valuable assets throughout the process, especially during the institutionalization phase. Cultivation of heroes and storytellers needs to take place early in the process if they are to be an asset by the end of the process. This is yet another indication of the importance of considering this process as integrated, rather than step-by-step or sequential.

Diagnostic Checklist

Here are a few questions you can address in assessing whether a change has been *institutionalized*:

1. Has the evaluation process indicated that the change has been *effective*?
2. Has the foundation been established by involving the *heroes and storytellers* early in the process?
3. Has the change been incorporated into the institution's *catalogs, manuals, and handbooks*?
4. Have the heroes and storytellers been encouraged to *participate* in institutionalizing the change?

CONCLUSION

W. Edwards Deming said that healthy organizations are ones that are continually improving. The same thing can be said of individuals. Continuous improvement assumes change. Therefore, if the heroic follower is to be effective, he or she must become an agent of change, or at the very least be tolerant of change. Thus, the habit of flexibility or adaptability is essential.

Mastering the change process in one's professional and personal lives requires the follower to know and understand the steps involved in planning a successful transformation. If the change can take place in an atmosphere of mutual trust and respect, its chances for success are maximized.

A common model for effecting change is to assess the organization or the individual to ascertain the need for change, to diagnose the forces that influence change, and to implement the change by maximizing the forces in favor of the change and minimizing the forces opposing the change. Once the change is made, a thorough evaluation of its effectiveness precedes the final step of institutionalizing the change, which ensures its continuation even after the change agent is no longer present.

The key step in the process is the diagnosing of the forces influencing change. A useful technique in assessing these factors is called Force Field Analysis. This technique allows one to determine the forces both in favor of and opposed to change, and to plan interventions that would mobilize the forces in favor of change and mitigate the forces opposing change. If one can effectively orchestrate this step of the process, the desired change will most likely occur. In many ways, successfully effecting the process of change necessitates the collective use of all of the heroic follower's abilities and skills. It can be seen as the culminating activity of a highly effective follower.

John Kuhn and Joel Barker share an insight into why most individuals are resistant to change that may be helpful in understanding this phenomenon. They contend that it is all about *paradigms.* A paradigm is a way of thinking. We all have a collection of paradigms or models for the way we perceive and do things. We have a card deck paradigm, for example, that defines what a card deck looks like. We have a car-making paradigm that defines how an automobile is built and operated. Once we get used to a certain paradigm or way of doing things, we habitualize the behavior and are reluctant to change it because it has been so effective in the past. However, Kuhn and Barker claim that in holding on to a paradigm even in the face of new evidence that supports a change can be a symptom of *paradigm paralysis*—an unreasonable fear of change. They further claim that most of the population has this disease and is therefore resistant to change. This common sense understanding of our reflexive resistance to change resonates with our experience, does it not? Thus, what we need to do is train ourselves to be counterintuitive and be open to new paradigms even though our instincts militate against it.

Joel Barker offers us a compelling example of the power of paradigms. He reminds us of the dominance that the Swiss had in the watchmaking industry for more than 100 years. In the last twenty years, the Japanese have dominated the watchmaking industry because of their perfection of the quartz watch. The Swiss had 80 percent of the market until 1980, when it began to change. Now, Japan has 80 percent of the market. How did the Swiss, who had dominated the watchmaking industry for a century, suddenly lose their market share so significantly? The answer is paradigms. The Swiss were so engrained in their watchmaking paradigm that they could not see any other way of doing things. So, when one of their own watchmakers presented them with the quartz mechanism, they sent him away unceremoniously. How could such a watch work? It had no mainsprings; it did not have to be wound. It did not meet the Swiss watchmaking paradigm. Thus rebuffed, the Swiss watchmaker showed his new watch at the International Watchmakers Exposition where Texas Instruments and Seiko of Japan saw it, and the rest is history. You see, Texas Instruments and Seiko were not inhibited by the Swiss watchmaker paradigm. Being computer companies, their paradigm allowed them to see possibilities to which the Swiss watchmakers were blind.

Another phenomenon resulting from our unreasonable attachment to our paradigms is that when an organization is caught in a paradigm shift, it goes back to zero. No matter how excellent the company might have been in the past, when a new paradigm takes effect, that excellent company becomes outdated almost overnight. The Swiss watchmaking industry is a prime example of this phenomenon. After dominating the watchmaking industry for over 100 years, once the paradigm shifted, they went back to zero.

The importance of the heroic follower possessing the habit of flexibility and openness to change was also demonstrated by Hersey and Blanchard. They developed a situational leadership theory based on the concept that appropriate leadership behavior is a function of the readiness or maturity of the follower. According to Hersey and Blanchard, if the follower is inexperienced and has a low readiness level, the appropriate leadership behavior would be a "telling" style. If the follower is experienced and effective, and therefore at a high readiness level, the appropriate leadership style is "delegating." Thus if the follower wishes to be dealt with in a delegating rather than telling style, he or she needs to acquire and display the six habits that Hersey and Blanchard suggest in their book.[19]

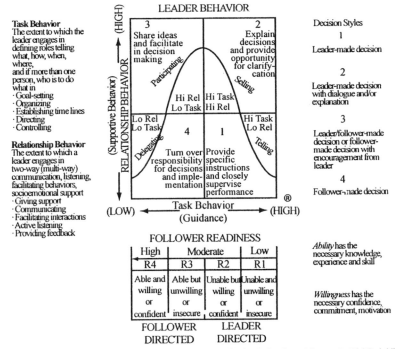

Figure 5.5.   Model of Situational Theory

NOTES

1. Robert H. Palestini, *Ten Steps to Educational Reform*, (Lanham, MD: Scarecrow Press, 2000).

2. E. Mark Hanson, *Educational Administration and Organizational Behavior* (Boston: Allyn and Bacon, 1991).

3. Max De Pree, *Leadership Is an Art* (New York: Dell Publishing, 1989).

4. E. Mark Hanson, *Educational Administration*.

5. Richard Carlson, Barriers to change in public schools, in *Change Processor in Public Schools*, ed. Richard Carlson et al. (Eugene: University of Oregon, Center for the Advanced Study of Educational Administration, 1965).

6. Goodwin Watson, "Resistance to Change," in *The Planning of Change*, ed. Warren Bennis et al. (New York: Holt, Rinehart and Winston, 1969), 488.

7. Michael G. Fullan, Coordinating top-down and bottom-up strategies for educational reform, *The Governance of Curriculum Journal* 28 (1995): 30–48.

8. S. Sarason, *The Predictable Failure of Educational Reform* (San Francisco: Jossey-Bass, 1990).

9. Ibid.

10. D. Taylor and C. Teddlie, Restructuring and the classroom: A view from a reform district (paper presented at the Annual Meeting of the American Education Research Association, San Francisco, 1992).

11. V. H. Vroom and P. W. Yetton, *Leadership and Decision Making* (Pittsburgh: University of Pittsburgh Press, 1973).

12. Robert H. Palestini, *Educational Administration: Leading With Mind and Heart* (Lancaster, PA: Technomic Publishing, 1999).

13. Robert H. Palestini, *The Human Touch in Educational Leadership*, (Lanham, MD: Rowman and Littlefield, 2003).

14. David A. Nadler, *Champions of Change* (San Francisco: Jossey-Bass, 1990).

15. Judith R. Gordon, *Organizational Behavior*, 4th ed. (Boston: Allyn and Bacon, 1993).

16. Robert H. Palestini, *Ten Steps to Educational Reform.*

17. Petra Snowden and Richard Gorton, *School Leadership and Administration*, 6th ed. (New York: McGraw-Hill, 2002).

18. Peter Senge, The leader's new work: Building learning organizations, *Sloan Management Review*, Fall 1990, 7–23.

19. Ken Blanchard, The extra minute, *Executive Excellence*, May 1994, 6–8.

6

DO UNTO OTHERS . . .!

They cannot take away our self-respect if we do not give it to them.

—Mahatma Gandhi

The next important habit of the heroic follower is trustworthiness or respectfulness. And one of the best ways of developing both respectfulness and trustworthiness is by adhering to the Golden Rule. Recall that the Golden Rule (*Do unto others as you would have them do unto you.*) is a proactive principle. It is not good enough to avoid unfair and inequitable treatment of peers; the Golden Rule calls on us to do all we can in our relationships with others to attain the common good. Thus, any individual good that does not undermine the common good of the individual or the organization ought to be pursued since it will cultivate trust, openness, respect, and esprit de corps.[1]

The Golden Rule is grounded in the belief that if individuals are left to their own devices, they will usually do the right thing. It is based on a faith in humanity. If you treat people well, they will treat you well. This rose-colored glasses approach does not deny that there is evil in the world. However, we cannot allow these rare exceptions to dissuade us from pursuing the common good. This approach is difficult at times, because people can be hurtful to one another on occasion. But, in the long run, one's faith in humanity is not misplaced. We should protect ourselves from these hurtful people in the future, but we should not allow the exception to obviate the rule.

For example, as a young high school teacher I worked for a principal who routinely treated people according to the tenets of the Golden Rule. Although most of the teachers and staff reacted to him in kind, one teacher, in particular, did not. This teacher bordered on being incompetent but that did not keep him from constantly belittling the principal's actions and programs when interacting with his colleagues. He never missed a chance to undermine the principal's initiatives. One day I asked the principal how he could continue to treat this teacher according to the Golden Rule, when my own instinct would have been to "fight fire with fire." He said something that I have never forgotten: "I behave toward him according to who I am, not according to who he is."

We spoke earlier about the need for heroic followers to have a sense of purpose in the form of a mission and a personal and professional strategic plan. How can the Golden Rule be applied to a strategic plan? I would suggest that it can be done by making use of the following commitments:

1. Consider actions in terms of not only satisfying one's own needs, but also satisfying the needs of others.
2. Concentrate on others' strengths rather than their weaknesses.
3. Recognize others' whole person rather than their particular skill set.
4. Resolve conflicts by collaboration (win/win) rather than compromise or forcing (win/lose).
5. Trust others until they give you a reason not to, rather than taking the position that they have to earn your trust.

These commitments, if held by a great majority of the workforce, can refocus the entire culture of an organization. If people in an organization would practice these commitments, it would improve communication, creativity, and esprit de corps; in effect, it would create a culture of mutual trust and respect. It can transform an organization from one that is rife with turf battles and politics to one that is committed to innovation, imagination, and the spirit of adventure. In order for this transformation to take place, all we need to do is sublimate our own egos and elevate our motives to an appreciation of human dignity. In other words, if we can practice the principles of the Golden Rule, it will liberate us to fully utilize our natural talents and skills in more productive and creative ways. To the contrary, if the Golden Rule is not adopted, the organization may very well witness the following signs of heartlessness:

- when there is a tendency to merely "go through the motions"
- when a dark tension exists among key individuals
- when a cynical attitude prevails among employees
- when finding time to celebrate accomplishments becomes impossible
- when stories and storytellers cease
- when there is the view that one person's gain needs to be at another's expense
- when mutual trust and respect erode
- when leaders accumulate power rather than distribute it
- when attainment of short-term goals becomes detrimental and preferential to the attainment of long-term goals
- when individuals abide by the letter of the law, but not its spirit
- when people treat customers as impositions
- when the accidents become more important than the substance
- when a loss of grace, style, and civility occurs
- when leaders use coercion to motivate employees
- when administrators dwell on individuals' weaknesses rather than strengths
- when individual turf is protected to the detriment of institutional goals
- when diversity and individual charisms are not respected
- when communication is only one-way
- when employees feel exploited and manipulated
- when arrogance spawns top-down decision making
- when leaders prefer to be served rather than to serve

So, effective people, teams, and organizations require not only skills and structures (mind), but also trust, respect, and spirit (heart) because these qualities are necessary for open communication, common cause, and synergy. When organizations fail to inspire esprit de corps among their workers, the workers tend to perform to the lowest common denominator rather than be self-actualized, self-motivated, empowered, adaptable, creative, and communicative.

Why is there seemingly so little time spent on the establishment of trust and respect in an organization? For one thing, it is intangible and therefore easily ignored in a world concerned about the bottom line. Secondly, it is not easily quantifiable and for that reason is not perceived as hard science but rather as one of the "soft," and less prestigious, social sciences. Finally, because trust and respect involve human dynamics, which is a difficult area to deal with, many individuals in an organization shy away from the challenge and remain in the comfort zone of processes, technology, and product innovation.

Still, both leaders and followers need to focus on these intangibles if they wish to be highly effective. And, even though they do not seem to affect the bottom line, in fact, they do. *Opportunity costs* is a commonly used term in business to account for the costs of lost opportunities. The opportunity costs for failing to consider developing a strong sense of trust and respect in an organization can be considerable. For example, if employees lack a sense of trust in the organization, they may engage in cavalier customer relations, wastefulness, and shoddy production. And since these opportunity costs are intangible, they go unnoticed because they are not evident in the bottom line

On the contrary, if the organization fosters a community of trust and respect, the organizational debilitators of fear, compulsive ego, passive aggression, resentment/anger, and suspicion will decrease. Performance objectives, empowerment, and self-accountability need no longer be threatening to anyone who has the skills and intentions to contribute to the organization's common cause. Highly effective followers can frequently identify and assist those who have problems with skills and intentions. Highly effective followers will be more willing to work with their peers on connecting, communicating, and moving toward a common cause by listening to and acting on feedback, and on building self-motivated, self-accountable, openly communicative, creative, and synergistic behaviors.[2]

ETHICS AND TRUST

Good ethics is good business. Ethical behavior not only keeps business out of court, but also creates a culture of trust, peace of mind, and high morale. To the contrary, a disregard for ethics does just the opposite.

But how do we define ethical behavior in ourselves and in our institutions? I believe that we need to develop a principle-based ethics rather than a practical-based one. In today's world, the majority of the population believes in and practices situational ethics. What is right or wrong depends on the situation. Collectively, we seem to believe that there is nothing that is intrinsically wrong—wrong in all situations. Rather, what is right or wrong is relative—relative to the situation. This philosophy opens the door to widespread rationalization, which as a population we tend to use very liberally. "Under-reporting income on our IRS forms is not cheating; everyone does it."

The only way of reversing this disturbing trend is to return to principle-based ethics. Without underlying principles, the current fad of absolving ourselves of blame by unmitigated rationalization will only increase. With the world becoming more complex, and with greater and greater ambiguity, or gray areas, we will be able to find an excuse to justify practically anything.

What are the inviolate principles on which principle-based ethics is based? Before addressing this question, it may be beneficial to consider the ethical systems and processes that are currently being used. When we try to categorize the criteria individuals use to determine if an action is right or wrong, two ethical systems emerge: 1) utilitarianism/consequentialism and 2) deontology.[3]

Utilitarianism/Consequentialism is an ethical system concerned with measuring harms versus benefits—sort of a cost/benefits analysis. If the consequences of a particular action produce more harm than good, the action is unethical. Consequentialists add to this process a belief that no particular actions are intrinsically evil—that is, evil under any circumstances. They do not believe that killing is intrinsically wrong, for example. It is only wrong if the consequences are demonstrated to be more harmful than not killing in a particular situation. Furthermore, utilitarians do not believe that actions are intrinsically good. Thus, virtues such as justice, honesty, and truthfulness are not good in and of themselves (intrinsically). It depends on whether pursuing them leads to more good than harm. For example, if redistributing the wealth in a first-world country would bring about anarchy, the utilitarians might argue that doing so would not be ethical. That is not to say that the utilitarians would argue that ethical rules are of no use. They would agree that the pursuit of honesty or justice would be generally good, because most of the time more good than bad would result. But they would not take the leap of agreeing that pursuing these goals would always be good.

There are at least two problems with this ethical process. First, it allows one to use any means to achieve a good end. Second, it can allow quantity to be more important than quality. For example, utilitarians might think it ethical to cause great harm to one person to prevent minor harm to ten people. A host of social revolutions have used this logic to justify killing large numbers of aristocrats, for example, to achieve a great social good for the working class.

Deontology, on the other hand, is an ethical process that espouses the promotion of intrinsic good and the avoidance of intrinsic evil. Hence, it is always bad to kill, and it is always good to tell the truth, even if some harmful effects result. Thus, the deontologists see virtue as good in and of itself, while the consequentialists view virtue as good only if it brought about greater good than harm. The deontologists would have no problem with principle-based ethics, a commitment to which the utilitarians would be harder to convince. However, no matter your ideology, there are certain ethical principles on which virtually all reasonable people can agree.

Six such principles are:

1. Avoid jeopardizing the life or safety of others.
2. Avoid infringing upon another person's custody over his own person or actions unless he is threatening others.
3. Avoid stealing.
4. Avoid cheating.
5. Avoid exploiting the vulnerable and the helpless.
6. Avoid breaking your word.[4]

WHY ACT ETHICALLY?

What is the motivation behind acting ethically? We started the discussion on ethics by stating that "good ethics is good business." The implication of this statement is that there is an enlightened self-interest in being ethical. Doing so will build a sense of trust and respect in you as an individual and, ultimately, help you to be successful either as a follower or a leader. Whether one has a belief in a Supreme Being is inconsequential. Regardless of one's religious beliefs, an argument could be made that acting ethically is in one's own best interest. It is safe to say that we all have a degree of self-interest. I would argue that even if egocentrism is our only motive, acting ethically makes sense.

If practical reasoning begins with something wanted, to show that it is rational to act morally would involve showing that in acting morally we achieve something we want. If we hold that it is rational to act in our long-term interests irrespective of what we happen to want at the present moment, we could show that it is rational to act morally by showing that it is in our long-term interests to do so. There have been many attempts to argue along one or other of these lines, ever since Plato, in *The Republic*, portrayed Socrates as arguing that to be virtuous is to have the different elements of one's personality ordered in a harmonious manner, and that this is necessary for happiness.[5]

People often say that to defend morality by appealing to self-interest is to misunderstand what ethics is all about. In other words, we can never get people to act morally by providing reasons of self-interest, because if they accept what we say and act on the reasons given, they will only be acting self-interestedly, not morally. In the words of Aristotle, "Virtue is its own reward."

One reply to this objection, however, would be that the substance of the action—what is actually done—is more important than the motive. People might give money to famine relief because their friends will think better of them, or they might give the same amount because they think it their duty. Those saved from starvation by the gift will benefit to the same extent either way. To deliberate over the ultimate reasons for doing what is right in each case would impossibly complicate our lives; it would also be inadvisable because in particular situations we might be too greatly influenced by strong but temporary desires and inclinations, and so make decisions we would later regret.

Aristotle, Plato, Aquinas, Spinoza, Butler, and Hegel all make broad claims of what makes individuals happy. Some were able to fall back on a belief that virtue will be rewarded and wickedness punished in a life after our bodily death. Philosophers cannot use this argument if they want to carry conviction these days, nor can they adopt sweeping psychological theories based on their own general experience, as philosophers used to do when psychology was a branch of philosophy.

So, what facts about human nature could show that ethics and self-interest coincide? One theory is that we all have benevolent or sympathetic inclinations that make us concerned about the welfare of others. Another relies on a natural conscience that gives rise to guilt feelings when we do what we know to be wrong. But how strong are these benevolent desires or feelings of guilt? Is it possible to suppress them? If so, is it not possible that in a world in which humans and other animals are suffering in great numbers, suppressing one's conscience and sympathy for others is the surest way to happiness?

Abraham Maslow, of whom we spoke earlier, asserts that human beings have a need for self-actualization, which involves growing towards courage, kindness, knowledge, love, honesty, and unselfishness. When we fulfill this need we feel serene, joyful, filled with zest, sometimes euphoric, and generally happy. When we act contrary to our need for self-actualization, we experience anxiety, despair, boredom, shame, and emptiness, and we are generally unable to enjoy ourselves.

The existence of psychopathic people counts against the contention that benevolence, sympathy, and feelings of guilt are present in everyone. It also appears to count against attempts to link happiness with the possession of these inclinations. But let us pause before we accept this conclusion. Must we accept the psychopaths' own evaluations of their happiness? They are, after all, notoriously persuasive liars.

So, "Why act morally?" cannot be given an answer that will provide everyone with overwhelming reasons for acting morally. Ethically indefensible behavior is not always irrational. We will probably always need the sanctions of the law and social pressure to provide additional reasons against serious violations of ethical standards. On the other hand, those reflective enough to ask the question we have been discussing in this section, that is, heroic followers, are also those most likely to appreciate the reasons that can be offered for taking the ethical point of view. Hence, we fall back on the opening argument that *good ethics is good business.*

VIRTUE ETHICS

Virtue is good behavior. In the best of situations, virtue becomes a habit whereby an individual's reflexive response to a situation will be to act in a virtuous way. If acting in a virtuous way is repeated and reinforced, it will become a habit. We are suggesting that making a habit of acting in a virtuous way will go a long way toward establishing a culture of trust and respect in an organization.

According to Plato, there are four cardinal virtues: wisdom, fortitude, temperance, and justice. Over the years, other virtues such as magnanimity, humility, love, and forgiveness, among others, have been added to the mix. All of these virtues are important to the heroic follower if trust and respect is one of his or her objectives. They are particularly important if one is attempting to actualize the Golden Rule.

The virtue of wisdom is important for understanding why we select the mission, goals, and objectives that adds purpose to our lives. The virtue of justice is explicit in all the principles and questions regarding fairness and unfairness, while the virtues of magnanimity and love are explicit in the personal commitments integral to the Golden Rule. The virtues of courage or fortitude, temperance or self-control, humility, and forgiveness are worth going into in some detail as they relate to the pursuit of the Golden Rule.

Courage or fortitude is a requisite for emulating the Golden Rule in that it keeps us from giving in to peer pressure, fear of retaliation, fear of embarrassment, or loss of popularity. Courage allows us to have the strength of our convictions and to be comfortable that our convictions are noble enough to withstand outside criticism. However, we must not confuse courage with fearlessness, which can be an end in itself. Evel Knievel is fearless, but not courageous. He does not do what he does out of principle or to promote the common good. True courage, however, is a virtue that will enable us to take an ethical stand even in the face of criticism and pressure.

Temperance is also important for those seeking to lead a virtuous life. If we do not have the will to deny satisfaction of our prurient interests, we will be destined to a life of hedonism. Basically, temperance is the victory of mind or will over matter. For example, breaking a smoking habit is a difficult process, as many Americans know. Not having the will to break the habit, however, is a classical example of matter over mind. From what people who have been successful in breaking a smoking habit tell me, their greatest victory is knowing that something material like a cigarette no longer has control over them. Conversely, they now have control over an inanimate object. Human dignity would not seem to allow for something nonhuman or inanimate to have control over something human. Hence, self-control or temperance ceases to be a passionate denial of passion and becomes a vehicle and a result of the purpose that makes life worth living, and an ethical path worth pursuing.

Forgiveness may be the most difficult of all virtues to master because it asks one to temper or eliminate vengeance. Vengeance seems always to be justifiable. "An eye for an eye" or "a tooth for a tooth" seems much more satisfying to most than "turning the other cheek." We usually feel intense hurt or betrayal when someone treats us unfairly. This hurt causes us to seek equal, if not greater, hurt on the other party. At this point, we move from redressing a justifiable claim to vengeance. But violence begets violence, and vengeance begets vengeance. Each party desires to hurt the other a little bit more for the previous hurt caused them, until a relatively small hurt has escalated into a major incident. Needless to say, vengeance not only undermines family life, it can undermine organizational life.

In order to avoid such escalations, followers will want to detach themselves from taking the unfairness personally. Hence, forgiveness can be looked upon as a subset of humility. Reacting in this way is tantamount to "giving oneself up for the team." In other words, the goals of the organization are seen as more important than your own personal feelings. This, of course, is a very pragmatic view of forgiveness. Those steeped in the Judeo-Christian culture would go a step further and be asked not only to forgive the offending person, but also to love the person.

As we pointed out earlier, however, the motivation behind being ethical and virtuous is somewhat inconsequential to the outcome of the action. As long as forgiveness is taking place, whether one loves the perpetrator of the hurt is not all that important. It is most effective, however, when it arises out of selfless love (agape), because it allows the heroic follower to redress the injustice while still caring for the instigator. This behavior will be noticed not only by the perpetrator but also by one's peers. Thus, the heroic follower is not only engaging in appropriate behavior, but also modeling such behavior for others to follow. Hence, the by-product of such behavior is the building of considerable trust and respect for the heroic follower.

Practicing the virtue of forgiveness, however, does not mean that the heroic follower totally ignores unfairness and conflict. The difference between the follower and the heroic follower is that the heroic follower deals with the unfairness and conflict in a way that respects the dignity of the individual. The notion of agape can sometimes affect the way individuals deal with others who have harmed them in some way, but it always affects their tone of voice, their expressions, and their openness. This approach can have dramatic effects in one's cultivation of trust and respect.

ETHICAL DILEMMAS

We encounter ethical dilemmas daily in our personal and professional lives. How do we deal with them? Ethical precedents can be extraordinarily helpful in resolving dilemmas. But before resorting to ethical precedents, it would be useful for the heroic follower to engage in a process of resolving the dilemma first and then checking the result with any precedents that might apply. This approach would give them a deeper understanding of how the ethical precedents were derived, while helping them to see the potential differences between their situation and some other.

Whenever an ethical dilemma is presented, one should try to resolve it by achieving clarity around the following questions:

1. What principles might be violated on either horn of the dilemma?
2. How do we prioritize these principles?
3. What is the level of harm that will be done on each horn of the dilemma?
4. What are the quantities of harm done on each horn of the dilemma?[6]

In using this formula, however, one should be careful not to invert the process because if we find in step four, for example, that the organization is going to lose $100 million, it may affect the decision we make. Thus, it is important to first identify the principles involved, prioritize them, and only then determine the costs to the organization so that a more objective and more ethical decision can be made.

Using the field of education as an example, all educators face three areas of dilemmas: control, curriculum, and societal. Control dilemmas involve the resolution of classroom management and control issues, particularly the issue of who is in charge and to what degree. Control dilemmas center around four questions: (1) Do you treat the child as a student, focusing narrowly on cognitive goals, or as a whole person, focusing more broadly on intellectual, aesthetic, social, and physical dimensions? (2) Who controls classroom time? In some classrooms, children are given latitude in scheduling their activities; in others, class activities follow a strict and mandatory schedule. (3) Who controls operations or what larger context of what it means to be human and how we resolve what inevitably goes on in the classroom? Some school districts have very tight standards, but others allow teachers much more latitude to be reflective practitioners in determining how to deal with students, what they teach, and how they teach it. (4) Who controls the standards and defines success and failure?

Similar dilemmas occur in the curricular domain and relate to whether the curriculum is considered as received, public knowledge or private, individualized knowledge of the type achieved through discoveries and experiments. These curricular difficulties also depend on whether one conceives of the child as a customer or as an individual. The customer receives professional services generated from a body of knowledge, whereas the individual receives personal services generated from his or her particular needs and context.

A final set of dilemmas has to do with what children bring to school and how they are to be treated once there. One concerns the distribution of teacher resources. Should one focus more resources on the less talented in order to bring them up to standards or on the more talented in order for them to reach their full potential? The same question arises regarding the distribution of justice. Should classroom rules be applied uniformly without regard to the differing circumstances of each child or should family background, economic factors, and other sociological influences be considered? Should a teacher stress a common culture or ethnic differences and subculture consciousness?

Much of teaching involves resolving such dilemmas by making a variety of decisions throughout the school day. Such decisions can be made, however, in a *reflective* or an *unreflective* manner. An unreflective manner means simply teaching as one was taught, without considering available alternatives. A reflective approach involves an examination of the widest array of alternatives. Thus, reflective teaching suggests that dilemmas need not be simply resolved but can be transformed so that a higher level of teaching expertise is reached.

This same logic can be applied to administration. Administration involves the resolution of various dilemmas and the making of moral decisions. One set of dilemmas involves control. How much participation can teachers have in the administration of the school? How much participation can parents and students have? Who evaluates whom, and for what purpose? Is the role of administration collegial or authority-centered? The area of the curriculum brings up similar questions. Is the school oriented to basic skills, advanced skills, social skills, or all three? Should the curricula be teacher-made or national-, state-, or system-mandated? Should student evaluation be based on teacher assessment or standardized tests? What is authentic assessment? Finally, an additional set of dilemmas pertains to the idea of schooling in society. Should the schools be oriented to ameliorate the apparent deficits that some students bring with them or should they see different cultures and groups as strengths? Should schools be seen as agents of change, oriented to the creation of a more just society, or as socializers that adapt the young to the current social structure?

Often, these questions are answered unreflectively and simply resolved on an "as needed" or emotional basis. This approach often resolves the dilemma but does not foster a real *transformation* in one's self, role, or institution. If evolving into a heroic follower encompasses transformation, and I would argue that it should, then an ethical lens must be developed through which these questions can be viewed.

TRUST AND COMMUNICATION

Another way for the heroic follower to be perceived as trustworthy is to communicate in a supportive and honest way. Supportive communication emphasizes congruence between thoughts, feelings, and communication. An individual who feels unappreciated by a supervisor, for example, must communicate that feeling to the supervisor, rather than deny it or communicate it inaccurately. Communication must also validate an individual's importance, uniqueness, and worth. Nondefensive communication recognizes the other person's existence; recognizes the person's uniqueness as an individual, rather than treating him or her as a role or a job; acknowledges the worth of the other person; acknowledges the validity of the other person's perception of the world; and expresses willingness to be involved with the other person, at least during the communication.

Interpersonal communication can be improved by encouraging individuals to communicate using as complete knowledge of themselves and others as possible. The Johari window provides an analytical tool that individuals can use to identify information that is available for use in communication. Figure 6.1 illustrates this model of interpersonal knowledge.[7]

Note that information about an individual is represented along two dimensions: (1) information known and unknown by the self and (2) information known and unknown by others.

Together these dimensions form a four-category representation of the individual. The open self is information known by the self and known by others. The blind self is information unknown by the self and known by others, such as others' perceptions of your behavior or attitudes. The concealed self is information known by you and unknown by others; secrets we keep from others about ourselves fall into this category. Finally, the unconscious self is information that is unknown to the self and unknown to others. To ensure quality communication, in most cases an individual should communicate from his or her open self to another's open self and limit the amount of information concealed or in the blind spot. Guarded communication occurs, however, if one party has violated trust in the past, if the parties have an adversarial relationship, if power and status differentials characterize the culture, if the relationship is transitory, or if the corporate culture does not support openness. Nevertheless, the more one can communicate from the open self to another's open self, the more chance that an environment of trust and respect can be nurtured and sustained.

	Known by Self	Unknown by Self
Known by Others	Open Self	Blind Self
Unknown by Others	Concealed Self	Unknown Self

Figure 6.1. Johari Window

DIAGNOSTIC CHECKLIST

Here are some questions that will help you assess the *trust and respect* in your environment:

1. Do you try consciously to surround yourself with an *aura of trust and respect*?
2. Is there an *ethical code* or value system that you use as the basis for your behavior?
3. Do you respect the gift of *diversity*?
4. Do you focus on peoples' *strengths* rather than their weaknesses?
5. Do you encourage *group participation* whenever feasible?

NOTES

1. Robert J. Spitzer SJ, *The Spirit of Leadership: Optimizing Creativity and Change in Organizations* (Provo, UT: Executive Excellence, 2000).

2. Robert H. Palestini, *Educational Administration: Leading with Mind and Heart* (Lanham, MD: Rowman and Littlefield, 1999).

3. C. S. Lewis, *The Four Loves* (New York: Harcourt, Brace, Jovanovich, 1960).

4. Joseph Fletcher, *Situation Ethics: The New Morality* (Philadelphia: Warminster Press, 1966).

5. Peter Singer, *Practical Ethics* (Cambridge, England: Cambridge University Press, 1979).

6. Robert J. Spitzer, SJ, *The Spirit of Leadership* (Provo, UT: Executive Excellence, 2000).

7. Robert H. Palestini, *The Ten-Minute Guide to Educational Leadership* (Lancaster, PA: Technomic Publishing, 1998).

7

HAVE A HEART!

In dealing with others, primary objective must always be *cura personalis*, care of the whole person.

—Ignatius of Loyola

The final habit of the heroic follower is *sensitivity*. Whether the heroic follower develops sensitivity toward others depends largely on one's philosophy of life regarding how human beings behave in the workplace. One extreme of the continuum might be those who believe that human beings are basically lazy and will do the very least that they need to do to "get by" in the workplace. On the other end are those who believe that people are basically industrious and, if given the choice, would opt for doing a quality job. I believe that today's most effective individuals hold the latter view. I agree with Max De Pree, owner and CEO of the highly successful Herman Miller Furniture Company. Writing in his book, *Leadership Is an Art,* he says that a leader's function is to "liberate people to do what is required of them in the most effective and humane way possible."[1] Instead of catching people doing something wrong, our goal as enlightened leaders is to catch them doing something right. I would suggest, therefore, that in addition to the other skills needed to become a heroic follower, a truly enlightened follower follows with sensitivity or heart.

Too often, leaders underestimate the skills and qualities of their followers. I remember Bill Faries, the chief custodian at a high school at which I was assistant principal in the mid-1970s. Bill's mother, to whom he had been extraordinarily close, had passed away after a long illness. The school was a religiously affiliated one, and the school community went "all out" in its remembrance of Bill's mother. We held a religious service in which almost 3000 members of the school community participated. Bill, of course, was very grateful. As a token of his gratitude, he gave the school a six-by-eight-foot knitted quilt that he had sewn himself. From that point on, I did not know if Bill was a custodian who was a quilt weaver, or a quilt weaver who was a custodian. The point is that it took the death of his mother for us to realize how truly talented our custodian was. So our effectiveness as followers begins with sensitivity to the diversity of people's gifts, talents, and skills. When we think about the variety of gifts that people bring to organizations and institutions, we see that following with heart lies in cultivating, liberating, and enabling those gifts.

HEROIC FOLLOWERS AND HEROIC LEADERS

I believe that in order for followers to flourish, there needs to be a highly effective, even heroic, leader in place. The first responsibility of this leader is to define reality through a vision. The last is to say thank you. In between, the leader must become the servant of the servants. Being a leader means having the opportunity to make a meaningful difference in the lives of those who allow leaders to lead. This summarizes what I call leading with sensitivity or heart. In a nutshell, leaders don't inflict pain; they bear pain.

Whether one is a successful leader, therefore, can be determined by looking at the followers. Are they reaching their potential? Are they learning? Are they able to change without bitterness? Are they able to achieve the institution's goals and objectives? Can they manage conflict among themselves? Where the answers to these questions is an emphatic "yes," is where a heroic leader resides.

I prefer to think about leadership in terms of what the gospel writer Luke calls the "one who serves." The leader owes something to the institution he or she leads. The leader is seen in this context as steward rather than owner or proprietor. Leading with heart requires the leader to think about his or her stewardship in terms of legacy, direction, effectiveness, and values.

LEGACY

Too many of today's leaders are interested only in immediate results that bolster their career goals. Long-range goals are left to their successors. I believe that this approach fosters autocratic leadership, which often produces short-term results but militates against creativity and its long-term benefits. In effect, this approach is the antithesis of leading with heart.

On the contrary, leaders should build a long-lasting legacy of accomplishment that is institutionalized for posterity. They owe their institutions and their followers a healthy existence and the relationships and reputation that enable continuity of that healthy existence. Leaders are also responsible for future leadership. They need to identify, develop, and nurture future leaders to carry on the legacy.

VALUES

Along with being responsible for providing future leaders, leaders owe the individuals in their institutions certain other legacies. Leaders need to be concerned with the institutional value system, which determines the principles and standards that guide the practices of those in the organization. Leaders need to model their value systems so that the individuals in the organization can learn to transmit these values to their colleagues and to future employees. In a civilized institution, we see good manners, respect for people, and an appreciation of the way in which we serve one another. A humane, sensitive, and thoughtful leader will transmit his or her value system through his or her daily behavior. This, I believe, is what Peter Senge refers to as a "learning organization."[2]

DIRECTION

Leaders are obliged to provide and maintain direction by developing a vision. We made the point earlier that effective leaders must leave their organizations with a legacy. Part of this legacy should be a sense of progress or momentum. A CEO, for instance, should imbue his or her institution with a sense of continuous progress: a sense of constant improvement. Improvement and momentum come from a clear vision of what the institution ought to be, from a well-planned strategy to achieve that vision, and from carefully developed and articulated directions and plans that allow everyone to participate and be personally accountable for achieving those plans.

EFFECTIVENESS

Leaders are also responsible for effectiveness by being enablers. They need to enable others to reach their potential both personally and institutionally. I believe that the most effective way of enabling one's colleagues is through participative decision making. It begins with believing in the potential of people: believing in their diversity of gifts. Leaders must realize that to maximize their own power and effectiveness, they need to empower others. Leaders are responsible for setting and attaining the goals in their organizations. Empowering or enabling others to help achieve those goals enhances the leader's chances of attaining the goals, ultimately enhancing the leader's effectiveness. Paradoxically, giving up power really amounts to gaining power. Hence, in these ways heroic followers and heroic leaders have a *symbiotic* relationship.

What are the skills and characteristics that heroic followers need to have in order to follow with heart? How do we become sensitive to the needs of others? Rather than proposing a series of steps whereby followers would miraculously become sensitive, I would opine that having a heart is more of a state of mind than a set of skills. In cultivating this state of mind, considering the following concepts may be helpful: (1) employees as owners, (2) starting with trust and respect, (3) the value of teamwork, (4) employees as volunteers, and (5) the value of heroes.

EMPLOYEE OWNERS

We often hear managers suggest that a new program does not have a chance of succeeding unless the employees take "ownership" of the program. Most of us agree to the common sense of such an assertion. But how can employee ownership be promoted? Let me suggest four steps as a beginning. I am certain that you can think of several more.

1. *Respect people.* As we have indicated earlier, this starts with appreciating the diverse gifts that individuals bring to the workplace. The key is to dwell on the strengths of your coworkers rather than on their weaknesses. Try to turn their weaknesses into strengths.

2. *Let belief guide policy and practice.* We spoke earlier of developing a culture of civility in an institution. If there is an environment of mutual respect and trust, I believe that the organization will flourish. Both leaders and followers need to let their belief or value systems guide their behavior. Developing a personal and professional mission statement will facilitate this process.

3. *Recognize the need for covenants.* Contractual agreements cover such things as salary, fringe benefits, and working conditions. They are part of organizational life and there is a legitimate need for them. But in today's organizations, where the best people working for these institutions are like volunteers, we need covenantal relationships. There are agreements and understanding that go beyond the contract. Our best workers may choose their employers. They usually choose the institution where they work based on reasons less tangible than salaries and fringe benefits. They do not just need contracts, they need covenants.

   Covenantal relationships enable educational institutions to be civil, hospitable, and understanding of individuals' differences and unique charisms. They allow us to recognize that treating everyone equally is not necessarily treating everyone equitably and fairly.

4. *Understand that culture counts more than structure.* Interpersonal relations based on mutual respect and an atmosphere of goodwill are what create a culture of trust. Would you rather work as part of a company with an outstanding reputation or work as part of a group of outstanding individuals? Many times these two charac-

teristics go together, but if one had to make a choice, I believe that most people would opt to work with outstanding individuals.

If an institution is to be successful, everyone in it needs to feel that he or she "owns the place." "This is not the boss' company; it is not the shareholders'; it is my company." Taking ownership is a sign of one's love for an institution. In his book, *Servant Leadership*, Robert Greenleaf says, "Love is an undefinable term, and its manifestations are both subtle and infinite. It has only one absolute condition: unlimited liability!"[3] Although it may run counter to our traditional notion of American capitalism, employees should be encouraged to act as if they own the place. It is a sign of love—and cultivating employee ownership is a sign of sensitivity or heart.

IT STARTS WITH TRUST AND SENSITIVITY (HEART)

These are exciting times in American business. Revolutionary steps are being taken to restructure essential production and management processes. The concepts of empowerment, total quality management, the use of technology, and strategic planning are becoming the norm. However, while these activities have the potential to influence the workplace in significantly positive ways, they must be based upon a strong foundation to achieve their full potential.

Achieving professional and personal effectiveness is an incremental, sequential improvement process. This improvement process begins by building a sense of security within each individual so that he or she can be flexible in adapting to changes within his or her life. Addressing only skills or techniques, such as communication, motivation, negotiation, or empowerment, is ineffective when individuals in an organization do not trust its systems, themselves, or each other. An institution's resources are wasted when invested only in training programs that assist administrators in mastering quick-fix techniques that, at best, attempt to manipulate, and at worst, reinforce mistrust.

The challenge is to transform relationships based on insecurity, adversarialism, and politics to those based on mutual trust. Trust is the beginning of effectiveness and forms the foundation of a principle-centered learning organization that places emphasis upon strengths and devises innovative methods to minimize weaknesses. The transformation process requires an internal locus of control that emphasizes individual responsibility and accountability for change and for promoting effectiveness.

TEAMWORK

For many of us, there is a dichotomy between how we see ourselves as persons and how we see ourselves as workers. But consider the words of a Zen Buddhist:

> The master in the art of living makes little distinction
> between his work and his play, his labor and his leisure,
> his mind and his body, his education and his recreation,
> his love and his religion. He hardly knows which is which.
> He simply pursues his vision of excellence in whatever he does, leaving
> others to decide whether he is working or playing. To him he is always doing both.

Work can be and should be productive, rewarding, enriching, fulfilling, and joyful. Work is one of our greatest privileges, and it is up to all of us as a team to make certain that work is everything that it can and should be.

One way to think of work is to think of how a philosopher would lead an organization, rather than how an executive would lead an organization. Plato's *Republic* speaks of the "philosopher-king," a king who would rule with the philosopher's ideals and values.

Paramount among the ideals that we all need to recognize in an organization is the notion of teamwork and the valuing of each individual's contribution to the final product. The synergy produced by an effective team is greater than the sum of its parts.

The foundation of the team is the recognition that each member needs every other member and no individual can be successful without the cooperation of others. As a young boy, I was a very enthusiastic baseball fan. My favorite player was the Hall of Fame pitcher Robin Roberts of the Philadelphia Phillies. During the early '50s, his fastball dominated the National League. My uncle, who took me to my first ballgame, explained that opposing batters were so intimidated by Roberts' fastball that they were automatic outs even before they got to the plate. My uncle claimed that Robin Roberts was unstoppable. Even as a young boy, I intuitively knew that no one was unstoppable by himself. I said to my uncle that I knew how to stop Robin Roberts: "Make me his catcher." The point is that none of us, in and of ourselves, can be highly effective people. It takes teamwork to reach the ultimate goal. Realizing the value of teamwork will help one treat others with sensitivity or habit.

EMPLOYEES AS VOLUNTEERS

Our institutions will not amount to anything without the people who make them what they are. And the individuals most influential in making institutions what they are, are essentially volunteers. Our very best employees can work anywhere they please. So in a sense, they volunteer to work where they do. As leaders, we would do far better if we looked upon and treated our employees with the deference that we show volunteers. We made the point earlier that we should treat our employees as if we had a covenantal relationship, rather than a contractual relationship, with them.

Alexander Solzhenitsyn, speaking to the 1978 graduating class of Harvard College, said this about legalistic relationships: "A society based on the letter of the law and never reaching any higher, fails to take advantage of the full range of human possibilities. The letter of the law is too cold and formal to have a beneficial influence on society. Whenever the tissue of life is woven of legalistic relationships, this creates an atmosphere of spiritual mediocrity that paralyzes men's noblest impulses." And later: "After a certain level of the problem has been reached, legalistic thinking induces paralysis; it prevents one from seeing the scale and the meaning of events."[4]

Covenantal relationships, on the other hand, induce freedom, not paralysis. As the noted psychiatrist William Glasser explains, "Coercion only produces mediocrity; love or a sense of belonging produces excellence."[5] Our goal as leaders and followers is to encourage a covenantal relationship of love, warmth, and personal chemistry among our employee volunteers. Shared ideals, shared goals, shared respect, a sense of integrity, a sense of quality, a sense of advocacy, a sense of caring: these are

the basis of an organization's covenant with its employees—and they are
the basis for leading and following with heart.

THE VALUE OF HEROES

Leading and following with heart requires that an organization have its
share of heroes, both present and past. We have often heard individuals
in various organizations say that so-and-so is an "institution" around
here. Heroes such as these do more to establish the organizational culture of an institution than any manual or policies and procedures handbook ever could. The senior faculty member who is recognized and respected for his or her knowledge as well as his or her humane treatment
of students is a valuable asset to an educational institution. He or she is
a symbol of what the institution stands for. It is the presence of these heroes that sustains the reputation of the institution and allows the workforce to feel good about itself and about the workplace. The deeds and
accomplishments of these heroes need to be promulgated and become
part of the folklore of the institution.

The deeds of these heroes are usually perpetuated by the "tribal storytellers" in an organization.[6] These are the individuals who know the
history of the organization and relate it through stories of its former and
present heroes. Effective organizations encourage the tribal storytellers,
knowing that they are serving an invaluable role in an organization. They
work at the process of institutional renewal. They allow the institution
to continuously improve. They preserve and revitalize the values of the
institution. They mitigate the tendency of institutions, especially educational institutions, to become bureaucratic. These concerns are concerns of everyone in the institution, but they are the special province of
the tribal storyteller. Every institution has heroes and storytellers. It is
the job of leaders and followers alike to see to it that things like manuals and handbooks don't replace them.

THE HEART OF THE HEROIC FOLLOWER

We have made the point that the heart of the heroic follower is as important as the mind in the developmental process by which a follower

matures into a heroic follower. I have dealt with the heroic follower's mind in four respects: (1) the need to have a *purpose* in life, (2) the need to be *responsible* or accountable for one's behavior, (3) the need to be *communicative*, and (4) the need to be *flexible* and adaptable to change. The last two chapters have dealt with the heroic follower's heart in two respects: (1) the need to be (and to be viewed as) *trustworthy*, and (2) the need to be *sensitive* to others' needs.

Ideally, then, the heroic follower will demonstrate a balance between following with mind and following with heart. Both aspects are important. If the follower has a heart of gold but is incompetent, he or she will not be highly effective. On the other hand, a highly competent individual who is not sensitive to the needs of others is equally deficient. When both mind and heart are present, they complement and liberate each other. Each becomes stronger through the influence of the other.

Effectiveness rises out of the minds and hearts of heroic followers. It depends on their internal disposition that allows for a commitment to ethical behavior and the establishment of trust, and sensitivity to the needs and concerns of others. In his book, *The Spirit of Leadership*, Robert J. Spitzer calls this essential internal disposition "freedom from ego-compulsion."[7]

To help us understand this phenomenon, he describe four levels of motivators that drive most of us toward the ultimate goal of happiness: Level 1, immediate physical gratification; Level 2, ego gratification; Level 3, making a contribution; and Level 4, being involved with something of ultimate significance. The degree of happiness achieved by an individual depends on the level at which the person operates. And, in turn, the higher the degree of happiness, the more effective the person is in his or her personal and professional life.

Level 1: Immediate physical gratification. The first level of happiness is achieved through the pleasure produced by an external stimulus. The reward is immediate, but it does not endure for very long. It could be produced by a material possession, like a new automobile, or by some kind of sensual pleasure, like a hug from your grandchild. Thus, the Level 1 form of happiness provides immediate gratification from the pleasure or the possession of the external stimulus, followed almost immediately by a desire and need for more. According to Spitzer, very few of us are satisfied with this level of happiness.

Level 2: Ego gratification. The second level of happiness is called ego gratification; this refers to one's inner world of memories, choices, thoughts, and feelings. Ego gratification usually comes in the form of achievement, comparative advantage, recognition, and power. For example, when a student receives his or her bachelor's degree, the individual has a sense of achievement that makes him or her happy. Further, if I beat an opponent in a round of golf, I not only have a sense of achievement, I have emerged as a winner in a game of comparative advantage.

This second level of happiness can be either positive or negative. When accompanied by other kinds of happiness, it can be healthy. We have to satisfy our achievement, recognition, and power needs in order for us to be motivated to reach our ultimate potential. If we are to be productive as a nation, we need our citizens to be motivated by the satisfaction of these needs. If we want to live in a world of progress, we need a motivated society. Hence, in this case, attaining the second level of happiness can be very positive.

On the other hand, if Level 2 happiness is the only kind of happiness to which an individual aspires, it can become compulsive and negative. For example, if the desire for achievement in the form of advancement is one's only drive, we can see that it could lead to compulsive behavior. If one becomes compulsive over achievement, the first time that the person does not get the job that he or she is seeking, or is demoted, he or she is apt to go into severe depression. Such compulsive behavior can produce anger, jealousy, fear, suspicion, and contempt for those whom we perceive as our rivals.

The same can be said for competitiveness. In a market economy, healthy competition is what leads to effectiveness and efficiency. Competitiveness is invaluable to the pursuit of excellence. However, if competition is the only thing that will give us happiness and meaning in our lives, we are leaving ourselves open to destructive emotions when we do not "win." If Level 2 happiness is to be healthy, it cannot be an end in itself. It must have an additional end. In short, one cannot live for achievement or competitiveness alone. A higher goal must be involved. For example, if I am achievement oriented so that I can support my family, it is healthy. If I am competitive because it motivates me to hone my skills to be a better teacher or a better physician, it is healthy. Unfortunately, in our society, there are estimates that as many as 75 percent of us are fixated at this level of happiness, and many of us see achievement and competitiveness as goals in and of themselves.

Level 3: Making a contribution. The third level of happiness involves the satisfaction that one gets in making a contribution to someone or something beyond him- or herself. It is the converse of Level 2 happiness. This level of happiness requires an investment of one's inner world in something broader, such as making a difference in our society. Individuals operating at this level believe that their life has a greater meaning, and they create a sense of self-worth and self-value by serving others, especially those in need.

Notice that the feeling of happiness in Level 3 is significantly different from that of Levels 1 and 2. Level 3 (spirit, hope, positivity, connectedness, horizon, etc.) feels quite different than Level 2 (self-possession, control, influence, being fulfilled through achievement, winning, etc.), which, in turn, feels quite different than Level 1 (the new computer). They feel different and they have different results, but all of them give us happiness.

Level 3 happiness can keep Level 2 happiness from being an end in itself. Remember that Level 2 happiness, if it is an end in itself, can lead to fear, anger, and other destructive emotions when the achievement need is not satisfied. If we add Level 3 happiness to our motives, there is a higher motive driving our behavior and our needs are more likely to be satisfied even in the event of a "loss." "We fought the good fight," and we get satisfaction and happiness from that.

Level 4: Being involved with something of ultimate significance. This level of happiness is brought about by being involved in something of ultimate significance. For example, understanding the ultimate truth or experiencing unconditional love could be considered Level 4 happiness. Even though our expectations are often disappointed, for example when unconditional love turns out to be not so unconditional, individuals at this level of happiness, much like Don Quixote, will not let temporary setbacks negatively influence their continuing pursuit of the ideal. One might ask, what is it within us that makes us believe that perfection can be attained?

For those with faith, the capacity to seek perfection, the ultimate truth, the ultimate good, unconditional love, is rooted in a belief in a Supreme Being. In the Judeo-Christian culture, the Supreme Being is seen as the Truth, the Light, and the Way. In essence, God is perfect and His followers are called to seek the same perfection. They seek to be one with God. Thus, it is relatively easy for those who believe in God to aspire to Level 4 happiness.

For those without faith in a personal God, the same desire for Level 4 happiness is often based in the ideal of humanism. Human dignity demands that we seek the perfect truth, goodness, love, and beauty. These desires differentiate us from lower forms of animals. Thus, if an individual has an ideology like humanism, it is relatively easy to aspire to Level 4 happiness. Absent such ideals, however, an individual will have difficulty appreciating the significance of Level 4 happiness and will most likely be satisfied with a lower level of happiness.

THE COMPARISON GAME

Robert Spitzer points out that if a person does not hold an ideology that will encourage him or her to aspire to Level 3 or Level 4 happiness, he or she may become fixated at Level 2 happiness. In this case, happiness is derived only from winning at some kind of competition. Spitzer refers to this individual as being caught in the "comparison game."

As we noted earlier, achievement through competitiveness is a Level 2 form of happiness. But if achievement and competition are ends in themselves, it can be destructive. It is those who see achievement and competition as ends in themselves and are obsessed with winning that Spitzer says are involved in the comparison game.

Participants in the comparison game are constantly concerned with who is achieving more and who is achieving less. Every event in life is reduced to who wins and who loses. The losers, of course, are looked upon as being inferior and the winners are considered superior. One problem with this approach is that even when one is the winner in one instance, the pressure remains to continue winning.

Spitzer claims that 70 percent of the children in the United States are involved in one formal or another of the comparison game, while 73 percent of the adults are engaged in the game. For those in this category, the options that the comparison game present are not attractive. For example, if one wins, the stakes are increased for the next inning of the game. The emotional result can be emptiness, contempt, isolation, and resentment of oneself and others. If one plays the game to a draw, the emotional results are a fear of ultimately losing and suspicion of others. Finally, if one loses in the comparison game, depression, jealousy, anger, and inferiority are the result. The moral of the comparison game metaphor is that we cannot afford to get bogged down at the Level 2 form of happiness. In order for a follower to evolve into a heroic follower, he or she must move beyond Level 2 happiness (competition) and progress to Levels 3 and 4 (collaboration). When the follower behaves out of the Level 3 and 4 models of happiness, the follower is more likely to be manifesting the habit of *sensitivity* or *heart*.

EMOTIONAL INTELLIGENCE

Individuals who manifest the habit of sensitivity or heart are said to have a high degree of emotional intelligence. Most of us are familiar with the current notion of multiple intelligences; that is, individuals have a number of intelligences in addition to cognitive intelligence (Intelligence Quotient or IQ). Among these intelligences is emotional intelligence. Several theories within the emotional intelligence paradigm seek to understand how individuals perceive, understand, utilize, and manage *emotions* in an effort to predict and foster personal effectiveness.[8]

An awareness of the origins and motivations of each of these theories provides additional insight into why the specific constructs, and methods used to measure them, vary among the major theories. The first of the three major theories to emerge was that of Bar-On. In his doctoral dissertation, he coined the term emotional quotient (EQ) as an analogue to intelligence quotient (IQ). The timing of the publication of his dissertation in the late 1980s was consistent with an increasing interest in the role of emotion in social functioning and well-being, but before interest in emotional intelligence enjoyed the widespread interest and popularity that it does today. Bar-On currently defines his model in terms of an array of traits and abilities related to emotional and social knowledge that influence our overall ability to effectively cope with environmental demands; as such, it can be viewed as a model of psychological well-being and adaptation. This model includes the ability to be aware of, to understand, and to express oneself; the ability to be aware of, to understand, and to relate to others; the ability to deal with strong emotions and to control one's impulses; and the ability to adapt to change and to solve problems of a personal or social nature. The five main domains in this model are *intrapersonal skills, interpersonal skills, adaptability, stress management*, and *general mood*. If the reader sees a similarity between Bar-On's work and the underlying theory of this book, it is not coincidental.

The EQ-I, which Bar-On constructed to measure the model, is a self-report measure that specifically measures emotionally and socially competent behavior; this tool estimates an individual's emotional and social intelligence, as opposed to traditional personality traits or cognitive capacity. The use of the self-report measure to assess individuals on this model is consistent with established practice within personality psychology, where self-report measures represent the dominant, though certainly not the only, method of assessment.

Emotional intelligence as formulated in the theory of Mayer and Salovey has been framed within a model of intelligence. The motivation to develop a theory of emotional intelligence, and instruments to measure it, came from a realization that traditional measures of intelligence failed to measure individual differences in the ability to perceive, process, and effectively manage emotions and emotional information. The use of this frame is significant, as it defines emotional intelligence more specifically as the *ability* to perceive emotions, to access and generate emotions to assist thought, to understand emotions and emotional knowledge, and to reflectively regulate emotions to promote emotional and intellectual growth. Like other intelligences, emotional intelligence is defined as a group of mental abilities, and it is best measured using a testing situation that is performance- or ability-based. This focus on objective, performance-based assessment is similar in spirit to the methods used to measure traditional intelligence. For example, to measure spatial reasoning ability (traditionally seen as a type of cognitive intelligence), it makes sense to present an individual with a set of spatial reasoning tasks of varying difficulty in order to gauge his or her ability on this type of intelligence. Performance-based measures of emotional intelligence take a similar approach. For example, if you want insight into an individual's ability to perceive emotions in others, it makes sense to present the individual a variety of visual images, such as faces, and ask him or her to identity the emotions present.

The most recent addition to theory within the emotional intelligence paradigm is the framework of emotional intelligence put forward by Goleman in his book, *Working with Emotional Intelligence*.[9] This theory represents a framework of emotional intelligence that reflects how an individual's potential for mastering the skills of self-awareness, self-management, social awareness, and relationship management translates into success in the workplace. Goleman's model of emotional intelligence offers these four major domains. He then postulates that each of these domains becomes the foundation for learned abilities, or competencies, that depend on underlying strength in the relevant EI domain. The EI domain of self-awareness, for example, provides the underlying basis for the learned competency of "accurate self-assessment: of strengths and limitations pertaining to a role such as leadership." The competency level of this framework is based on a content analysis of capabilities that have been identified through internal research on work performance in several hundred companies and organizations worldwide. Goleman defines an emotional "competence" as "a learning capability based on emotional intelligence that results in outstanding performance at work." The fact that such competencies are learned is a critical distinction. Where emotional intelligence is defined by the other theories as our *potential* for achieving mastery of specific abilities in this domain, the emotional competencies themselves represent the degree to which an individual has *mastered* specific skills and abilities that build on EI and allow them greater effectiveness in the workplace. In this context, emotional intelligence might predict the ease by which a given individual will be able to master the specific skills and abilities of a given emotional competence. Grounding his theory specifically within the context of work performance separates Goleman's model from those of Bar-On and of Mayer and Salovey.

The above information begs the question: can emotional intelligence be developed, or is it innate? One of the factors contributing to the popularity of theories of emotional intelligence is the assumption that, unlike IQ, emotional intelligence can be developed. While it is acknowledged that genetics likely plays an important role in the development of emotional intelligence, it is also noted that geneticists themselves challenge as naïve the assumption that nurture does not impact nature in this case. However, without sustained effort and attention, individuals are unlikely to improve greatly a given aspect of their emotional intelligence. That is why we are stressing the importance of developing this habit if one wishes to become a heroic follower. Perhaps the knowledge of its importance will motivate followers to place a concerted effort toward developing their emotional intelligence.

Another question that arises when exploring the dimensions of emotional intelligence is an ethical one. Can individuals use their emotional intelligence in an unethical way? No intelligence is moral or immoral in and of itself. For example, Abraham Lincoln used his intelligence in a laudable way, whereas Adolph Hitler used his in a hateful way. Nevertheless, there are significant issues to explore at the intersection of ethics and emotional intelligence. Ordinarily, one would think that emotional intelligence would promote pro-social behavior. For example, empathy, a form of emotional intelligence, appears to be an essential step in fostering altruism and compassion. On the other hand, there is no doubt that there are Machiavellian types who use emotional intelligence abilities like empathy and persuasion to manipulate others. However, there is research to support the idea that those with a Machiavellian personality tend to have diminished rather than enhanced empathy abilities, focusing most clearly in areas related to their self-interest (Level 2 happiness).[10] Hence, it is safe to conclude that, like cognitive intelligence, emotional intelligence is ethically neutral. How one *utilizes* his or her emotional intelligence has ethical implications.

DIAGNOSTIC CHECKLIST

Here are some questions that will help your assess your *sensitivity* or heart:

1. Do you see yourself as an *employee-owner*?
2. Do you treat your colleagues with the deference that you would show a *volunteer*?
3. Do you have a *concern for others* rather than being egocentric?
4. Do you give a voice to those who are traditionally *underrepresented* in our society?
5. Do you nurture and cultivate your *emotional intelligence*?

NOTES

1. Max De Pree, *Leadership Is an Art* (New York: Dell Publishing, 1989).

2. P. M. Senge, *The Fifth Discipline: The Art and Practice of the Learning Organization* (New York: Doubleday, 1990).

3. Max De Pree, *Leadership Is an Art*.

4. A. Solzhenitsyn, *A World Split Apart* (New York: Harper and Row, 1978), pp. 17–19.

5. William Glasser, *Control Theory: A New Explanation of How We Control Our Lives* (New York: Harper and Row, 1984).

6. Lee Bolman and Terrence Deal, *Reframing Organizations: Artistry, Choice, and Leadership* (San Francisco: Jossey-Bass, 1991).

7. Robert J. Spitzer, SJ, *The Spirit of Leadership*, (Provo, UT: Executive Excellence, 2000).

8. Robert Emmerling and Daniel Goleman, Emotional intelligence: Issues and common misunderstandings, *Consortium for Research on Emotional Intelligence in Organizations* (Toronto: October 2003).

9. Daniel Goleman, *Working With Emotional Intelligence* (New York: Bantam Books, 1998).

10. M. Davis and L. Kraus, Personality and empathic empathy, *Empathic Accuracy*, ed. H. Ickes (New York: Guilford Press, 1997).

8

PUTTING IT ALL TOGETHER . . .
AND KEEPING IT GOING!

When people get busy producing or "sawing" they often neglect to
sharpen the saw. Regularly sharpening the saw means having a bal-
anced systematic program for self-renewal.

—Stephen Covey

In this chapter, I am suggesting a model for "putting it all together" or
integrating the six habits of the heroic follower. Furthermore, I will rec-
ommend some strategies for nurturing and sustaining these habits over
time. I have made the point that in order for a follower to develop into
a heroic follower and ultimately into a heroic leader, he or she would
have to nurture and manifest six habits of the mind and heart: purpose,
responsibility, communication, flexibility, trustworthiness, and sensitivity. We explored the ramifications of each of these habits in detail and
made suggestions regarding how they may be developed and sustained.

Along the heroic follower continuum, we demarcated the journey
with the stages of dependence, independence, and intradependence.
Once the follower perfected the habits of the mind, namely, purpose,
responsibility, communication, and flexibility, he or she would have pro-
gressed from the stage of dependence through the stage of independence where he or she could effectively interact with those in his or her
immediate environment. The path was completed when the follower

perfected the habits of the heart, namely, trust and sensitivity, arriving at the stage of intradependence where he or she could effectively interact with those in both the internal and external environment. At this point the follower has been transformed and self-actualized into the heroic follower and is poised to become the heroic leader.

What we would like to do next is suggest a lens through which the follower can view his or her behavior as the follower engages in the process of acquiring and perfecting the six habits of the heroic follower. The lens that we will suggest is that of the Ignatian vision. This lens has a distinctly moral tone to it. Hence, we will first make the argument that the process of maturing into the heroic follower be looked upon as a moral science rather than a purely empirical science.

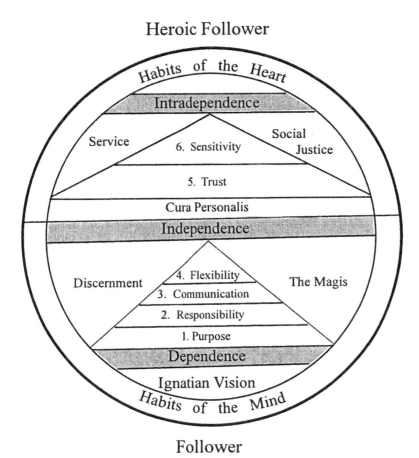

Figure 8.1.   Heroic Follower Wheel

HEROIC FOLLOWERSHIP AS A MORAL SCIENCE

Earlier, I made the point of the need to follow with both mind and heart. Until recently, the focus on becoming a highly effective person has been on the habits of the mind. The process of developing these habits traditionally has been looked upon as an empirical science. However, I suggest that a post-positivist follower follow in the humanist tradition, that is, being primarily concerned with the whole person and matters of both mind and heart.

Dissatisfaction with current approaches for examining social life stems from empirical science's inability to deal with questions of value and morality and its inability to fulfill its promise. For example, Griffiths criticizes orthodox theories because they "ignore the presence of unions and fail to account for the scarcity of women and minorities in top administrative positions."[1] The empiricist research program modeled on the natural sciences fails to address issues of understanding and interpretation.[2] This failure precludes researchers from reaching a genuine understanding of the human condition. It is time, they argue, to treat social science research as a moral science.

The term "moral" is being used here in its cultural, professional, spiritual, and ethical sense, not in a religious sense. The moral side of followership has to do with the *dilemmas* that face us each day. All followers face at least three areas of dilemmas: control, competency, and societal. Control dilemmas center around four questions: (1) Do you treat peers as robots, focusing narrowly on cognitive goals, or as a whole persons, focusing more broadly on intellectual, aesthetic, social, spiritual, and physical dimensions? (2) Who controls the workday? In some organizations, employees are given latitude in scheduling their activities; in others, class activities follow a strict and mandatory schedule. (3) Who controls operations or what larger context of what it means to be human and how we resolve conflicts in the workplace? (4) Who controls the standards and defines success and failure? Is the decision making unilateral or participative?

Similar dilemmas occur in the competency domain and relate to whether one's abilities and skills are considered as received, determined knowledge or whether it is considered private, individualized knowledge, of the type achieved through discoveries and experiments: the age-old question of nature versus nurture. These difficulties also depend on whether one conceives of the worker as an employee or as an individual.

The employee receives professional development generated from a body of knowledge, whereas the individual receives personal and professional development generated from his or her particular needs and context.

A final set of dilemmas has to do with what followers bring to the workplace and how they are to be treated once there. One concerns the distribution of resources. Should one focus more resources on the less talented in order to bring them up to standards or on the more talented, in order for them to reach their full potential? The same question arises regarding the distribution of justice. Should rules be applied uniformly without regard to the differing circumstances of each person or should family background, economic factors, and other sociological influences be considered? Should a supervisor stress a common culture or ethnic differences and subculture consciousness?

Much of human dynamics involves resolving such dilemmas by making a variety of decisions throughout the workday. Such decisions can be made, however, in a *reflective* or an *unreflective* manner. An unreflective manner means simply behaving as one was trained, without considering available alternatives. A reflective approach involves an examination of the widest array of alternatives. Thus, reflective followership suggests that dilemmas need not be simply resolved but can be transformed so that a higher level of expertise is reached.

This same logic can also be applied to leadership. Leadership involves the resolution of various dilemmas, that is, the making of moral decisions. One set of dilemmas involves control. How much participation can employees have in the operation of the organization? How much participation can customers have? Who evaluates whom, and for what purpose? Is the role of management collegial or authority-centered? Finally, an additional set of dilemmas pertains to the idea of the place of the organization in society. Should organizations be oriented to ameliorate the deficits that some employees bring with them or should they see different cultures and groups as strengths? Should organizations be seen as agents of change, oriented to the creation of a more just society, or as socializers that duplicate the current social structure?

Often, these questions are answered unreflectively and simply re-solved by a "knee-jerk reaction." This approach often resolves the dilemma but does not foster a real *transformation* in one's self, role, or institution. If the habits of leaders and followers are to encompass trans-formation, and I would argue that they should, then an additional lens to traditional model of structural functionalism must be found through which these questions can be viewed. I suggest that the additional lens be in the form of the Ignatian vision. In this context, then, the study of followership and leadership can be viewed as a moral science.

THE IGNATIAN VISION REVISITED

In chapter 2 we suggested that the Ignatian vision be considered as a lens through which the heroic follower would develop his or her pur-pose or mission in life. Here we suggest that the Ignatian vision be con-sidered as an integrating force in connecting the six habits of the heroic follower and moving along the continuum from dependence to interde-pendence, and finally, to intradependence.

Ignatius of Loyola, a young priest born to a Spanish aristocratic fam-ily, founded the Society of Jesus, the Jesuits, and wrote his seminal book, *The Spiritual Exercises*.[3] In this book, he suggested a "way of life" and a "way of looking at things" that has been propagated by his religious com-munity and his other followers for almost five centuries. His principles have been utilized in a variety of ways. They have been used as an aid in developing the spiritual life of the individual; they have been used to formulate a way of learning that has become the curriculum and in-structional method employed in the sixty high schools and the twenty-eight Jesuit colleges and universities in the United States; and recently they have been used by Chris Lowney in his book, *Heroic Leadership*, as guidance for developing one's own managerial style. Together, these principles comprise the *Ignatian vision*.[4]

We mentioned five Ignatian principles that serve as a foundation for developing a model of behavior for the heroic follower: (1) Ignatius' con-cept of the *magis*, or the "more"; (2) implications of his notion of *cura personalis*, or "care of the person"; (3) the process of *inquiry* or *discern-ment*; (4) the development of *men and women for others*; and (5) service to the *underserved* and marginalized, or his concept of *social justice*.

The first two will be helpful in our efforts to develop the habits of the mind (purpose, responsibility, communication, flexibility), and the other three will do likewise in our efforts to develop the habits of the heart (trust and sensitivity).

At the core of the Ignatian vision is the concept of the *magis,* or the "more." Ignatius spent the greater part of his life seeking perfection in all areas of his personal, spiritual, and professional life. He was never satisfied with the status quo. He was constantly seeking to improve his own spiritual life, as well as his secular life as leader of a growing religious community. He was an advocate of "continuous improvement" long before it became a corporate slogan.

The idea of constantly seeking "the more" implies change. The *magis* is a movement away from the status quo, and moving away from the status quo defines change. The Ignatian vision requires individuals and institutions to embrace the process of change as a vehicle for personal and institutional improvement. For Ignatius' followers, frontiers and boundaries are not obstacles or ends, but new challenges to be faced, new opportunities to be welcomed. Thus, change needs to become a way of life. Ignatius further implores his followers to "be the change that you expect in others." In other words, we are called to model desired behavior—to live out our values, to be of ever-fuller service to our communities, and to aspire to the more universal good. Ignatius had no patience with mediocrity. He constantly strove for the greater good.

The *magis* principle, then, can be described as the main norm in the selection of information and the interpretation of it. Every real alternative for choice must be conducive to the advancement toward perfection. When some aspect of a particular alternative is *more* conducive to reaching perfection than other alternatives, we have reason to choose that alternative. Earlier in this book, we spoke of the "dilemmas" that we face during every working day. The *magis* principle is a "way of seeing" that can help us in selecting the better alternative.

At first hearing, the *magis* principle may sound rigid and frightening. It is absolute, and Ignatius is unyielding in applying it, but not rigid. On the one hand, he sees it as the expression of our love of humanity, which inexorably seeks to fill all of us with a desire not to be content with what is less good for us. On the other hand, he sees that humanity not only has its particular gifts, but also has its limitations and different stages of growth. If a choice would be more humane in the abstract than in the concrete, that choice would not be seen as adhering to the *magis* principle.

In every case, then, accepting and living by the *magis* principle is an expression of our love of humanity. So, whatever the object for choice, the measure of our love of neighbor will be the fundamental satisfaction we will find in choosing and acting by the *magis* principle. Whatever one chooses by this principle, no matter how undesirable in some other respect, will always be what one would most want as a moral and ethical member of the human race.

Closely related to the principle of the *magis* is the Ignatian principle of *inquiry* and *discernment*. In his writings, Ignatius urges us to challenge the status quo through the methods of inquiry and discernment. To Ignatius, the need to enter into inquiry and discernment is to determine God's will. However, this process is of value for the purely *secular* purpose of deciding on which "horn of a dilemma" one should come down. To aid us in utilizing inquiry and discernment as useful tools in challenging the status quo and determining the right choice to be made, Ignatius suggests that the ideal disposition for inquiry and discernment is humility. The disposition of humility is especially helpful when, despite one's best efforts, the evidence that one alternative is more conducive to the betterment of society is not compelling. When the discerner cannot find evidence to show that one alternative is more conducive to the common good, Ignatius calls for a judgment in favor of what more assimilates the discerner's life to the life of poverty and humiliation. Thus, when the *greatest* good cannot readily be determined, the *greater* good is more easily discerned in position of humility. These are very demanding standards, but they are consistent with the *magis* principle and the tenets of critical humanism.

In addition to the *magis* principle norm, taking account of what has been said about the norm of humility as a disposition for seeking the greater good, the relationship of the greater good norm to the greatest good norm can be clarified. The latter is absolute, overriding, always primary. The greater good norm is secondary; it can never, in any choice, have equal weight with the first *magis* principle. It can never justify a choice of actual poverty and humiliation over riches and honors if the latter are seen to be more for the service of humanity in a particular situation for choice. In other words, if being financially successful allows one to better serve the poor and underserved, financial success would be preferred to actual poverty. Both the principle of the *magis* and the discernment norms speak to the habits of the *mind* of the heroic follower and move the heroic follower from dependence to independence where he or she is able to interact effectively with the immediate environment.

Ignatius presents us with several other supplemental norms for facing our "dilemmas." In choices that directly affect individuals who are underserved or marginalized, especially the poor, Ignatius urges us to give preference to those in need. This brings us to his next guiding principle, *cura personalis*, or care of the person.

Another of Ignatius' important and enduring principles is his notion that, despite the primacy of the common good, the need to care for the individual person should never be lost. From the very beginning, the *cura personalis* principle has been included in the mission statement of virtually every high school and college founded by the Jesuits. In the Ignatian vision, the care of the person is a requirement, not only on a personal needs basis, but also on a "whole person" basis.

This principle also has implications for how we conduct ourselves as heroic followers. Ignatius calls us to value the gifts and charisms of our colleagues and to address any deficiencies that they might have and turn them into strengths. For example, during the employee evaluation process, Ignatius would urge us to focus on the formative stage (correcting weaknesses) of the evaluation far more than on the summative stage (firing or disciplining the employee). This would be one small way of applying *cura personalis* theory to practice.

The fourth principle that we wish to consider is the Ignatian concept of service. Once again, this principle has been propagated from the very outset. The expressed goal of virtually every Jesuit institution is "to develop men and women for others." Jesuit institutions are called on to create a culture of service as one way of ensuring that the students, faculty, and staffs of these institutions reflect the educational, civic and spiritual values of the Ignatian vision.

Institutions following the Ignatian tradition of service to others have done so through community services programs, and more recently, through service learning. Service to the community provides students with a means of helping others, a way to put their value systems into action, and a tangible way to assist local communities. Although these are valuable benefits, until recently there was no formal integration of the service experience into the curriculum and no formal introspection concerning the impact of service on the individual. During the last ten years, there has been a movement toward creating a more intentional academic relationship. Service has evolved from a modest student activity into an exciting pedagogical opportunity. In the past, service was viewed as a cocurricular activity; today it plays an integral role in the learning process.

Since many institutions are situated in an urban setting, service gives them a chance to share resources with surrounding communities and allows reciprocal relationships to form between the institution and local residents. Immersion into different cultures—economic, racial, educational, social, and religious—is the vehicle by which students make connections. Working side-by-side with people of varying backgrounds significantly influences individuals, forcing them outside of their comfort zones and into the gritty reality of how others live. Through reflection, they have the opportunity to integrate these powerful experiences into their lives, opening their eyes and hearts to the larger questions of social justice.[5]

At Ignatian institutions, service learning is a bridge that connects faculty, staff, and students with community partners and their agency needs. It connects academic and student life views about the educational value of experiential learning. It also connects students' textbooks with human reality, and their minds and hearts with values and action. The programs are built on key components of service learning including integration into the curriculum, a reciprocal relationship between the community agency and student, and structured time for reflection, which is very much related to the Ignatian principle of *discernment* discussed earlier.

Participation in service by high school and college students, whether as a cocurricular or a course-based experience, correlates to where they are in their developmental process. Service work allows students to explore their skills and limitations; to find what excites and energizes them; to put their values into action; and to use their talents to benefit others, to discover who they are, and who they want to become. By encouraging students to reflect on their service, these institutions assist in this self-discovery. The reflection can take many forms: an informal chat, a facilitated group discussion, written dialogue, journal entries, reaction papers, or in-class presentations of articles. By integrating the service experience through critical reflection, students develop self-knowledge of the communities in which they live and knowledge about the world that surrounds them. It is only after the unfolding of this service-based knowledge that the students are able to synthesize what they have learned into their lives. Through this reflection, the faculty members also have an opportunity to learn from and about their students. Teachers witness the change and growth of the students first-hand. In short, "service to others" changes lives.

The implications of "service to others" for the heroic follower are clear. Followers can enhance their effectiveness, not only by including the idea of service to others in the workplace, but also by modeling it in their personal and professional lives.

The Ignatian concept of "service" leads into his notion of solidarity with the underserved (poor) and marginalized and his principle of *social justice*. We begin with an attempt to achieve some measure of clarity on the nature and role of social justice in the Ignatian vision. According to some, Ignatius defined justice in both a narrow and wide sense.[6] In the *narrow* sense, it is "justice among men and women." In this case, it is a matter of "clear obligations" among "members of the human family." The application of this kind of justice would include not only the rendering of material goods but also immaterial goods such as "reputation, dignity, the possibility of exercising freedom."

Many of Ignatius' followers also believe he defined justice in a *wider* sense "where situations are encountered which are humanly intolerable and demand a remedy." These situations may be a product of "explicitly unjust acts" caused by "clearly identified people" who cannot be obliged to correct the injustices even though the dignity of the human person requires that justice be restored, or they may be caused by nonidentifiable people. It is precisely within the structural forces of inequality in society where injustice of this second type is found, where injustice is "institutionalized." In other words, injustice is built into economic, social, and political structures both national and international, causing people to suffer from poverty and hunger; from the unjust distribution of wealth, resources, and power.

It is almost certain that Ignatius did not only concern himself with injustices that were purely economic. He often cites injustices about "threats to human life and its quality," "racial and political discrimination," and loss of respect for the "rights of individuals or groups."[7] When one adds to these the "vast range of injustices" enumerated in his writings, one sees that the Ignatian vision understands its mission of justice to include "the widest possible view of justice," involving every area where there is an attack on human rights. We can conclude, therefore, that although Ignatius was to some degree concerned about commutative justice (right relationships between private persons and groups) and distributive justice (the obligations of the state to render to the individual what is his or her due), he is most concerned about what is generally called today social justice, or "justice of the common good." Such justice is comprehensive; it includes the above strict legal rights and duties, but it is more concerned about the natural rights and duties of individuals, families, communities, and the community of nations toward one another as members of the human family. Every form of justice is included in and presupposed by social justice, but with social justice, it is the social nature of the person that is emphasized, as well as the social significance of all earthly goods, the purpose of which is to aid all members of the human community to attain their dignity as human beings. Many of Ignatius' followers believe that this dignity is being undermined in our world today, and their main efforts are aimed toward restoring that dignity.

In the pursuit of social justice, Ignatius calls on his followers to be "in solidarity with the poor." The next logical question might then be, who are the poor? The poor are usually thought to be those who are economically deprived and politically oppressed. Thus, we can conclude that the promotion of justice means to work to overcome the oppressions or injustices that cause poverty. The fallacy here, however, is that the poor are not necessarily oppressed or suffering injustice, and so Ignatius argues that our obligation toward the poor must be concerned with "inhuman levels of poverty and injustice." It is not primarily concerned with the "lot of those possessing only modest resources," even though those of modest means are often poor and oppressed. So, we conclude that the poor include those "wrongfully" impoverished or dispossessed.[8]

An extended definition of the poor, one that Ignatius would espouse, would include any of these types of people:

First would be those who are economically deprived and socially marginalized and oppressed, especially those with whom one has immediate contact and who one is in a position to assist.

The second group would include the "poor in spirit," that is, those who lack a value system or an ethical and moral sense.

The third group would include the emotionally poor; those who have psychological and emotional shortcomings and are in need of comfort.

In defining the poor in the broadest way, Ignatius exhorts us to undertake social change in our role as leaders, to do what we can do to bring an end to inequality, oppression, and injustice. These last three norms, *cura personalis*, service to others, and a concern for social justice, speak to the habits of the heart of the heroic follower and move the heroic follower from independence to intradependence and self-actualization.

IMPLICATIONS FOR THE HEROIC FOLLOWER

Each of the principles of the Ignatian vision noted above has a variety of implications for the heroic follower. The *magis* principle has implications for followers in that it calls for us to continually seek perfection in all that we do. In effect, this means that we must seek to continually improve. And, since improvement implies change, we need to be champions of needed change in our personal and professional lives. This means that we have to model a tolerance for change and embrace not only our own change initiatives but also those in other parts of the organization.

The Ignatian process of *discernment* requires educational administrators to be reflective practitioners. It calls on us to be introspective regarding our administrative and leadership behavior. We are asked to reflect on the ramifications of our decisions, especially in light of their cumulative effect on the equitable distribution of power and on the marginalized individuals and groups in our communities. In effect, the principle of discernment galvanizes the other principles embodied in the Ignatian vision. During the discernment process, we are asked to reflect upon how our planned behavior will manifest the *magis* principle, *cura personalis*, and service to the community, especially the underserved, marginalized, and oppressed.

The principle of *cura personalis* has additional implications. To practice the Ignatian vision, one must treat people with dignity under all circumstances. *Cura personalis* also requires us to extend ourselves in offering individual attention and attending to the needs of all those with whom we come in contact. Being sensitive to each individual's unique needs is particularly required. Many times in our efforts to treat people equally, we fail to treat them fairly and equitably. Certain individuals have greater needs than do others, and many times these needs require exceptions to be made on their behalf. As mentioned earlier, if a colleague does not complete an assignment on time, but the tardiness is because he or she is going through some personal trauma, the principle of *cura personalis* calls on us to make an exception in this case. It likely that many would consider such an exception to be unfair to those who made the effort to complete the assignment in a timely manner, or they might say that we cannot possibly be sensitive to the special needs of all of our colleagues. However, as long as the exception is made for anyone in the same circumstances, Ignatius would not perceive this exception as being unfair. In fact, the exception would be expected if one is practicing the principle of "care of the person."

The development of men and women for others requires the heroic follower to have a sense of service toward those with whom he or she interacts as well as to develop this spirit of service in others. The concept of "servant leadership" requires us to encourage others toward a life and career of service and to assume the position of being the "servant of the servants." Ignatius thinks about both followers and leaders in terms of what the gospel writer Luke calls the "one who serves." The leader owes something to the institution he or she leads

The implications of Ignatius' notion of social justice are myriad for the both the follower and the leader. Being concerned about the marginalized among our constituencies is required. We are called to be sensitive to those individuals and groups that do not share equitably in the distribution of power and influence. Participative decision making and collaborative behavior are encouraged among heroic followers and leaders imbued with the Ignatian tradition. Equitable representation of all segments of the community should be provided whenever feasible. Behavior such as this will assure that the dominant culture is not perpetuated to the detriment of the minority culture, rendering the minorities powerless.

THE HABIT OF RENEWAL

In the spirit of the *magis*, our pilgrimage toward perfection is never quite complete. Thus, we must engage in continual renewal and progress. As the Stephen Covey quote at the beginning of this chapter indicates, there is a need for the heroic follower to continually "sharpen the saw."[9]

Sharpening the saw refers to the allegory of the woodsman who is so intently immersed in chopping down as many trees as possible in the shortest amount of time that he refuses to take time out to sharpen his dull saw. As a result, it takes him longer to chop down the trees. The obvious moral to the story is that in order to maximize our productivity, we should pause from time to time to reflect on how effective we have been in pursuing our goals. As the former New York mayor Ed Koch used to say to his constituents, "How am I doing?" This is an example of what we have previously referred to as the *reflective practitioner.*

Taking the holistic approach of Ignatius of Loyola, we should engage in a weekly or monthly process of examining and renewing the four dimensions of our nature: physical, mental, psychological, and spiritual. We need to enter into a wellness program that involves proper nutrition, adequate exercise, and rest, as well as a program of stress management. Our minds also need exercise. We should continually engage our minds through reading, writing, and critical thinking. Psychologically, we need to continually develop our emotional intelligence by honing our coping skills and refining our interpersonal skills. Finally, our spirit must continually be renewed, whether it be through prayer and religious activities or through meditation, reflection, and the pursuit of beauty and virtue.

Another approach to sharpening the saw is to systematically and frequently review your progress in developing and nurturing each of the six habits of the heroic follower. Once again, ask yourself, "How am I doing?" with your sense of *purpose, responsibility, communication, flexibility, trustworthiness,* and *sensitivity.* The Diagnostic Checklists supplied at the end of each chapter may be useful in this endeavor. Whichever approach you take, however, be sure that you take time out occasionally to "sharpen the saw."

CONCLUSION

The role of the follower is rarely studied despite the fact that everyone, including leaders, must assume the role of a follower at one time or another. Sometimes, we even assume the role of the follower concomitantly with that of the leader. For example, the CEO of General Electric is a leader when dealing with other employees of the company, but he is a follower when interacting with the chairman of the board of General Electric. Until now, I had been as guilty as anyone of focusing exclusively on the leader and ignoring the follower. I had written five books on various aspects of leadership before it dawned on me that leaders are nothing without followers, and that there is a desperate need for a guidebook for followers.

After much research, I have laid out what I believe is a helpful recipe for what the makeup of an ideal follower should be. Much of what I have presented is common sense. Its value, however, is in the systematic way it is presented. Developing the six habits of the heroic follower and showing how the follower progresses along the continuum of dependency, independency, and intradependency gives one a clear path to arriving at the goal of being a highly effective follower—all the while, examining one's performance through the lens of the Ignatian vision. I have included the Diagnostic Checklists as well as the Mind & Heart Survey (appendix I) as aids in this developmental process.

All of what I have suggested in this book is research-based. This is not popular science; it is empirical and moral science. In addition to my own research, I have relied heavily on the theories and writings of such respected scholars as Abraham Maslow, Scott Martin, Robert Spitzer, Stephen Covey, Chris Lowney, Jim Collins, Peter Senge, and Thomas Sergiovanni. An amalgam of their research has resulted in the development of the six habits of the heroic follower approach that I have presented here. I have found this approach to be effective in my own personal and professional lives, and in those of many of my colleagues. It is my hope that this approach will be successful in developing you into a heroic follower, and if you choose, into a heroic leader.

NOTES

1. D. Griffiths and Peter Ribbins, *Leadership matters in education regarding secondary headship* (inaugural lecture, University of Birmingham, Edgbaston, 1995).

2. F. Erickson, School literacy, reasoning, and civility: An anthropologist's perspective, *Review of Educational Research* 54, (1984), 525–546.

3. Andre Ravier, SJ, *Ignatius of Loyola and the Founding of the Society of Jesus* (San Francisco: Ignatius Press, 1987).

4. Chris Lowney, *Heroic Leadership: Best Practices from a 450 Year-Old Company that Changed the World* (Chicago: Loyola Press, 2003).

5. Martin R. Tripole, SJ, *Faith Beyond Justice* (St. Louis: The Institute of Jesuit Sources, 1994).

6. Jules J. Toner, SJ, *Discerning God's Will: Ignatius of Loyola's Teaching on Christian Decision Making* (St. Louis: The Institute of Jesuit Sources, 1991).

7. Christopher Chapple, *The Jesuit Tradition in Education and Missions* (Scranton, PA: University of Scranton Press, 1993).

8. *Documents of the 34th General Congregation of the Society of Jesus* (St. Louis: Institute of Jesuit Sources, 1995).

9. Stephen Covey, *The 8th Habit: From Effectiveness to Greatness* (New York: Free Press, 2004).

IMPLICATIONS FOR
ORGANIZATIONAL DEVELOPMENT

The effective functioning of social systems from the local PTA to the United States of America is assumed to be dependent on the quality of their leadership.

—Victor H. Vroom

Since many heroic followers will aspire to be leaders, it is important for them to not only be concerned with how they can personally contribute to their organizations as a loyal and effective follower, but they also need to concern themselves with the big picture in preparation for becoming heroic leaders.

Practitioners are often critical of the theoretical concepts such as humanism and the Ignatian vision because, although these principles are acceptable and even laudable, their proponents never seem to suggest meaningful ways of applying these principles. In this chapter, I suggest ways of effectively applying these theories to the development of an organization. I am suggesting here that the organizational health of an institution is determined by how effectively the following aspects of the organization are developed and operationalized:

1. Organizational structure
2. Organizational culture

3. Organizational leadership
4. Motivation
5. Communication
6. Conflict management
7. Decision making
8. Distribution of power
9. Strategic planning
10. Change

We will suggest that these components of the institution be addressed using research-based structural functionalist strategies and examined through the lens of Ignatian vision, in other words, leading with both mind and heart.

ORGANIZATIONAL STRUCTURE

All institutions are essentially organized according to one of three basic structures: the classical structure, the social systems structure, or the open systems structure. Despite being primarily organized around one of these structures, most organizations reflect certain aspects of each of these models.[1]

Classical theorists believe that an application of a bureaucratic structure and process will promote rational, efficient, and disciplined behavior, making possible the achievement of well-defined goals. Efficiency, then, is achieved by arranging positions and jurisdiction and by placing power at the top of a clear chain of command. The conceptual model of the classical theory has had a significant impact on business and industry. Virtually every institution in the United States is organized according to the tenets of the classical theory. For example, classical theory calls for a hierarchy with graded levels of authority. Every corporation has its organizational chart. Even nonprofits such as schools have responded to this aspect of classical theory by setting up levels of control beginning with the school board and flowing down to the superintendent, the principals, the teachers, and the students.

Within the classical theory framework, the individual is regarded as an object, a part of the bureaucratic machine. This is the antithesis of the Ignatian vision. A more acceptable organizational structure would be one based on social systems theory. Historically, researchers found that the impact of social-psychological variables within the worker group was significant. The study of behavior in social system settings intensified, and a greater sophistication developed about how and why group members behave as they do under given conditions. In time, a natural social systems orientation to the analysis of behavior evolved in the literature as an alternative to the rational or classical systems approach.

The conceptual perspective of the social systems model suggests that an organization consists of a collection of groups (social systems) that collaborate to achieve system goals. Coalitions among subgroups within the organization—for example, the elementary grade teachers—form to provide power bases upon which positive or negative action can be taken; for example, "Let's lobby the principal for introducing technology in the primary grades." As with the classical organizational theory, both for-profit and not-for-profit organizations have been profoundly influenced by the social systems model.

A newer theory that is a growing influence on institutions, especially businesses, is the open systems model. The classical and social systems theories tend to view organizational life as a closed system, isolated from the surrounding environment. In contrast, open system theory treats an organization as a set of interrelated parts that interact with the environment. It receives "input" such as human and material resources, values, community expectations, and societal demands; transforms them through a production process (producing a computer, for example), and exports the product in the form of "output" into the environment (businesses, the military, homes, etc.) with "value added." The organization receives a return (revenue and profits) for its efforts so it can survive and prosper. Then the cycle begins once again with some of the profits being invested for new and improved products.

Through the perspective of open systems theory, a new logic on issues of organizational governance has emerged. It emphasizes the relationship of the organization to its surrounding environment and thus places a premium on planning and programming for events that cannot be controlled directly. The key to making an open system work effectively and efficiently is its ability to gather, process, and utilize information. In a business, then, the ease with which a need is discovered, a goal is estab-

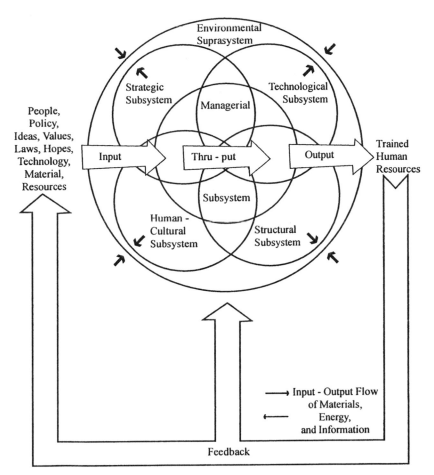

Figure 9.1.   Open System Model

lished, and resources are coalesced to meet that need will determine the effectiveness and efficiency of that company.

Knowing how one's organization is structured within the context of these three models is the first step in a leader's quest to truly "know the territory" of the institution. The very latest research indicates that none of these models, in and of itself, is an effective organizational structure. On the contrary, a *combination* of these models has been shown to be most effective. There is a need in most institutions for roles to be defined (classical theory), but there is also a need for relationships to be considered (social systems theory) and for groups to collaborate (open

systems theory). It is the responsibility of the leader to develop the organizational structure that is appropriate and effective in his or her situation. By doing so, the leader will have take the first step in the process
of ensuring the organizational good health of the institution.

Diagnostic Checklist

Here are some questions that can be addressed in assessing your institution's organizational *structure* through the lens of structural functionalism and the Ignatian vision:

- Is there appropriate division of labor and is it flexible?
- Is the division of labor conducive to reaching organizational goals?
- Is the structure of the organization well designed?
- Do workgroups operate and communicate effectively?
- Are the best aspects of the classical, social systems, and open sys-
  tems organizational models present?
- Does the organization's structure respond to the external and in-
  ternal environmental contingencies?
- Does the structure of the organization marginalize various individ-
  uals and/or groups?
- Does the structure of the organization serve to treat people hu-
  manely?
- Does the structure ensure the equitable distribution of power and
  influence?
- Is the structure flexible enough to adapt to continuous progress
  and change?

ORGANIZATIONAL CULTURE

The next consideration in ensuring the organizational good health of an
institution is its organizational culture. Organizational culture can be defined as the shared beliefs, expectations, values, and norms of conduct
of its members. In any organization, the informal culture interacts with
formal structure and control system to produce a generally clear understanding of the "way things are done around here." Even more than the

forces of bureaucracy, the organization's culture is the glue that binds people and groups together.

Anyone who has visited a number of educational institutions, for example, develops a sense of their different "personalities" or culture. Walking the hallways and campus of an educational institution, an astute observer can see physical manifestations of an underlying set of values: perhaps a huge trophy case in the entrance lobby; classroom desks bolted to the floor; a clean and attractive campus; football, basketball and band programs that overshadow academic programs; faculty and staff constantly patrolling the halls; clandestine meetings of students and/or faculty. The same observations can be made of virtually any organization.

The above are tangible aspects of the organization's culture. The intangible aspects often parallel those values. Businesses attempting to develop shared values and enculturate them often illustrate them by symbols frequently found around the institution: "Knowledge is Power," "Wildcat Pride," "When EF Hutton talks, people listen," "Just Say No," "Coke is the One," and so forth. Other symbols of an organization's culture are the heroes and storytellers that we spoke of earlier. Another important component of an organization's culture is the dominant attribution process in the institution. Do individuals tend to have an internal or external locus of control? Do they tend to blame outside forces for their deficiencies, or do they internalize the blame and try to improve?

The attitude of the management and staff, along with how they perceive their environment, are other important components of the institution's culture. Do they have a positive or negative predisposition? Do perceptual distortions, like stereotyping, projection, and the halo effect proliferate?

Another important component of organizational culture is the learning processes in an institution. Just as students have different learning styles, so do adults. So the question is, how can managers encourage their own and others' learning in the workplace, and how can they transform the workplace into what Peter Senge calls the "learning organization?"[2] They can ensure that appropriate conditions for learning exist; providing appropriate stimuli (e.g., professional development materials) should facilitate acquisition of the skills or attitudes desired. Administrators should reinforce desired learned behaviors. They should also provide environmental cues that encourage learning. Structuring a context that supports learning is essential. In effect, just as we advise teachers to adapt their teaching styles to the learning styles of their students, administrators must adapt their management styles to the variety of learning styles that are present in their organizations.

Leaders can use the following modeling strategy. First, the administrator should identify the goal or target behaviors that will lead to improved performance; for example, "A more extensive use of collaborative learning strategies will lead to improving employees' social skills." Second, the administrator must select the appropriate model and determine whether to present the model through a live demonstration, videotape, other media, or a combination of all of these. Third, the administrator must make sure the employees are capable of meeting the technical skill requirements of the target behavior. For example, further training might be necessary. Fourth, the administrator must structure a favorable and positive learning environment to increase the likelihood that the employees will learn the new behavior and act in the desired way. Starting collaborative learning with a particularly skilled trainer and a cooperative group of employees will ensure success. Fifth, the administrator must model the target behavior and carry out supporting activities such as role-playing. Conducting a meeting using collaborative learning techniques would be an example of such a strategy. Sixth, the administrator should positively reinforce reproduction of the target behaviors both in training and in the workplace. Employee-of-the-month awards are an example of this strategy. Once the target behaviors are reproduced, administrators must maintain and strengthen them through a system of rewards until the behavior is institutionalized, that is, part of the organizational culture.

Although all of the above considerations are important in assessing and improving an institution's culture, perhaps the most important component of organizational culture is the presence of, or the lack of, trust and respect among the organization's members, especially between the administration and the staff. Achieving effectiveness is an incremental, sequential improvement process. This improvement process begins by building a sense of security within each individual so that he or she can be flexible in adapting to changes within the organization. Addressing only skills or techniques, such as communication, motivation, negotiation, or empowerment, is ineffective when individuals in an organization do not trust its systems, themselves, or one another. An institution's resources are wasted when invested only in training programs that assist administrators in mastering quick-fix techniques that, at best, attempt to manipulate and, at worst, reinforce mistrust.

The challenge is to transform relationships based on insecurity, adversarialism, and politics to those based on mutual trust. Trust is the beginning of effectiveness and forms the foundation of a principle-centered learning environment that places emphasis upon strengths and devises innovative methods to minimize weaknesses. The transformation process requires an internal locus of control that emphasizes individual responsibility and accountability for change and for promoting effectiveness.

Diagnostic Checklist

Here are some questions that can be addressed in assessing your institution's organizational *culture* through the lens of structural functionalism and the Ignatian vision:

- Does the organization exhibit a culture of mutual trust and respect?
- Do perceptual distortions proliferate?
- Does the workforce exhibit an internal locus of control?
- Is the institution a learning organization?
- Are the various learning styles being addressed in the management process?
- What beliefs and values do the individuals in the organization have?
- Do the beliefs and attitudes conform to the principles of critical theory and the Ignatian vision?
- How do these beliefs and values influence individual attitudes?
- What functional and dysfunctional behaviors result from the individuals' attitudes?
- Is there a climate of participative decision making?
- Is there a caring atmosphere present?
- Is there a respect for diversity in all of its expressions?
- Is the management interested in continuous progress (*magis*)?

ORGANIZATIONAL LEADERSHIP

In recent years, a plethora of research studies have been conducted on leadership and leadership styles. The overwhelming evidence indicates that there is no single leadership style that is most appropriate in all situations. Rather, an administrator's leadership style should be adapted to the situation so that, at various times, task behavior or relationship behavior might be appropriate. At other times and in other situations, various combinations of both task and relationship behavior may be most effective.

The emergence of transformational leadership has seen leadership theory come full circle. Transformational leadership theory combines aspects of the early trait theory perspective with the more current situational or contingency models. The personal charisma of the leader, along with his or her ability to formulate an educational vision and to communicate it to other, determines the transformational leader's effectiveness.

Since the effective leader is expected to adapt his or her leadership style to an ever-changing environment, administration becomes an even more complex and challenging task. However, a thorough knowledge of leadership theory can make some sense of the apparent chaos that the administrator faces on an almost daily basis.

From a structural/functionalist viewpoint, the transformational leaders would simply need to practice the research-based skills that have been found to be effective. Thus, they would develop a mission and a vision, establish goals and objectives, and implement them by employing leadership behaviors that are appropriate to the situation. However, the followers of Ignatian pedagogy would posit that if a leader confines his or her thinking to the technical aspects of leadership, the leader will not maximize his or her impact. They would suggest that in addition to involving the *mind* in determining their behavior, leaders should also involve the *heart* and *soul* in the process. Thus, such concerns as "care of the person," equitable distribution of power and influence, social justice, and identification with the oppressed and marginalized should be considered in determining one's leadership behavior.

Diagnostic Checklist

Here are some questions that can be addressed in assessing your institution's *leadership* through the lens of structural functionalism and the Ignatian vision:

- Do the administrators display the behaviors required for effective leadership?
- Do the leaders encourage the appropriate amount of participation in decision making?
- Does the leadership adapt to the task and the maturity level of the followers?
- Do transformational leaders exist?
- Do they operate in the various frames of leadership?
- Do they articulate a vision and a strategic plan?
- Are they sensitive to the needs of individuals?
- Are they inclusive in their dealings with the followers?
- Do they view the institution as a vehicle for social change?

MOTIVATING EMPLOYEES

The next step in preparing oneself to be an effective leader is to adopt an approach to motivate one's colleagues to attain the corporate vision that has been jointly developed. To begin the process, you might ask yourself what motivates individuals to behave, think, or feel in certain ways. What factors make you or others more willing to work, to be creative, to achieve, and to produce? Theory and research in the area of motivation provide a systematic way of diagnosing the degree of motivation and of prescribing ways of increasing it. There are two main views of motivation. One view posits that individuals are motivated by inherited, conflicting, and unconscious drives. This view, which was popularized by Freud and Jung, and more recently by Skinner, Maslow, and Glasser, is operationalized through the so-called *content* theories of motivation, such as the various needs theories.

The other view of motivation says that an individual is basically rational and is normally conscious of his or her pursuit of goals. Plato and Aristotle, and more recently Jerome Bruner, are associated with this view. This perspective has spawned the so-called *process* theories of motivation, including the equity theory, expectancy theory, and goal-setting theory.

Suppose the CEO of a company earns $250,000 per year and the vice president for marketing earns $175,000. And suppose this company decided to base part of its annual salary increase on whether it met its sales quota. Why would such a company think this policy might motivate its executives who are not directly involved in sales? Early motivation theorists would explain such a situation by saying that the company expects the new policy to meet the employees' *needs*—their basic requirement for living and working productively. As the workforce in organizations becomes more diverse, recognizing the individuality of needs becomes paramount; identifying and responding to them becomes a critical issue in effective management.

How do we identify employees' needs? To do a good job of identifying them, we probably would need to spend a great deal of time talking with the employees and observing their behavior both in and out of the work environment. Many times, determining employees' needs outside of the work environment is conjecture. But the effort should be made so that the leader has a better change of identifying, and then meeting, the needs of his or her colleagues.

In 1935, Abraham Maslow developed the first needs theory, which is still one of the most popular and well-known motivation theories. Maslow stated that individuals have five needs, arranged in a hierarchy from the most basic to the highest level: physiological, safety, belongingness and love, esteem, and self-actualization.[3]

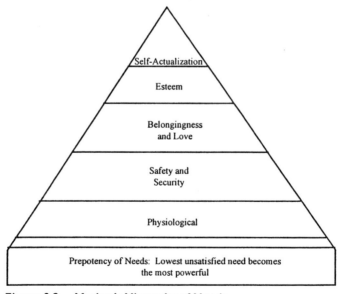

Figure 9.2.   Maslow's Hierarchy of Needs

Physiological needs are the most basic needs an individual has. These include, at a minimum, a person's requirement for food, water, shelter, sex, the ability to care for his or her children, and medical and dental coverage. Safety needs include a person's desire for security or protection. This translates most directly into concerns for short-term and long-term job security, as well as physical safety at work. Belongingness and love needs focus on the social aspects of work and nonwork situations. Virtually all individuals desire affectionate relationships or regular interaction with others, which can become a key facet of job design. Esteem needs relate to a person's desire to master his or her own work, demonstrate competence and accomplishments, build a reputation as an outstanding performer, hold a position of prestige, receive public recognition, and feel self-esteem. Self-actualization needs reflect an individual's desire to grow and develop to his or her fullest potential. An individual often wants the opportunity to be creative on the job or desires autonomy, responsibility, and challenge.

According to needs theory, organizations must meet unsatisfied needs in order for employees to be motivated. In Maslow's scheme, the lowest unsatisfied need, starting with the basic physiological needs and continuing through safety, belonging and love, esteem, and self-actualization needs, becomes the *prepotent* need, the most powerful and significant need. Although the order may vary in certain special circumstances, generally the prepotent need motivates an individual to act to fulfill it; satisfied needs do not motivate. If, for example, a person lacks sufficient food and clothing, he or she will act to satisfy those basic physiological needs; hence, this person would most likely work to receive pay or other benefits to satisfy those needs. On the other hand, a person whose physiological, safety, and belongingness needs are satisfied will be motivated to satisfy needs at the next level, the esteem needs. For this person, pay will not motivate performance unless it increases esteem, but a promotion or other changes in job title or status, which satisfy esteem needs, are likely to motivate.

Administrators should understand that the popularity of this theory of motivation stems primarily from its simplicity and logic, not from strong current research support. In general, research indicates that two or three categories of needs, rather than five, exist, and that the relationships, relative importance, and sequences are not consistent from one individual to another. In addition, the ordering of needs may vary in different cultures; thus Maslow's theory may not be generalized across cultures.

Consider again the example of the company that attached some of the salary increases to whether it reached its sales goals. To use Maslow's theory to diagnose the likely effectiveness of the new policy, we can ask three questions: (1)Which needs have already been satisfied? (2) Which unsatisfied need is lowest in the hierarchy? (3) Can this need be satisfied with the new policy? If, for example, the physiological and safety needs have been satisfied, then the social needs become prepotent; if the new policy can satisfy those needs (which is unlikely), then, according to Maslow's theory, it would be motivating.

There are a number of needs-based theories including Alderfer's ERG theory, McClelland's theory, Herzberg's two-factor theory, and Glasser's control theory. However, they are all rooted in Maslow's theory and only differ from it in idiosyncratic ways.[4]

The second major type of motivation theory evolved from social comparison theory. Lacking objective measures of performance or appropriate attitudes, individuals assess and compare their performance and attitudes to those of others. Equity theory assumes that people assess their job performance and attitudes by comparing both their contribution to work and the benefits they derive from work to the contributions and benefits of a comparison "other," an individual whom the person selects and who in reality may be like or unlike the person. A female employee, for example, might reasonably compare her effort and rewards to those of a male employee in a comparable position.

Equity theory further states that a person is motivated in proportion to the perceived fairness of the rewards received for a certain amount of effort. You may have heard a student complain, "I'm going to stop studying so hard. Scott is brighter than I am and he never seems to study and still gets As." This student has compared his effort with Scott's and perceived an inequity in this school situation. In fact, no actual inequity may exist, but the perception of inequity influences the student's subsequent actions.

Specifically, this student compared his perceptions of two ratios: (1) the ratio of his outcomes to his inputs to (2) the ratio of another's outcomes to inputs. Outcomes may include pay, status, and job complexity;

inputs may include effort, productivity, age, sex, or experience. Thus, a person may compare his or her pay-to-experience ratio to another's ratio, or his or her status-to-age ratio to another's. For example, employee A may feel that he receives $25 for each hour of effort. In contrast, he may assess that employee B receives $50 for each hour of effort. Employee A perceives that his ratio of outcomes to inputs (25 to 1) is less than employee B's (50 to 1). In fact, employee B may only receive $15 for each hour of effort he contributes to the job. According to equity theory, the facts do not influence motivation; perceptions of the situation do. Recent research suggests, however, that equity calculations may be difficult because of cognitive differences in assessment and performance. Instead, individuals look for long-term rather than short-term parity in work situations; they compare their rank order on merit and rank order on a scale of reward outcomes, and see equity as a goal to work for over time.

According to equity theory, individuals are motivated to reduce any perceived inequity. They strive to make these ratios equal by changing either the outcomes or the inputs. The student referred to above, for example, might reduce his inputs (his effort) to make his ratio the same as Scott's. If he cannot change his own inputs or outcomes, he might adjust either his perception of Scott's outcomes or inputs or his attitude toward the situation by reevaluating his effort. He might also obtain more accurate information about Scott's grades and study habits, and adjust the ratio accordingly.

In theory, the same adjustment process occurs when a person perceives that he or she receives too much reward for the input or has too complex a job in comparison to others. Thus, if a person believes that he or she is overpaid, the individual should either increase his or her effort or ask that his or her pay be decreased. Although early studies suggested that this would happen, recent research has questioned whether this overjustification effect really occurs.

While equity theory makes strong intuitive sense, the empirical evidence has been mixed. The concept of equity sensitivity in part explains these findings by suggesting that individuals have different preferences for equity (e.g., a preference for higher, lower, or equal ratios) that cause them to react consistently but differently to perceived equity and inequity.

In a sense, equity theory oversimplifies the motivational issues by not explicitly considering individual needs, values, or personalities. This oversimplification becomes particularly important as the workforce becomes more diverse. Cross-cultural differences may occur in preferences for equity, as well as in the preferred responses to inequitable situations.

To determine whether equity exists in the workplace, we can use a questionnaire such as the Organizational Fairness Questionnaire.[5] If nothing else, equity theory makes a strong case for fairness in the workplace, which would please the critical theorists as well as those espousing the Ignatian vision.

Another process theory worth considering is expectancy theory. It has dominated research on motivation for some time because it has strong empirical support, integrates diverse perspectives on motivation, and provides explicit ways to increase employee motivation. Perhaps more than the preceding theories, expectancy theory offers a comprehensive view of motivation that integrates many of the elements of the needs, equity, and reinforcement theories. The research done in education regarding teacher expectations and students of all ages fulfilling these expectations is a compelling example of expectancy theory in practice.[6]

Victor Vroom popularized the expectancy theory in the 1960s with his model, which stated that motivation is a function of expectancy, valence, and instrumentality:

$$\text{Motivation} = \text{Expectancy} \times \text{Valence} \times \text{Instrumentality}$$

This simple formulation identifies the three basic components of expectancy theory. *Expectancy* refers to a person's perception of the probability that effort will lead to performance. For example, a person who perceives that if he or she works harder, then he or she will produce more, has a high expectancy. An individual that perceives that if he or she works harder, he or she will be ostracized by other employees and will not receive the cooperation necessary for performing, has a lower expectancy. If expectancy is zero, motivation will be lower than if expectancy is positive.

Instrumentality refers to a person's perception of the probability that certain outcomes, positive or negative, will be attached to that performance. For example, a person who perceives that he or she will receive greater pay or benefits if he or she produces has a high instrumentality. Motivation is a function of the degree of instrumentality, in addition to expectancy and valence.

Valence refers to a person's perception of the value of specific outcomes; that is, how much the person likes or dislikes receiving these outcomes. An individual with high esteem needs generally will attach a high valence to a new job title or a promotion. When valence is high, motivation is likely to be higher than when valence is less positive or is negative.

Let us examine the case of a college professor using this formulation of motivation. If the college professor perceives that devoting more time to scholarly research will result in his or her performing better, expectancy will be positive. If the professor perceives that he or she will receive a promotion and a pay raise if he or she performs the job well, then the instrumentality is positive. If the professor likes receiving a promotion and a raise, then the valence will be positive. We can operationalize this equation by arbitrarily assigning values to each variable.

Because performance can lead to multiple outcomes, each with different valences or values, each performance-to-outcome expectancy is multiplied by the corresponding valence. For example, consider a new employee who knows that if he or she demonstrates an effort to be productive in the workplace, he or she can depend on continued employment; this results in a positive performance-to-outcome expectancy. But the employee also knows that if he or she puts in too much time and effort, the employee may be ostracized by coworkers for being a "pawn of the administration" or "union buster"; this performance-to-outcome expectancy is much less positive and probably approaches zero. These products are summed before being multiplied by the effort-to-performance expectancy. If the sum of the formula is positive, the work environment is motivating. If there is a negative sum, the work environment is not motivating.

Although evidence for the validity of the expectancy model is mixed, managers can still use it to diagnose motivational problems or to evaluate effective motivation by asking the following questions: (1) Does the individual perceive that effort will lead to performance? (2) Does the individual perceive that certain behaviors will lead to specified outcomes? (3) What values do individuals attach to these outcomes?

Answers to these questions should help administrators determine the level of an employee's work motivation, identify any deficiencies in the job situation, and prescribe remedies. The expectancy perspective implies the value of equity in the work situation, as well as the importance of consistent rewards; in fact, both equity and reinforcement theory have been viewed as special cases of expectancy theory. It also addresses the issue of individual differences and offers the opportunity for quantification of the various facets of motivation. Hence, expectancy theory, more than any other theory presented thus far, offers a comprehensive diagnostic tool.

Other process theories of motivation such as reinforcement theory, goal-setting theory, and redesign of work have also been found to be effective. Given the number of motivation theories available, which can be very perplexing, perhaps the best approach for the heroic follower or leader is to be situationally selective. Steers and Porter write: "In recent years . . . the notion of a multiple strategy using different approaches to motivation at one time or another depending upon the nature of the organization, its technology, its people, and its goals and priorities has come to be labeled a 'contingency approach' to management."[7]

Diagnostic Checklist

Here are some questions that might be addressed in assessing your institution's *motivational* process through the lens of structural functionalism and the Ignatian vision:

- Do the rewards satisfy the variety of individual needs?
- Are rewards both intrinsic and extrinsic?
- Are they applied equitably and consistently?
- Do individuals value the rewards they receive?
- Do they perceive that their efforts correlate with performance?
- Do individuals set goals as a source of motivation?
- Are the rewards and incentives effective in motivating desired behaviors?
- Does the rationale for motivation benefit *both* the institution and the individual?

THE COMMUNICATION PROCESS

One of the perennial complaints of employees is a lack of communication between themselves and another segment of the work community, frequently the administration. If the transformational leader is to be effective, therefore, he or she must master the skill of effective communication.

Feedback is perhaps the most important aspect of the communications process. Feedback refers to an acknowledgement by the receiver that the message has been received; it provides the sender with information about the receiver's understanding of the message being sent.

Often, one-way communication occurs between administrators and their colleagues. Because of inherent power differences in their positions, administrators may give large quantities of information and directions to their staffs without providing them the opportunity to show their understanding or accurate and clear receipt of the information. These managers often experience conflict between their role as authorities and a desire to be liked by their colleagues. Other administrators have relied on the use of written memoranda as a way of communicating with faculty and staff. In addition to the inherent lack of feedback involved in this method, the use of a single channel of communication also limits the effectiveness of communication. The proliferation of the use of e-mail has alleviated this problem somewhat by providing a relatively facile feedback mechanism. Of course, the misuse and overuse of e-mail presents its own set of problems.

Why do administrators sometimes not involve their staff members in two-way communication? In some instances, administrators do not trust their colleagues to contribute effectively. In other situations, the lack of self-confidence on the part of the administrator makes him or her appear uninterested in others' opinions. Or administrators are sure that their staff members have the same goals as they do and thus feel that input from colleagues is not required or would not add anything of significance to the process. Of course, none of these attitudes is consistent with critical theory and the Ignatian vision. Encouraging feedback from others helps show them that you are concerned about them as individuals in ways that go beyond merely ensuring that they produce.

So-called subordinates also have a responsibility for encouraging two-way communication. While managers may attempt to protect their power positions, subordinates attempt to protect the image their supervisor holds of them. Frequently, for example, employees withhold negative information about themselves and their departments for fear that it may reflect negatively on them. Or they may fail to inform the leader about their needs and values. Other subordinates mistrust their superiors and so withhold information from them. Why do these situations arise? Some subordinates may assume that they and their supervisors have different goals and agendas. Others mistrust their supervisors because of past behavior. Still others lack persistence in seeking responses from their supervisors. Impression of management, therefore, plays a key role in whether individuals send feedback. They may assess how asking for feedback will be interpreted and how the resulting information will affect each person's public image. In order for effective communication to take place, then, subordinates must show that they, too, are willing to build relationships with their supervisors. Thus, as we discussed earlier, a culture of mutual trust and respect is required for effective communication.

What can individuals do to improve their communication in both formal and informal settings? There are at least three ways of improving communication effectiveness: creating a supportive communication climate, using an assertive communication style, and using active listening techniques.

In communicating with their faculties and staffs, administrators know they must create a trusting and supportive environment. Creating such a climate has the objective of shifting from evaluation to problem solving and formation in communication. They must avoid making employees feel defensive, that is, threatened by the communication. They can create such an atmosphere in at least six ways:[8]

1. They use descriptive rather than evaluative speech and do not imply that the receiver needs to change. An administrator may describe certain employee traits as areas in need of further development rather than as weaknesses.
2. They take a problem-solving orientation, which implies a desire to collaborate in exploring a mutual problem, rather than try to control or change the listener. An administrator can ask the employee what he or she hopes to achieve for the fiscal year rather than setting out a list of goals for the employee.

3. They are spontaneous, honest, and open, rather than appearing to use "strategy" than involves ambiguous and multiple motivations. A CEO might share with the corporate community the need for restructuring and the possible areas of downsizing rather than keeping these concerns secret.

4. They convey empathy for the feelings of their listener rather than appearing unconcerned or neutral about the listener's welfare. They give reassurance that they are identifying with the listener's problems rather than denying the legitimacy of the problems. When reviewing a union grievance with an employee, the manager may indicate sensitivity to the employee's position even though the decision may ultimately go against the employee.

5. They indicate that they feel equal rather than superior to the listener. Thus, they suggest that they will enter a shared relationship, not simply dominate the interaction. A college dean may come out from behind his or her desk and sit next to a colleague to indicate a relationship of equality.

6. Finally, they communicate that they will experiment with their own behavior and ideas rather than be dogmatic about them. They do not give the impression that they know all the answers and do not need help from anyone. An administrator can concede that he or she does not know if his or her suggestion will work, but asks the employee in question "give it a try."

In addition, supportive communication emphasizes congruence between thoughts, feelings, and communication. An individual who feels unappreciated by a supervisor, for example, must communicate that feeling to the supervisor, rather than deny it or communicate it inaccurately. Communication must also validate an individual's importance, uniqueness, and worth. Nondefensive communication recognizes the other person's existence; it recognizes the person's uniqueness as an individual, rather than treating the person only as a role or a job; it acknowledges the worth of the other person; it acknowledges the validity of the other person's perception of the world; and it expresses willingness to be involved with the other person during the communication.

Interpersonal communication can be improved by encouraging individuals to communicate using as complete a knowledge of themselves and others as possible. The Johari window provides an analytical tool that individuals can use to identify information that is available for use in communication.[9] In the Johari window (Fig. 6.1), information about an individual is represented along two dimensions: (1) information known and unknown by the self and (2) information known and unknown by others.

Together these dimensions form a four-category representation of the individual. The open self is information known by the self and known by others. The blind self is information unknown by the self and known by others, such as others' perceptions of your behavior or attitudes. The concealed self is information known by you and unknown by others. Secrets we keep from others about ourselves fall into this category. Finally, the unconscious self is information that is unknown to the self and unknown to others. To ensure quality communication, in most cases an individual should communicate from his or her open self to another's open self and limit the amount of information concealed or in the blind spot. Guarded communication may be appropriate, however, if one party has violated trust in the past, if the parties have an adversarial relationship, if power and status differentials characterize the culture, if the relationship is transitory, or if the corporate culture does not support openness. Of course, this last situation should not exist in an institution inspired by the Ignatian vision.

Another approach in improving communication is using an assertive communication style. An assertive style, which is honest, direct, and firm, is contrasted to an aggressive style at one extreme and a nonassertive style at the other. With this style, a person expresses needs, opinions, and feelings in honest and direct ways and stands up for his or her rights without violating the other person's rights. Assertive behavior is reflected in the content and the nonverbal style of the message. The assertive delegator, for example, "is clear and direct when explaining work to subordinates, doesn't hover, [and] . . . criticizes fairly, objectively, and constructively."[10]

Consider the situation of a supervisor whose assistant has missed two important deadlines in the past month. How would she respond assertively? She might say to her assistant, "I know you missed the last two deadlines. Is there an explanation I should know? It is important that you meet the next deadlines." Her assertive response can include the expression of anger, frustration, or disappointment, but it is expressed in terms that would allow the employee to explain the behavior. This distinguishes it from an aggressive style, which is inappropriate behavior.

We can further contrast the assertive approach to nonassertive and aggressive styles. Nonassertive communication describes behavior in which the sender does not stand up for personal rights and indicates that his or feelings are unimportant; the person may be hesitant, apologetic, or fearful. In the situation of a missed deadline, nonassertive behavior might involve saying nothing to your assistant, hoping the situation would not recur. Individuals might act nonassertively because they mistake assertion for aggression, mistake nonassertion for politeness or being helpful, refuse to accept their personal rights and responsibilities, experience anxiety about the negative consequences of assertiveness, or lack assertiveness skills.[11]

Aggressive communication is standing up for an individual's rights without respecting the rights of the other person. Aggressive behavior attempts to dominate and control others by sounding accusing or superior. In the situation of the missed deadlines, an aggressive response might be. "You always miss deadlines. You're taking advantage of me and the situation. If you miss another deadline, disciplinary action will be taken." While such a response may result in the desired behavior in the short run, its long-term consequences likely will be dysfunctional, resulting in distrust between the individuals involved. Ultimately, such behavior will reduce productivity and will especially affect the submission of creative and innovative solutions offered to management by the employee. Finally, such behavior is inconsistent with the Ignatian vision.

Active listening, which requires understanding both the content and the intent of a message, is still another way of improving communication. It can be facilitated by paraphrasing, perception checking, and behavior description.

The receiver can paraphrase the message conveyed by the sender. For example, if the sender states, "I don't like the work I am doing," the receiver might paraphrase it as, "Are you saying that you are dissatisfied with the profession of education? Or are you dissatisfied with the grade that you teach? Or do you wish to be reassigned to another school?" Note that these ways of paraphrasing the original message suggest very different understanding of the original statement. The sender, upon receiving this feedback from the receiver, can then clarify his or her meaning.

Alternatively, the receiver may perception-check; that is, describe what he or she perceives as the sender's inner state at the time of communication to check his or her understanding of the message. For example, if the sender states, "I don't like the work I am doing," the receiver might check his or her perception of the statement by asking "Are you dissatisfied with the way you are being treated?" or, " Are you dissatisfied with me as a supervisor?" Note that the answers to these two questions will identify different feelings.

A third way of checking communication is through behavior description. Here, the individual reports specific, observable actions of others without making accusations or generalizations about their motives, personality, or characteristics. Similarly, description of feelings, where the individual specifies or identifies feelings by name, analogy, or some other verbal representation can increase active listening. For example, to help others understand you as a person, you should describe what others did that affects you personally or as a group member. Then you can let others know as clearly and unambiguously as possible what you are feeling.

Moving beyond individual communication, let us now address the communication networks that are prevalent in many businesses. Communication is embedded in all business structures. In the traditional, classical, or bureaucratic model, formal communication channels, or networks, traverse the institution through the hierarchy of authority. In most organizations, there are formal communication channels and every member of the institution reports to someone. For instance, marketing directors report to the Vice President for Marketing, who, along with the CFO, reports to the CEO. The lines of communication from the CEO to the directors go through several hierarchical levels. Every layer can be a source of inaccurate communication.

With all organizations, formal restrictions on the communication process are apparent. "Making certain to go through proper channels" and "following the chain of command" are two common expressions that are a reflection of communication in organizations. Three characteristics of school bureaucracies seem particularly critical in communication. They are centralization in the hierarchy, the organization's shape or configuration, and the level of information technology.[12]

The degree to which authority is not delegated, but concentrated in a single source in the organization, is important to the effectiveness of communication systems. In centralized schools, a few positions in the structure have most of the information-obtaining ability. For example, the CEO and the other executives in our above illustration would gather most of the information for the formal system of communication. If the corporation is decentralized or loosely coupled, however, the information-obtaining potential is more or less spread across all of the positions. Research examining the different information-obtaining abilities supports the finding that centralized structures are more efficient for communication when the problems and tasks are relatively simple and straightforward. When the tasks become more complex, however, decentralized hierarchies appear to be more efficient.

The number of hierarchical levels, or tallness versus flatness of the school organization, also affects the communication processes. Hierarchical levels and size are structural characteristics that are commonly associated with the shape of an organization. A company with five levels differs from systems with more or fewer levels in its ability to communicate across levels and from top to bottom. The number of levels can be seen as the distance a message must travel. As the distance increases, the chance of message distortion increases, and the satisfaction with communication decreases. Employees will generally express less satisfaction with messages from CEOs than from their immediate supervisors. In addition, organizational size is negatively related to communication quality; as the corporation becomes larger, communication becomes more impersonal or formal and quality declines. This is part of the reason that the subdividing of large corporations into smaller companies, Wal-Mart notwithstanding, is proliferating. For communication and other purposes, smaller is sometimes better.

To overcome some of the problems inherent in the classical structure of most organizations, matrix or mixed designs have evolved to improve mechanisms of lateral communication and information flow across the organization. The matrix organization, originally developed in the aerospace industry, is characterized by a dual-authority system. There are usually functional and program or product-line managers, both reporting to a common superior and both exercising authority over workers within the matrix. Typically, a matrix organization is particularly useful in highly specialized technological areas that focus on innovation. But that certainly does not preclude their use in those educational settings where creativity is fostered. The matrix design allows program managers to interact directly with the environment vis-à-vis new developments. Usually each program requires a multidisciplinary team approach; the matrix structure facilitates the coordination of the team and allows team members to contribute their special expertise.

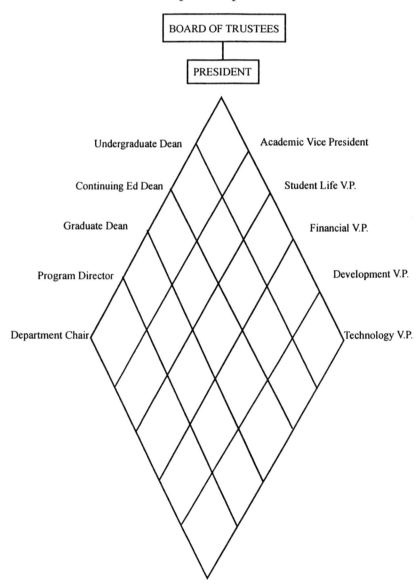

Figure 9.3.   Matrix Design

The use of matrix design is not very common, but it is a viable way of organizing when communication needs to occur outside the "proper channels." The popularity of open system organizational theory that espouses inter- and intradepartmental cooperation has caused an increased interest in matrix design. Many organizations are *informally* organized in a matrix design. It would most likely serve these institutions well to consider matrix design as a *formal* organizational structure, especially in cases when communication problems are evident.

Technology also appears to have a significant effect on organizational communication, though that effect remains somewhat speculative. We are living in a creative and dynamic era that is producing fundamental changes, as are apparent in such advances as computer networks, electronic mail, computer conferences, communication satellites, data-handling devices, and the various forms of distance education. Until recently, electronic information exchange has largely been adapted to convey voice, vision, text, and graphics as distinct and separate types of communication. During the next few years, simultaneous and instantaneous transmission of voice, vision, text, and graphics to many locations will be common. Even imagining these technologies together with the geographic distribution of participants does not adequately capture the differences between these and traditional media. Consequently, the potential influence of such technologies on all aspects of communication in schools is probably underestimated.

Next, we need to make a distinction between the internal and external communication and the appropriate communication network for each. I have suggested that for internal communication purposes, a loosely structured communication network is most effective. Although the principles of effective communication still prevail when dealing with the outside community, some nuances need to be stressed. Perhaps the most important aspect of communication to consider when dealing with the public is the uniformity of the message. The message must be clear and consistent and must emanate from a single source. In these cases, the chain of command and channels of communication need to be well-defined and structured along the lines of the classical model. It is imperative that the company "speak with one voice." Someone in the company should be designated as the clearinghouse for all external communication. This individual, or office, should review all external communication for clarity and accuracy, and all personnel should be keenly aware of the company's policy with regard to external communication. Examples abound of the communications nightmares caused by organizations that did not speak with one voice to external audiences. Thus, although a more loosely structured communication system is very appropriate for internal communication, a more tightly structured one is necessary for effective external communication. Recall the story of the plumber seeking advice on cleaning pipes. Although the information he initially received from Washington was technically accurate, it was not an effective communication. Only when the Bureau scientists considered their audience when conveying their message did the plumber finally understand that hydrochloric acid "eats the hell out of pipes."

Communicating with ease and clarity is no simple task. There are, however, various theories about how it can be most effectively carried out. Classical theory, social system theory, and open system theory all incorporate a perspective toward the communication process; that is, who should say what through which channel to whom and to what effect. Classical theory stresses that the communication process exists to facilitate the manager's command and control over the employees in a formal, hierarchical, and downwardly directed manner. The purpose is to increase efficiency and productivity.

The social system orientation suggests that to be effective, communication has to be two-way and that the meaning of the message is as much to be found in the psychological makeup of the receiver as of the sender. The channels can be informal as well as formal and include anyone who has an interest in a particular subject.

The open system orientation emphasizes the communication process working toward drawing the various subsystems of an organization into a collaborating whole, as in a matrix system or communication. Also, drawing the organization's actions into a close fit with the needs of its environment is an essential outcome of the process. This orientation emphasizes that between senders and receivers, the communication process must penetrate social class differences, cultural values, time orientations, and ethnocentrism of all types. In this way, open system communications encompass the spirit of critical theory and the Ignatian vision.

None of the conceptual frameworks, by itself, escapes the barriers to communication. The story of the plumber illustrates the problems of message coding, decoding, and transmission. We have suggested that in order for communication to be effective, we should adapt the process to the situation. We have suggested that when communicating with the outside community, a structured process may be appropriate, while when communicating with the inside community, a less structured process may be appropriate. This situational approach is in concert with one of the underlying themes of effective leadership; that is, whether we are speaking about organizational structure, leadership, motivation, or communication, we need to adapt the approach or model to the situation in which we find ourselves. Thus, the structural functionalist organizational models need to be adapted to the situation, while the principles of critical theory and the Ignatian vision are applicable no matter what the situation.

Diagnostic Checklist

Here are some questions than can be addressed in assessing your institution's *communication* process through the lens of structural functionalism and the Ignatian vision:

- How effective is the communication process at your institution?
- What barriers to communication exist?
- Is the correct communication structure utilized in a given situation?
- Does communication include feedback, where appropriate?
- Is there a climate of mutual trust and respect to facilitate the communication process?
- Are active listening and other techniques that improve communication being used?
- Do individuals use assertive, rather than nonassertive or aggressive, communication styles?
- Are individuals communicating from the open self?

CONFLICT MANAGEMENT

A few years ago we invited Dr. Janet Baker, well-known authority on conflict, to address a group of principals at a Principal's Academy, which was offered at Saint Joseph's University in Philadelphia. We introduced Dr. Baker's topic as "conflict resolution." Upon taking the podium, Dr. Baker quickly corrected us and said that she was there to talk about "conflict management, not conflict resolution." "If your goal as a manager is to resolve all conflict, you will be doomed to frustration and failure," she said. "The best that you can hope for is to manage conflict."

Conflict is the result of incongruent or incompatible potential influence relationships between and within individuals, groups, or organizations. Conflict can be public or private, formal or informal, rational or irrational. The likelihood of conflict increases when parties have the chance to interact, when the parties see their differences as incompatible, and when one or both parties see some utility in engaging in conflict to resolve incompatibility.

Conflict most commonly results from four circumstances. First, when mutually exclusive goals or values exist, or are perceived to exist, by the groups involved, conflict can occur. In the collective bargaining process, for example, the teachers' union may perceive that the administration's goals may conflict with those of the teachers. Second, behavior designed to defeat, reduce, or suppress the opponent may cause conflict. Again, union and management have historically experienced conflict for this reason. Third, groups that face each other with mutually opposing actions and counteractions cause conflict. For example, if the marketing manager does not do his or her job effectively, the sales manager will be negatively affected. Finally, if each group attempts to create a relatively favored position, conflict may occur. If the finance department attempts to show the CEO that it is superior to the other departments by demonstrating the others' ineptness, conflict occurs.

Conflict can have functional or dysfunctional outcomes. Whether conflict takes a constructive or destructive course is influenced by the sociocultural context in which the conflict occurs, because differences tend to exaggerate barriers and reduce the likelihood of conflict resolution. The issues involved will also affect the likely outcomes. Whether the parties have cooperative, individualistic, or competitive orientations toward conflict will affect the outcomes as well. Obviously, those with cooperative attitudes are more likely to seek a functional outcome. The characteristics of the conflicting parties also affect conflict behavior. Finally, misjudgments and misperceptions contribute to dysfunctional conflict.

Effective managers learn how to create functional conflict and manage dysfunctional conflict. They develop and practice techniques for diagnosing the causes and nature of conflict and transforming it into a productive force in the organization. Many colleges, for example, have a healthy competition among schools within the university for the recruitment of the most qualified students.

Some conflict is beneficial. It can encourage organizational innovation, creativity, and adaptation. We saw earlier that at least a low level of conflict is needed to spur on needed change. Capitalism, with its emphasis on private enterprise and competition, is an example of functional conflict fostering innovation. This phenomenon also occurs in the not-for-profit area. For example, a number of nonpublic school systems, and even some public school systems, allow schools within the system to compete for the same students. This "open enrollment" policy often spawns innovation in marketing techniques, and more importantly, in curriculum and programs. In these cases, conflict can result in more worker enthusiasm and better decisions. Can you think of a situation where such positive outcomes occurred? Perhaps during a disagreement with a colleague, you came to hold a different perspective on an issue or learned that your own perceptions or information had been inaccurate. Finally, in order to generate and implement the reforms suggested by critical theory and the Ignatian vision, often a sense of urgency or tension must exist.

On the other hand, conflict can be viewed as dysfunctional for organizations. It can reduce productivity, decrease morale, cause overwhelming dissatisfaction, and increase tension and stress in the organization. It can arouse anxiety in individuals, increase the tension in an organizational system and its subsystems, and lower satisfaction. In addition, some people, often the losers in a competitive situation, feel defeated and demeaned. As the distance between people increases, a climate of mistrust and suspicion may arise. Individuals or groups may focus more narrowly on their own interests, preventing the development of teamwork. Production and satisfaction may decline; turnover and absenteeism may increase. Diagnosing the location and type of conflict, as described next, is a first step in managing conflict so that it results in functional outcomes.

Administrators may encourage individuals or groups to use at least five behaviors or strategies for dealing with conflict: avoidance, accommodation, compromise, forcing, and collaborating. These differ in the extent to which they satisfy a party's own concerns and the other party's concerns. For example, a person or group that uses an avoiding mode is unassertive in satisfying its own concerns and uncooperative in satisfying others' concerns. In contrast, a person or group that uses a collaborating mode is assertive and cooperative (see table 9.1).

Each style is appropriate to different situations that individuals or groups face in organizations. Once again, the underlying theme of con-

Table 9.1. Uses of the Five Conflict Modes

Conflict Handling Modes	Appropriate Situations
Competing	1. When quick, decisive action is vital—e.g., emergencies. 2. On important issues where unpopular actions need implementing—e.g., cost cutting, enforcing unpopular rules, discipline. 3. On issues vital to institutional welfare when you know you are right.
Collaborating	1. To find an integrative solution when both sets of concerns are too important to be compromised. 2. When your objective is to learn. 3. To merge insights from people with different perspectives. 4. To gain commitment by incorporating concerns into a consensus. 5. To work through feelings that have interfered with a relationship.
Compromising	1. When goals are important, but not worth the effort or potential disruption of more assertive modes. 2. When opponents with equal power are committed to mutually exclusive goals. 3. To achieve temporary settlements to complex issues. 4. To arrive at expedient solutions under time pressure.
Avoiding	1. When an issue is trivial or more important issues are pressing. 2. When you perceive no chance of satisfying your concerns. 3. When potential disruption outweighs the benefits of resolution. 4. To let people cool down and regain perspective. 5. When gathering information supersedes immediate decision.
Accommodating	1. When you find you are wrong—to allow a better position to be heard, to learn, and to show your reasonableness. 2. When issues are more important to others than yourself—to satisfy others and maintain cooperation. 3. To build social credits for later issues. 4. To minimize loss when you are outmatched and losing. 5. When harmony and stability are especially important.

tingency theory applies. That is, there is rarely one single approach that is applicable at all times in all situations. Rather, the effective model or approach will change depending on the situation. What does remain constant, however, is the applicability of the principles of the Ignatian vision.

The behavior an individual or group chooses depends, therefore, on that party's experiences in dealing with conflict, his or her own personal disposition in interpersonal relations, and the specific elements of a particular conflict episode.

The first conflict management style to examine is that of *avoidance*. Individuals or groups may withdraw from the conflict situation. They act to satisfy neither their own nor the other party's concerns. Avoidance works best when individuals or groups face trivial or tangential issues, when they have little chance of satisfying their personal concerns, when conflict resolution will likely result in significant disruption, or when others can resolve the conflict more effectively. If two secretaries in the secretarial pool, for example, have an argument, the most appropriate strategy for managing the conflict may be avoidance. Let the secretaries resolve the conflict in their own ways. It is like the proverbial story of the next-door neighbors whose children get into an argument, and the adults try to intervene on behalf of their respective children. The adults end up being lifelong enemies, and the children begin playing with each other again within the hour.

Once the leader decides that avoidance is not the appropriate conflict management style, the leaders must then be proactive and decide which remaining style would be most effective in resolving the conflict. Individuals or groups who use *accommodation* demonstrate willingness to cooperate in satisfying others' concerns, while at the same time acting unassertively in meeting their own. Accommodating individuals often smooth over conflict. This mode builds social credits for later issues, results in harmony and stability, and satisfies others. A vice president for finance may capitulate on a disagreement with the vice president for marketing over a minor matter in hopes that he or she can prevail on a larger issue in the future, thus building political capital to be used later.

The *compromise* mode represents an intermediate behavior between the assertiveness and cooperation dimensions. It can include sharing of positions but not moving to the extremes of assertiveness or cooperation.

Hence, it often does not maximize satisfaction of both parties. This style works well when goals are important but not sufficiently important for the individual or group to be more assertive, when the two parties have equal power, or when significant time pressure exists. For example, if two marketing executives disagree over which ad campaign should be used, they may compromise and use some of each campaign's concepts.

Using the *competing* mode, a party tries to satisfy its own concerns while showing an unwillingness to satisfy the other's concerns to even a minimal degree. This strategy works well in emergencies, on issues calling for unpopular actions, and in cases when one party is correct in its position or has much greater power. For example, if a child threatens to commit suicide, the principal may wish to inform the parents immediately, and the guidance counselor may wish it to remain confidential. If the principal chooses to inform the parents, he or she is using a forcing behavior. The Ignatian vision would prompt us to use this conflict management style very infrequently.

The *collaboration* mode emphasizes problem solving with a goal of maximizing satisfaction for both parties. It means seeing conflict as natural, showing trust and honesty toward others, and encouraging the airing of every person's attitudes and feelings. Each party exerts both assertive and cooperative behavior. Parties can use it when their objectives are to learn, to use information from diverse sources, and to find an integrative solution. If the labor union and the human resources department establish a mutually satisfactory way of working together, they are taking a collaborative or problem-solving approach to resolve or avoid conflict. Unfortunately, the history of labor/management relations has been adversarial, featuring forcing, compromising, and accommodating behavior, rather than collaborative behavior. *A good rule of thumb in managing conflicts is to begin with a collaborative style, while using the other modes only when collaboration has not brought about the desired results.*

Diagnostic Checklist

Here are some questions that can be addressed in assessing your institution's *conflict management* process through the lens of structural functionalism and the Ignatian vision:

- Is the conflict in the institution functional or dysfunctional?
- Are mechanisms for effectively managing conflict and stress present?
- Do the mechanisms reflect the situational nature of conflict management?
- Are avoidance, compromise, competition, accommodation, and collaboration utilized in the appropriate situations?
- Is the competition or forcing style used sparingly or routinely?
- Is collaboration the preferred means of conflict management?
- Is the care of the individual an important impetus for conflict management?
- Are cultural differences and values considered in the conflict management process?

THE DECISION-MAKING PROCESS

According to Vroom and Yetton, the two most important aspects of a decision are its *quality* and its *acceptance*.[13] A good quality decision brings about the desired result while meeting relevant criteria and constraints. The quality of the decision depends on the level of the decision maker's technical or task skills, interpersonal or leadership skills, and decision-making skills. Technical or task skills refer to the individual's knowledge of the particular area in which the decision is being made. Interpersonal or leadership skills relate to the way individuals lead, communicate with, motivate, and influence others. Decision-making skills are the basic abilities to perform the components of the decision-making process. They include situational analysis; objective setting; and generation, evaluation, and selection of alternatives, discussed later in this chapter. The other important factor, acceptance, is the extent to which acceptance or commitment on the part of subordinates is crucial to the effective implementation of the decision. In addition to quality and acceptance, another factor that would be espoused in light of a commitment to critical theory and the Ignatian vision is the *ethics* or *morality* of the decision (figure 9.4).

The relationship of quality to acceptance is critical in determining the appropriate decision making strategy. For example, if a new law is passed regarding the package safety, and the administrator had to decide if and

The administrative and organizational theory literature (Maier, 1962; Bridges, 1967; Vroom and Yetton, 1973) are in total agreement about the two most important factors to be considered in determining the decision style which will produce the most effective decisions. While Vroom and Yetton's model adds the additional dimension of shared goals and conflict possibility, the two key elements are also stressed: QUALITY and ACCEPTANCE. The diagram below summarizes Maier's work in identifying the decision style which is most appropriate for particular problem types. The two key elements are defined as:

(1) Quality (Q) - The importance of quality, i.e., one solution is likely to be more rational than another.

The extent to which the leader possesses sufficient information/ expertise to make high-quality decisions by him or herself.

(2) Acceptance (A) - The extent to which acceptance or commitment on the part of subordinates is crucial to the effective implementation of the decision.

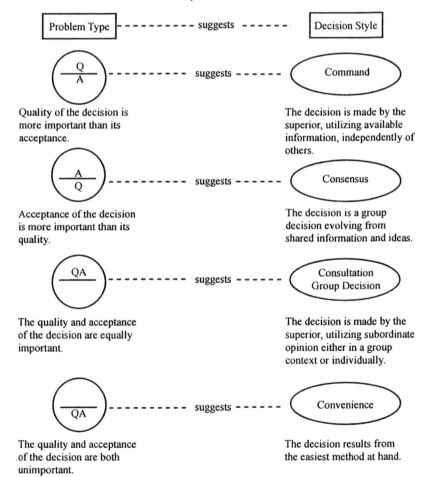

| Problem Type | ------ suggests ------ | Decision Style |

$\dfrac{Q}{A}$ --------- suggests ------ (Command)

Quality of the decision is more important than its acceptance.

The decision is made by the superior, utilizing available information, independently of others.

$\dfrac{A}{Q}$ --------- suggests ------ (Consensus)

Acceptance of the decision is more important than its quality.

The decision is a group decision evolving from shared information and ideas.

QA --------- suggests ------ (Consultation Group Decision)

The quality and acceptance of the decision are equally important.

The decision is made by the superior, utilizing subordinate opinion either in a group context or individually.

$\overline{QA}$ --------- suggests ------ (Convenience)

The quality and acceptance of the decision are both unimportant.

The decision results from the easiest method at hand.

Figure 9.4.   The Dimensions of Effective Decisions

how it should be implemented, the *quality* of the decision would be more important than the *acceptance*. Therefore, Vroom and Yetton would suggest that the appropriate decision style is *command*. In other words, the leader makes the decision alone. On the other hand, if acceptance is more important than quality, as in the development of a new employee evaluation instrument, the proper decision style would be *group consensus.*

If both the quality and acceptance are of equal importance, as in whether to adopt a new production process, *consultation* or group decision making would be the appropriate style. Finally, if neither the quality nor the acceptance is important, such as deciding what color to paint the rest rooms, *convenience* would be the applicable decision making style. Simply find out what color paint is available in the district warehouse.

While the administrative and organizational theory literature are in agreement about the two most important factors to be considered in determining the decision style that will produce the most effective decisions, there is far less agreement that the third factor, ethical fairness and justice, is as important. Consider, for example, a disastrous decline in quarterly profits. Top executives are faced with the decision of whether to risk stockholder outrage and the possible sell-off of equities by admitting the facts or manipulating the books to cover up the situation.

Administrators and staff can assess whether the decisions they make are ethical by applying personal moral codes or society's code of values. They can apply philosophical view of ethical behavior, or they can assess the potential harmful consequences of behaviors to certain constituencies. One way of thinking about ethical decision making suggests that a person who makes a moral decision must first, recognize the moral issue of whether the person's actions can hurt or help others; second, make a moral judgment; third, decide to attach greater priority to moral concerns than financial or other material concerns; and finally, act on the moral concerns of the situation by engaging in moral behavior.[14]

The decision-making processes described thus far can apply to decisions made by individuals or groups. Yet, group decision making brings different resources to the task than does individual decision making. When a group makes a decision, a synergy occurs that usually causes the group decision to be better than the sum of the individual decisions. The involvement of more than one individual brings additional knowledge and skills to the decision, and it tends to result in higher quality decisions. However, the same caveat holds true for decision making as with other processes discussed earlier. That is, decision making is situational, and the idiosyncrasies of the moment dictate the decision-making approach to be taken. For example, if the building is on fire, participative decision making is not appropriate (figure 9.5).

In most cases, using a rational, sequential decision-making process, often called the "rational decision-making process," increases the likelihood that a high-quality, acceptable, and ethical decision will result. It involves the five steps of situational analysis: objective setting, generation of alternatives, evaluation of alternatives, making the decision, and evaluation of the decision. Let us look at the five steps in turn, using a case study where a corporation is forced to restructure itself due to declining profits.

Decision making first requires the recognition that there is a problem to be solved or a decision to be made, followed by exploration and classification of the decision situation.[15] Decision making then requires asking such questions as; "What are the key elements of the situation?" "What constraints affect the decision?" and "What resources are available?" How will the leader answer these questions? The key elements include the past performance of various companies and branches, the reputation of each of the companies, the projected demographic information, the profit margin in each company or branch, any special needs in certain neighborhoods, the overhead costs for each company, and contractual issues, among others. The leader must consider his or her

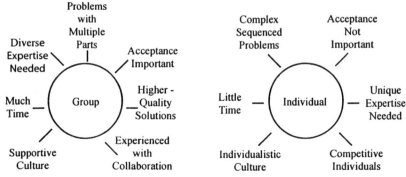

Figure 9.5.   Individual Versus Group Problem Solving

previous experience with restructuring and how the various components of the corporate community reacted to those efforts. The leader must then assess whether approaches successful in the past can be effective in the new situation.

Constraints on the decision will include the state and federal laws regarding staff downsizing as well as the local labor agreement constraints. While limitations on resources and constraints such as those mentioned can be debilitating, they can also generate creative alternatives. For example, if there are restrictions on layoffs, one can offer early retirement and voluntary severance packages to achieve the rightsizing objectives. From the situational analysis, the decision maker begins to formulate the issues to be addressed.

The way the decision makers frame the problem has a significant impact on its ultimate resolution. Subsequent steps may differ, for example, if the leader frames the goals as cost reduction, downsizing, or an opportunity to serve the constituencies in a more effective and efficient way that will ensure the long-range future of the corporation. Errors in problem definition may be hard to identify and even harder to correct. The decision maker should carefully identify the goals and objectives that the decision must accomplish and specify the criteria that will be used to assess its quality, acceptance, and ethical appropriateness. The accomplishment of these goals and objectives serves as one measure of the effectiveness of the decision and the decision-making process.[16]

Often, decision makers err at this step by confusing action plans with objectives. Decision makers must first set their goals and then determine ways of accomplishing them. For example, offering all eligible employees early retirement is one way of accomplishing the goal of rightsizing. In this case, the early retirement program is not the goal, but a means to a goal.

When possible, decision makers should establish objectives that specify observable and measurable results. Certainly, reducing absenteeism and costs or increasing profits by a specified percentage or amount are objectives that are observable and measurable. Objectives related to employee attitudes, such as satisfaction, commitment, or involvement, may be more difficult to measure and observe. Still, skillful crafting of the objectives by the decision maker can meet the need for quantifiable and observable results even in these difficult-to-measure instances.

The decision maker presents a set of realistic and potentially acceptable solutions to the problem, or ways of meeting the objectives, as part of the "searching for alternatives" phase. What alternatives are available in the downsizing example? The leader can offer early retirement incentives to decrease costs, close plants and lay off a number of employees, reduce an administrative layer, increase the per capita production, and/or increase efficiencies throughout the corporation. Techniques for generating alternatives, such as brainstorming, the Delphi Technique, and the Nominal Group Technique, are described later in this chapter.

The decision maker next appraises each alternative. Criteria for evaluation include the alternative's feasibility, cost, and reliability. In addition, the decision maker must assess the risks involved and the likelihood of certain outcomes for each alternative. What other criteria might be used in evaluating the alternatives? For example, what will the stockholders think of the alternatives? What about the board? Will local or national politicians prefer one alternative above another? Are there advocacy groups to be considered? All of these factors, and more, need to be considered before making a decision.

Quantifying the alternatives can systematize their evaluation, dramatizing difference among them and improving the quality of decision making. For example, we might score each of the alternatives on its feasibility, cost, potential adverse consequences, and probability of success. Summing the scores of each alternative would allow us to rank-order them and ultimately select the highest one. The process assumes that the criteria are equally weighted, that the numerical values are exact, and that ranks alone are sufficient to provide the best choice. More sophisticated statistical treatment can also be used for such an evaluation. Obviously, this approach to quantifying the evaluation of alternatives is highly subjective because the decision maker's rating of each criterion is incorporated into the overall evaluation. Recent research suggests that decision makers should evaluate alternatives using a compatibility test.[17] In decision making, which can be either intuitive or deliberative, the decision maker compares each alternative with a set of standards (such as values, moral, beliefs, goals, and plans) called "images." The decision maker rejects incompatible alternatives and adds compatible ones to the set of feasible alternatives.

The next step in the process is making the decision. Ideally, a decision maker should select the optimal, or best, alternative. Note, however, that the decision maker's knowledge, abilities, and motivation will affect the choice. In addition, each alternative had disadvantages as well as advantages. If the cost criterion outweighs all others, then closing plants and laying off employees would be the best solution. If a moderate cost reduction is acceptable and a lower likelihood of adverse consequences is desired, then offering early retirement or some other less drastic alternative may be acceptable. Of course, the moral and ethical implications of the various alternatives need to be considered through the lens of the Ignatian vision.

Next comes the evaluation of the decision. Review of the decision is an essential step in effective decision making. Too often, selecting an alternative and reaching a decision comprise the final step. Individuals must pause and recheck their decisions, as well as the process that led to them, as one way of increasing their effectiveness. Where possible, the decision maker might check his or her thinking with another person or group. Together, they can evaluate the planned implementation of the decision by assessing its likely or actual outcomes and comparing them to the objectives set earlier. Evaluation performed after implementation is part of management control and may call for corrective action and follow-up.

The next question one might logically ask is, how can decision makers overcome barriers, reduce biases, and make more effective decisions? There are at least three techniques that can improve decision making: brainstorming, the Nominal Group Technique, and the Delphi technique.

Most of us are familiar with brainstorming. Groups or individuals use brainstorming when creativity is needed to generate many alternatives for consideration in decision making. In brainstorming, the decision maker lists as many alternatives as possible without yet evaluating the feasibility of any alternative. The use of this technique is limited, however, to less complex decisions.

The Nominal Group Technique is a structured group meeting that helps resolve differences in group opinion by having individuals generate and then rank-order a series of ideas in the problem exploration, alternative-generation, and/or choice-making stages of group decision making. It has the advantage of being effective with more complex decision making.

The Delphi Technique can be used in making complex decisions. It involves four phases: exploration of the subject by individuals, reaching an understanding of the group's view of the issues, sharing and evaluation of any differences, and final evaluation of all information. In the conventional Delphi, a small group designs a questionnaire, which is completed by a larger respondent group. The results are then tabulated and used in developing a revised questionnaire, which is again completed by the larger group. Thus, the results of the original polling are fed back to the respondent group to use in subsequent responses. This procedure is repeated until the issues are narrowed, responses are focused, or consensus is reached.

Diagnostic Checklist

Here are some questions that can be addressed in assessing your institution's *decision-making* process through the lens of structural functionalism and the Ignatian vision:

- Do organizational members make high-quality, acceptable, and ethical decisions?
- Do decision makers follow the basic rational process of decision making?
- Is the group appropriately involved in decision making?
- What barriers to effective decision exist?
- What techniques are being used to overcome these barriers?
- What techniques are being used to improve decision making?
- Is participative decision making being used whenever possible?
- Are all components of the corporate community given opportunities for equitable input in decision making?
- Is the input from certain constituencies being marginalized?

POWER DISTRIBUTION

Jerome Martin was the new director of the Quality Control Circle effort at a major motorcycle manufacturing company. He met Beverly Wilson, the labor union representative, on her first day at the plant. Both were strong-willed individuals who had reached their respective positions by aggressively pursuing their professional goals. They were each intent on showing the other who was the boss.

The above scenario is not unlike many that occur at educational institutions of all levels. This situation reflects the exercise of power in an organization. Power is the potential or actual ability to influence others in a desired direction. An individual, group, or other social unit has power if it controls information, knowledge, or resources desired by another individual, group, or social unit. The presence of power and the distribution of power are important issues to followers of the Ignatian vision. These followers are concerned that the society has developed a power structure that perpetuates the dominant culture to the detriment of the minority culture. This concept is often called hegemony.

Who has the power in the situation described at this company? Recognizing, using, and dealing with power differences is implicit in negotiation, which is a process for reconciling different, often incompatible, interests among interdependent parties. In this instance, both Jerome Martin and Beverly Wilson have power. How well each of them uses his or her power and negotiation skills will determine their effectiveness.

Organizational researchers increasingly cite the value of identifying and using power behavior to improve individual and organizational performance, even calling its development and use "the central executive function."[18] Theorists and practitioners have transformed an early view of power, which considered it evil and as mainly stemming from coercion, into a model of viable political action in organizations. Yet, while functional and advantageous in many situations, power behavior can create conflict, which is frequently dysfunctional for the organization.

Different individuals and groups within and outside an organization can exert power. For example, individual employees, including top- and middle-management, technical specialists, support staff, and other non-managerial employees, can influence the actions an organization takes to reach its goals.[19] Thus, there are many sources of power. The three that we will discuss here are position power, personal power, and information or resource power.

By using position power, administrators can exert influence over others simply because of the authority associated with their jobs. It results in subordinates obeying the instructions given by a supervisor, for example, simply by virtue of the position that the supervisor holds. In most organizations, the union contract mitigates the supervisor's position power to a significant degree. Thus, it is inappropriate to rely on position as the only source of power. One study showed, for example, that as a supervisor's position power increased, a followers compliance increased, but his or her satisfaction with supervision decreased.[20] So in the long run, the abuse of position power can have diminishing returns.

Personal power is based on the knowledge or personality of an individual that allows him or her to influence the behavior of others. An individual who has unique or special knowledge, skills, and experience may use this expertise as a source of influence and as a way of building personal power. When the use of computers first made its impact on organizations, for example, the "computer guru" on the staff often wielded personal power based on special knowledge and skills. As schools and other organizations have become increasing technology-oriented, the technical support staff have acquired increased power and influence.

Access to resources or information provides a third major source of power. This differs from expert power in its greater transience. Expertise is more permanent than information-based power. For example, the first individuals to learn to use a new computer system may initially derive their power from having information that others do not possess, but if their power persists after even the average employee becomes computer literate, they have developed personal power based on expertise. Power may also come from the control of scarce resources, such as money, materials, staff, or information. In many organizations, the business manager or CFO has this type of power. Even the audiovisual director can have this type of power if there is a greater demand for than supply of these types of resources in an organization. Think of the many PowerPoint presentations that have been embarrassing disasters because the presenter did not have adequate knowledge of the technology.

Recent research suggests that individuals can increase their own power by sharing power with others. Administrators can facilitate such sharing by helping colleagues to understand and tap into the sources of power described above. They can also give them empowering information, such as providing emotional support, affirmation, serving as a role mode, and facilitating successful accomplishment of a task. Other strategies for the empowering process for administrators include providing a positive emotional atmosphere, rewarding staff achievements in visible and personal ways, expressing confidence in subordinates' abilities, fostering initiative and responsibility, and building on success.

The empowering of others leads us to a discussion of the legitimate or ethical use of power in organizations. Certainly, if the use of power is manipulative and autocratic, it raises questions about the ethics of power. The abuse of power is evident not only in politics and business but also in service agencies and other nonprofits. However, the use of power that does not abuse the rights of others is encouraged and even necessary in an organization. It helps administrators attain institutional goals, facilitate their own and others' achievements, and expedites effective functioning in the workplace. Power viewed in this way is an essential part of effective administration and leadership.

Administrators must establish guidelines for the ethical use of power in their organizations. They and other organizational members must emphasize its contribution to organizational effectiveness and control its abuses. Ensuring that the rights of all organizational members are guaranteed is one criterion for the ethical use of power. This is especially appropriate in institutions that are not unionized, where the employee handbook should outline employee rights in a way similar to that of a labor agreement. We spoke earlier of the importance of having covenantal in addition to, or in place of, contractual relationships.

Another concern is the equitable distribution of power between individuals and groups. Leaders must be particularly attuned to the needs of those individuals and/or groups that are systematically marginalized by our society. Leaders need to continually examine the power implications of their decisions. Even decisions that, on the surface, do not seem to have power distribution implications may in fact have immense implications for perpetuating the dominant culture. An example is whether to send business overseas in order to reap a grater profit. Whether to do so is usually determined by considering the bottom line. However, the manner in which such a policy affects the sustenance of the dominant culture rarely enters the decision-making process. Practitioners of the Ignatian vision must closely examine the social impact and the power implications of such decisions.

Perhaps nowhere is the importance of power distribution more critical than in the negotiation process. Negotiation is a process by which two or more parties attempt to reach an agreement that is acceptable to both parties about issues on which they disagree. Negotiations typically have four key elements. First, the two parties demonstrate some degree of interdependence. Second, some perceived conflict exists between the parties involved in the negotiations. Third, the two parties have the potential to participate in opportunistic interaction. Therefore, each party tries to influence the other through various negotiating strategies. Each party cares about and pursues its own interests by trying to influence decisions to its advantage. Finally, the possibility of agreement exists.

There are basically two bargaining paradigms in current use: distributive bargaining, which takes an adversarial or win/lose approach, and integrative bargaining, which takes a problem-solving or win/win approach.[21]

The classical view considers bargaining as a win/lose situation, where one party's gain is the other party's loss. Known also as a zero-sum type of negotiation, because the gain of one party equals the loss of the other and hence the net adds to zero, this approach characterizes the great majority of the negotiations taking place in business and industry today.

Recent research, let alone the Ignatian vision, encourages negotiators to transform the bargaining into a win/win situation. Here, both parties gain as a result of the negotiations. Known also as a positive-sum type of negotiation, because the gains of each party yield a positive sum, this approach has recently characterized the negotiations in a few companies, especially those that have had a history of strikes and are looking for an alternative to the classical mode of collective bargaining (table 9.2).

Table 9.2. Goldaber's Win/Win Contract Development Program

Phase	Activity
1	Both sides receive protocols governing the process.
2	Each side lists questions and concerns for Phase 3
	Weekend 1: The Communications Laboratory
3	All participants and the facilitator meet.
4	Issues are identified for inclusion in the contract and contract matter committees are appointed.
5	Committees discuss issues, finalize agreements, and list unresolved issues (approximately thirty days allowed).
	Weekend 2
6	All participants and the facilitator meet to reach agreement on the contract.
7	The writing committee writes the proposed contract.
8	All participants review the proposed contract and recommend its approval to their constituencies.
9	Each side votes on the proposed contract.
10	All participants meet to witness the signing of the contract.

Diagnostic Checklist

Here are some questions that can be addressed in assessing your institution's equitable distribution of *power* through the lens of structural functionalism and the Ignatian vision:

- Who has the power in the organization?
- From what sources does the power emanate?
- Is the power appropriately shared?
- Does the negotiation process tend to be distributive or integrative?
- Is empowerment taking place on a routine basis?
- Are distribution of power implications being considered in the decision-making process?
- Are the social implications of the distribution of power being considered?

THE STRATEGIC PLANNING PROCESS

The strategic planning process should be understood as a dynamic ebb and flow of events in the life of an educational institution. The so-called chaos theory tells us that life is a process, constantly changing and evolving. Therefore, it should not be surprising to see that some of the best-laid plans become obsolete before they see the light of day. As I suggested earlier, Mirror Lake is slowly drying up and evolving into a meadow. If you were planning strategically, you would do well to buy your grandchild a kite rather than a boat, if he or she lived near Mirror Lake.

The moral of the story, therefore, is to plan for the unexpected as well as the expected. Even though your institution may currently be prosperous and healthy, the only way to sustain this success is to plan for the possibility of difficult times. How do we know that the unexpected will eventually occur? One need only look at history.

What prevents us from planning accurately is our paradigm for how things are. We want to find order when the reality is chaos. We like to think that events occur in a linear way. This is how we have been trained. The positivistic theory leads us to believe that we can accurately predict outcomes. The reality is that events occur in sporadic and unpredictable ways. Our mission, then, is to find order in this apparent chaos. Thus, we must see our plans as constantly evolving and changing. The process is ongoing. The plans themselves change so frequently that they are of limited value. Dwight Eisenhower aptly pointed out that "[p]lanning is all, but plans are nothing." The primacy of the planning process over the plan itself is a notion that the astute administrator will constantly keep in mind.

So let us look at the planning *process.* Strategic planning is a process that was first developed and refined in business and industry, but has been adopted by a variety of education institutions throughout the nation. In some states, the process is mandated for all publicly funded educational institutions. Strategic planning begins with the development of a mission or vision statement. Goals and objectives are derived from the mission, and strategies are developed for achieving them. Although it may be built into existing structure, it is common practice to create a task force composed of representatives from all levels of the organization; the task force is responsible for planning and making decisions. The process must look forward to the future.

The process of developing a mission statement involves establishing a strong group consensus about the unique purposes of the educational institution and its place in the community that it serves. The process of developing the mission statement will set the tone for all further planning activity. Most often, educational institutions have an existing mission. However, the planning process should not begin until there is broad acceptance of the mission. Many times the mission statement needs to be revised to adapt to current realities before the process can continue.

The mission statement, then, must be developed through discussion among the various constituencies that make up the community, be an outgrowth of a discussion of unique institutional purposes, and reflect the unique character of the organization. The institutional vision is derived from the mission statement, but it is more futuristic in nature. It is often a concise summary of the mission.

The institution should next develop a set of goals that it deems appropriate in the accomplishment of its mission. Goals are more specific and give direction to the action that needs to take place to achieve them. The goals should be expressed in terms that promote easy assessment. It should be clear to an objective observer whether they have been achieved.

Thus, the goals should be behavioral; they should be measurable, make someone accountable for their attainment, and provide a timeline for their completion. It is hoped that the mission statement and goals of the institution will reflect the values and ideals of the Ignatian vision.

The planning process is completed by implementing the plan, evaluating its effectiveness, and institutionalizing it, that is, making it part of the institution's identity or character.

Diagnostic Checklist

Here are some questions that can be addressed in assessing your institution's *strategic planning* process through the lens of structural functionalism and the Ignatian vision:

- Does a mission statement exist?
- Does a vision statement exist?
- Does the mission reflect the values and ideals of the Ignatian vision?
- Does a strategic plan exist?
- Are the goals and objectives clear, measurable, and accountable, and is there a timeline for completion?
- Are the goals and objectives known and understood by the community?
- Is the planning process ongoing?

THE CHANGE PROCESS

Perhaps the most important element in an organization's development is how it responds and adapts to change. In order to bring about effective change, the leader must draw together his or her knowledge and skills in all the other components of organizational development. The process of change is so important to the development of an institution that I devoted the entire chapter 5 to the process. In an earlier work, *The Ten-Minute Guide to Educational Leadership*, I suggested that to be a highly effective leader or follower, one should take ten minutes each day to assess the organizational health of the workplace by evaluating each of the ten components of the organization that we have explored in this chapter. Individuals who wish to become heroic followers (and possibly even heroic leaders) would do well to adopt this research-based approach to improving both their personal and professional lives. It is my hope that this book will be of help in that process.

NOTES

1. Robert H. Palestini, *The Ten-Minute Guide to Educational Leadership* (Lancaster, PA: Technomic Publishing, 1998).

2. Peter Senge, The leader's new work: Building learning organizations, *Sloan Management Review* 32 (1990) 7–23.

3. Abraham H. Maslow, *Motivation and Personality*, 3rd ed. (New York: Harper & Row, 1987).

4. Abraham H. Maslow, *Motivation and Personality*.

5. E. L. Thordike, *Behaviorism* (New York: Norton, 1924).

6. B. A. Mellers, Equity judgment, a revision of Aristotelian views, *Journal of Experimental Psychology*, 111 (1982): 42–70.

7. R. Vance and A. Colella, Effects of two types of feedback on goal acceptance and personal goals, *Journal of Applied Psychology* 75 (1990): 68–76.

8. R. E. Zuker, *Mastering Assertiveness Skills: Power and Positive Influence at Work* (New York: AMACOM, 1983).

9. Judith R. Gordon, *A Diagnostic Approach to Organizational Behavior,* 4th ed. (Boston: Allyn and Bacon, 1995).

10. A. J. Lange and P. Jokubowski, *Responsible Assertive Behavior* (Champaign, IL: Research Press, 1976).

11. Robert H. Palestini, *Educational Administration: Leading with Mind and Heart* (Lancaster, PA: Technomic Publishing, 1999).

12. Wayne Hoy and Cecil Miskel, *Educational Administration*, 5th ed. (New York: McGraw-Hill, 1996).

13. V. H. Vroom and P. W. Yetton, *Leadership and Decision Making* (Pittsburgh: University of Pittsburgh Press, 1973).

14. L. K. Trevino, Ethical decision making in organizations: A person situation interactionist model, *Academy of Management Review* 11 (1986) 601–617.

15. J. S. Carroll and E. J. Johnson, *Decision Research: A Field Guide* (Newbury Park, CA: Sage, 1990).

16. P. C. Nutt, Types of organizational decision processes, *Administrative Science Quarterly* 29 (1984): 414–450.

17. Judith R. Gordon, *A Diagnostic Approach to Organizational Behavior*.

18. J. P. Kolter, Why power and influence issues are at the very core of executive work. In S. Srivastva et al., *Executive Power* (San Francisco: Jossey-Bass, 1986).

19. Henry Mintzberg, *Power In and Around Organizations*, (Englewood Cliffs, NJ: Prentice Hall, 1983).

20. R. M. Emerson, Power-dependence relations, *America Sociological Review* 27 (1962) 31–41.

21. R. Fisher and W. Ury, *Getting to Yes: Negotiating Without Giving In* (Boston: Houghton Mifflin, 1981).

APPENDIX A

THE MIND & HEART SMART
DIAGNOSIS MODEL

Just as there are vital signs in measuring *individual* health, I believe that there are vital signs in measuring the *organizational* health of institutions. This survey will help us to determine those vital signs. The purpose of the Mind & Heart Smart Diagnosis Survey, therefore, is to provide feedback data for intensive diagnostic efforts. Use of the questionnaire, either by itself or in conjunction with other information-collecting techniques such as systematic observation or interviewing, will provide the data needed for identifying strengths and weaknesses in the functioning of the heroic follower as well as his or her institution.

A meaningful diagnostic effort must be based on a theory or model of professional and personal development. This makes action research possible as it facilitates problem identification, which is essential to determining the proper functioning of an organization and its heroic followers. The model suggested here establishes a systematic approach for analyzing relationships among the variables that influence how an organization is managed. It provides for assessment of seven areas of formal and informal activity: *purpose, responsibility, communications, flexibility, trust, respect,* and *sensitivity*. The outer circle in the figure represents an organizational boundary for diagnosis. This boundary demarcates the functioning of the internal and external environments.

Since the underlying organizational theory upon which this survey is based is an open systems model, it is essential that influences from both the internal and external environment be considered for the analysis to be complete.

Purpose
Do the individual and
the institution have goals
and objectives?

Responsibility
Does the heroic follower
accept responsibility
and accountability?

INTERNAL

Communication
How effectively does
the heroic follower
communicate?

ENVIRONMENT

Flexibility
Is the heroic
follower tolerant
of change?

Sensitivity
Does the heroic
follower use both
Mind and Heart?

Trust
Is the heroic follower
using a
Code of Ethics?

Respect
Does the heroic
follower respect
diversity?

EXTERNAL ENVIRONMENT

Please think of your *present personal or professional environment*
and indicate the degree to which you agree or
disagree with each of the following statements.
A "1" is *Disagree* Strongly and a "7" is *Agree*
Strongly.

						Agree Strongly
					Agree	
				Agree Slightly		
			Neither Agree Nor Disagree			
		Disagree Slightly				
	Disagree					
Disagree Strongly						
1	2	3	4	5	6	7

1. My personal and professional goals are measurable.
2. The relationships among coworkers are harmonious.
3. I take responsibility for my actions.
4. My work at this institution offers me an opportunity to grow as a person.
5. I can always talk to someone at work if I have a work-related problem.
6. The employees actively participate in decisions.
7. When something goes wrong, my first instinct is to blame myself.
8. There is a strong fit between this institution's mission and my own values.
9. The faculty and staff are represented on most committees and task forces.
10. Staff development routinely accompanies any significant changes that occur in this institution.
11. The manner in which the tasks in this institution are distributed is a fair one.
12. I communicate clearly with my colleagues at work and my family at home.
13. I almost always communicate from my open self.
14. I listen before wanting to be understood.
15. There is open and direct communication among all levels of this institution.
16. Participative decision making is fostered at this institution.

Agree Strongly
Agree
Agree Slightly
Neither Agree Nor Disagree
Disagree Slightly
Disagree
Disagree Strongly

| 1 | 2 | 3 | 4 | 5 | 6 | 7 |

17. I almost always provide an opportunity for feedback to my communications.
18. Representatives of all segments of the community participate in the strategic planning process.
19. The employees have an appropriate voice in the operation of this institution.
20. This institution is not resistant to constructive change.
21. I consciously consider the resistances to change before I attempt to make a significant change.
22. I feel valued by this institution.
23. The administration encourages an appropriate amount of participation in decision making.
24. Employees are often recognized for special achievements.
25. There are no significant barriers to effective communication at this institution.
26. Favorable and opposing forces to change are addressed in the change process.
27. There are mechanisms at this institution to effectively manage conflict and stress.
28. Most of the employees understand the mission and goals of this institution.
29. The employees feel empowered to make their own decisions regarding their daily work.
30. Tolerance toward change is modeled by most everyone in this institution.
31. I try to treat everyone equitably and fairly.
32. Differences among people are accepted.
33. A sense of fairness is present in the workplace.
34. My ideas are encouraged, recognized, and used.

Agree Strongly

Agree

Agree Slightly

Neither Agree Nor Disagree

Disagree Slightly

Disagree

Disagree Strongly

| 1 | 2 | 3 | 4 | 5 | 6 | 7 |

35. Communication is carried out in a nonaggressive style.
36. Ethics and fairness are an important component of this institution.
37. I appreciate the diversity of peoples' gifts.
38. For the most part, the employees of this institution feel an "ownership" of its goals.
39. The employees are encouraged to be creative in their work.
40. When changes are made, they are implemented using a rational process.
41. This institution's organizational design responds well to changes in the internal and external environment
42. The staff and management get along with one another.
43. I focus on peoples' strengths rather than weaknesses.
44. The goals and objectives for the year are mutually developed by the staff and the management.
45. I believe that my opinions and ideas are listened to.
46. Usually, a collaborative style of decision making is utilized at this institution.
47. A collaborative approach to conflict resolution is ordinarily used.
48. This institution has a clear vision.
49. The employees can express their opinions without fear of retribution.
50. I feel confident that I would have an opportunity for input if a significant change were to take place in this institution.
51. This institution is "people-oriented."
52. Managers and staff have mutual respect for one another.
53. The managers give people the freedom to do their job.
54. I treat everyone with dignity and respect.
55. The opportunity for feedback is always available in the communications process.
56. The concern for employees here goes well beyond the contract.

Agree Strongly
Agree
Agree Slightly
Neither Agree Nor Disagree
Disagree Slightly
Disagree
Disagree Strongly

| 1 | 2 | 3 | 4 | 5 | 6 | 7 |

57. I am concerned that the voices of the underrepresented are heard.
58. This institution has a strategic plan for the future.
59. Most managers here use the power of persuasion rather than the power of coercion.
60. This institution is committed to continually improving through the process of change.
61. I believe that I am tolerant of change.
62. This institution exhibits grace, style, and civility.
63. I have developed a philosophy of life.
64. At this institution, employees are not normally coerced into doing things.
65. I share my goals with my family and with my colleagues at work.
66. I can constructively challenge the decisions in this institution.
67. A process to resolve work-related grievances is available.
68. There is an ongoing planning process at this institution.
69. There is a family atmosphere in which most people are concerned about each other.
70. The policies, procedures, and programs of this institution are periodically reviewed.

THE MIND & HEART SMART SCORING SHEET

Instructions: Transfer the numbers you circled on the questionnaire to the blanks below. Add each column and divide each sum by seven. This will give you comparable scores for each of the ten areas.

Purpose	*Responsible*	*Communication*	*Flexible*
1_____	3_____	5_____	10_____
8_____	7_____	12_____	20_____
18_____	16_____	13_____	21_____
28_____	19_____	14_____	26_____
38_____	29_____	15_____	30_____
48_____	34_____	17_____	40_____
58_____	39_____	25_____	41_____
63_____	44_____	35_____	50_____
65_____	61_____	45_____	60_____
68_____	66_____	55_____	70_____
Total _____	Total _____	Total _____	Total _____
Average____	Average____	Average____	Average____

Trust	*Respect*	*Sensitivity*
31_____	2_____	4_____
33_____	6_____	9_____
36_____	24_____	11_____
47_____	32_____	22_____
49_____	37_____	23_____
52_____	42_____	27_____
59_____	43_____	54_____
62_____	46_____	56_____
64_____	51_____	57_____
67_____	53_____	69_____
Total _____	Total _____	Total _____
Average____	Average____	Average____

Instructions: Transfer your average scores from the Scoring Sheet to the appropriate boxes in the figure below. Then study the background information and interpretation suggestions that follow.

BACKGROUND

The Mind & Heart Smart Diagnosis Survey is a survey-feedback instrument designed to collect data on the functioning of both an organization and the heroic follower. It measures the perceptions of individuals in an organization to determine areas of activity that would benefit from a professional development effort. It can be used as the sole data-collection technique or in conjunction with other techniques (interview, observation, etc.). The instrument and the model reflect a systematic approach for analyzing relationships among variables that influence how an organization is managed and how the heroic follower functions. Using the Mind & Heart Smart Diagnosis is the first step in determining appropriate interventions for professional and personal change efforts.

INTERPRETATION AND DIAGNOSIS

A crucial consideration is the diagnosis based upon data interpretation. The simplest diagnosis would be to assess the amount of variance for each of the seven variables in relation to a score of 4, which is the neutral point. Scores *below* 4 would indicate a *problem* with organizational and individual functioning. The closer the score is to 1, the more severe the problem would be. Scores *above* 4 indicate the *lack of a problem*, with a score of 7 indicating optimum functioning.

Another diagnostic approach follows the same guidelines of assessment in relation to the neutral point (score) of 4. The score of each of the seventy items on the questionnaire can be reviewed to produce more specific information on problematic areas, making the diagnosis more precise. For example, let us suppose that the average score on item number 50 was 1.4. This would indicate not only a problem in the organization's tolerance for change but also a more specific problem that the employees are not provided with the opportunity to have meaningful input into the change. This more precise diagnostic effort is likely to lead to a more appropriate intervention for the organization and/or the individual than the more generalized diagnostic approach described in the preceding paragraph.

Appropriate diagnosis must address the relationships between the boxes to determine the interconnectedness of problems. For example, if there is a problem with *communication*, it could be that the organizational *purpose* is not being promulgated effectively. This might be the case of the average score on communication is well below 4 (2.5 or lower) and the average score on purpose is also well below 4.

INDEX

ABOUT THE AUTHOR

Robert H. Palestini has been in education for more than 40 years as a teacher, principal, and superintendent of schools. He is currently the Dean of Graduate and Continuing Studies at Saint Joseph's University in Philadelphia.